Hollywood or History?

An Inquiry-Based Strategy for Using *The Simpsons* to Teach Social Studies

A Volume in Hollywood or History?

Series Editors

Scott L. Roberts
Central Michigan University

Charles J. Elfer
Clayton State University

Hollywood or History

Scott L. Roberts and Charles J. Elfer, Series Editors

Hollywood or History?:
An Inquiry-Based Strategy for Using
The Simpsons to Teach Social Studies (2024)
edited by Annie McMahon Whitlock

Hollywood or History?
An Inquiry-Based Strategy for Using Film to Teach World Religions (2023)
edited by Thomas E. Malewitz and Adam P. Zoeller

Hollywood or History?
An Inquiry-Based Strategy for Using Film to
Acknowledge Trauma in Social Studies (2022)
edited by Paul J. Yoder and Aaron P. Johnson

Hollywood or History?
An Inquiry-Based Strategy for Using Television Shows to
Teach Issue-Centered Curriculum (2022)
by Starlynn R. Nance

Hollywood or History?
An Inquiry-Based Strategy for Using Film to Teach About
Inequality and Inequity Throughout History (2022)
edited by Sarah J. Kaka

Hollywood or History?
An Inquiry-Based Strategy for Using Film to Teach World History (2021)
edited by Scott L. Roberts and Charles J. Elfer

Hollywood or History?
An Inquiry-Based Strategy for Using Film to
Teach United States History (2018)
edited by Scott L. Roberts and Charles J. Elfer

Hollywood or History?
An Inquiry-Based Strategy for Using *The Simpsons* to Teach Social Studies

Edited by

Annie McMahon Whitlock
Grand Valley State University

INFORMATION AGE PUBLISHING, INC.
Charlotte, NC • www.infoagepub.com

Library of Congress Cataloging-in-Publication Data

CIP record for this book is available from the Library of Congress
http://www.loc.gov

ISBNs: 979-8-88730-403-8 (Paperback)

979-8-88730-404-5 (Hardcover)

979-8-88730-405-2 (ebook)

Copyright © 2024 Information Age Publishing Inc.

All rights reserved. No part of this publication may be reproduced, stored in
a retrieval system, or transmitted, in any form or by any means, electronic,
mechanical, photocopying, microfilming, recording or otherwise, without written
permission from the publisher.

Printed in the United States of America

DEDICATION

To Mike, whose love for The Simpsons is legendary

CONTENTS

Acknowledgments...*xi*

Introduction: The Longevity and Complexity of *The Simpsons*
    Annie McMahon Whitlock ....*xiii*

1. Culture *1*

    Immigration: South Asian Stories From the Past and Present
    Ritu Radhakrishnan.. 3

    "A Bootable Offense:" Satire or Stereotype
    Annie McMahon Whitlock.. 20

    Whacking Away at Holiday Origins
    David A. Johnson.. 29

    For Further Viewing.. 37

2. Time, Continuity, and Change *41*

    "History Hath a Silver Tongue:" Protecting Our Ideals, or
    Refusing to Change?
    Martin Castro.. 43

    Lewis and Clark's Expedition to the West
    Amy Allen.. 56

    For Further Viewing.. 64

3. People, Places, and Environments *69*

    D'oh! Schools, Race, Segregation ... and Zip Codes?
    Timothy Monreal 71

    "I Don't Eat Anything That Casts a Shadow"
    Annie McMahon Whitlock.. 80

    For Further Viewing.. 88

viii CONTENTS

4. Individual Development and Identity...........................89

"You Don't Win Friends With Salad"
Annie McMahon Whitlock.. 91

"Ruthless Bader Ginsburgs"
Annie McMahon Whitlock.. 98

For Further Viewing.. 106

5. Individuals, Groups, and Institutions 109

"The Cause of, and Solution to, All of Life's Problems:"
The Simpsons and Prohibition
Jeffrey Koslowski 111

The Influence of Teachers' Unions Purple Monkey
Dishwasher
Annie McMahon Whitlock.. 120

For Further Viewing.. 128

6. Power, Authority, and Governance 131

The Simpsons State of Nature
Kymberli Wregglesworth 133

"Can't Someone Else Do It?" Experience in Governing
Annie McMahon Whitlock..143

For Further Viewing..151

7. Production, Consumption, and Distribution 155

Is Competition Always Good?
Timothy Constant.. 157

"No More PB or J for Me!" Microlending on *The Simpsons*
Annie McMahon Whitlock..170

For Further Viewing..183

8. Science, Technology, and Society 185

STEM, Human Capital, and the Future of Work
Erin C. Adams.. 188

"Trusting Every Aspect of Our Lives to a Giant Computer
was the Smartest Thing We Ever Did:" Are Smart
Technologies Worth the Cost?
Daniel G. Krutka.. 201

"Well, Kids, Aren't You Glad We Don't Believe in
Inoculations?" Does New Media Provide More "Real News?"
Daniel G. Krutka..214

For Further Viewing.. 228

Contents   ix

9. Global Connections *231*

"Is Anything in This Bar Made in America?"
Annie McMahon Whitlock...*233*

"It's My First Day!" The Creation of the United Nations
Annie McMahon Whitlock... 242

For Further Viewing...*251*

10. Civic Ideals and Practices *255*

Springfield and the History of American Immigration
Anthony Salciccioli.. 257

"Down With Homework!"
Annie McMahon Whitlock... 269

For Further Viewing... 278

11. Commentary on Public Education *281*

"Here's Your Scientifically Selected Career"
Tiffany Craigie 283

"Why Do We Take So Many Tests?" The Pros and Cons of
High Stakes Testing in the United States
Scott L. Roberts and Kate Van Haren 294

For Further Viewing... 306

About the Authors *311*

ACKNOWLEDGMENTS

This book wouldn't be possible without Scott Roberts's encouragement. Once I revealed to him my "dream project" over a meal in North Carolina, he asked me to be a part of his and Charles Elfer's Hollywood or History? series. Thank you for the opportunity to add to this long line of scholarship and dip my toes into the genre of film/TV studies for a fun deviation from my usual line of work.

To all of the authors who contributed to this volume, some of whom weren't even fully into *The Simpsons* until I made them watch an episode or two: Erin Adams, Amy Allen, Martin Castro, Tim Constant, Tiffany Craigie, Dave Johnson, Jeff Koslowski, Daniel Krutka, Timothy Monreal, Ritu Radhakrishnan, Scott Roberts, Anthony Salciccoli, Kate Van Haren, and Kymberli Wregglesworth.

A special thank you always goes to my family. First and foremost, my husband Mike who always works *Simpsons* quotes into everyday conversation with me. He was very happy to help me research and copyedit this book— way more so than anything else I've ever written. "Maybe it's the beer talking, but you've got a butt that won't quit." To my daughters, Maggie (who may or may not be named after *The Simpsons*) and McKenzie—thank you for watching episodes with me. Hopefully I created a new generation of fans.

And finally, to Matt Groening for creating the world of *The Simpsons* and for James L. Brooks, Sam Simon, Al Jean, and others for bringing the show into my life week in and week out, for 700+ weeks. Combining my love for *The Simpsons* and my love of social studies education has been a creative dream.

Hollywood or History?: An Inquiry-Based Strategy for Using The Simpsons to Teach Social Studies, pp. xi–xi
Copyright © 2024 by Information Age Publishing
www.infoagepub.com
All rights of reproduction in any form reserved.

INTRODUCTION

The Longevity and Complexity of *The Simpsons*

On Sunday night, December 17, 1989, I tuned in to the FOX network to watch a new animated show called *The Simpsons*. The episode began with the character of 10-year-old troublemaker Bart Simpson singing an inappropriate version of "Jingle Bells" at the school holiday concert and getting a "Mother" tattoo, which caused his mother Marge to spend the family's Christmas money on its removal. I was immediately captivated by what I considered to be the funniest and most scandalous show I had ever seen on TV in my short life up to that point. The episode, "Simpsons Roasting on an Open Fire" (Pond & Silverman, 1989), was revolutionary for many reasons—it was the first successful 30-minute animated program since *The Flintstones* and launched the new FOX network's popularity. Now *The Simpsons* has millions of fans around the world, its numerous characters are instantly recognizable, and it is the longest running American scripted series ever.

After more than 30 years and 700+ episodes later, I still tune in on Sunday nights. Over my years teaching social studies and social studies methods courses, I have found ways to incorporate clips of the show into my lessons. No matter the year or the age of my students, these clips are always engaging, funny, and help demonstrate social studies concepts for students. Once I found other educators who used the show in their classrooms, I was eager to put together a collection of the ways *The Simpsons*

Hollywood or History?: An Inquiry-Based Strategy for Using The Simpsons
to Teach Social Studies, pp. xiii–xix
Copyright © 2024 by Information Age Publishing
www.infoagepub.com
All rights of reproduction in any form reserved.

can be used to teach social studies concepts. There has been no shortage of episodes to choose from!

The world of Springfield, where the show takes place, has a large group of secondary characters that often have their own episodes or feature prominently in B-stories as they interact with the main family of Homer, Marge, Bart, Lisa, and Maggie Simpson. Homer works at the Springfield Nuclear Power Plant for the evil boss Mr. Burns. Many episodes that take place here could be used to teach economic concepts of organized labor, work, and management. The town is run by the corrupt Mayor Quimby and the incompetent police chief Clancy Wiggum. Any episode featuring these two and the governing of Springfield are excellent sources for teaching civics or political science. The show has also tackled environmental issues, particularly through the character of Lisa, and introduced the characters to cultures all over the world. *The Simpsons* also plays with reality and directly retells historical events using the characters in several episodes and in their Halloween "Treehouse of Horror" series of episodes. Bart and Lisa attend Springfield Elementary and their educational experience is satirized frequently, with episodes taking place at school and featuring their teachers, classmates, and administration—often with biting criticism of curriculum, privatization, and standardized testing, to name a few.

The Simpsons is unique in that the show itself is also a historical source, having been on the air since 1989. Issues that were current in the early 1990s at the height of popularity of *The Simpsons* are now considered historical, and there is room in classrooms to critically analyze with students about whether the show has adapted well to the 2020s, particularly with the show's use of cultural stereotypes. Not all the jokes told in episodes from the mid-1990s still hold up—many would not be acceptable today. As the show continues to air, they continually must face their past and adapt, such as when producers eliminated the practice of having white actors voice characters of color (Gelman, 2020). The potential for comparison between the show's early years and later years, or the show's depictions of social studies and reality make *The Simpsons* good source material for the *Hollywood or History?* Method.

THE *HOLLYWOOD OR HISTORY?* METHOD

The *Hollywood or History?* instructional strategy was developed by Scott L. Roberts and Charles Elfer as a way to bring historical thinking into their classrooms by having students engage with films as a source for inquiry (Roberts & Elfer, 2018). The first step in the *Hollywood or History?* strategy is typically to select the film(s) that students will analyze, taking care to choose films that are appropriate for the audience of students, are easily available, and most importantly—connect to social studies content standards. Even though this book is focused on one TV show, with over 700 episodes to choose from, educators still need to carefully curate how they will show *The Simpsons*.

Each of the authors in this book chose episodes or clips of episodes that could be used to teach social studies content standards in various states, Common Core ELA Standards, and the College, Career, and Civic Life (C3) Framework (NCSS, 2013). In some lessons, authors included alignment to the Social Justice Standards from Learning for Justice (https://www.learningforjustice.org/frameworks/social-justice-standards), the Next Generation Science Standards (https://www.nextgenscience.org/), and teacher preparation standards. Each episode of *The Simpsons* is roughly 22 minutes long, so some lessons have students watching an entire episode. However, other lessons in the book use clips. In many of these cases, clips are used because one or more of the storylines in the episode doesn't relate at all to content standards. Although *The Simpsons* is a cartoon, there are certain scenes and lines that are not appropriate to show students. Even high school students—some of the jokes may end up more of a distraction from the educational goals of the lesson. The authors in this book use exact timestamps of clips to avoid inappropriate content, but where that could not be avoided, there is a note to teachers about what to expect so they can prepare their students.

This book assumes that educators will access episodes of *The Simpsons* through the Disney+ streaming service. Disney+ has every episode of *The Simpsons* on the service, organized by season and episode. I recommend purchasing a subscription, not only to access *Simpsons* content, but to access a wide range of Disney movies that are also excellent sources for any *Hollywood or History?* lesson! (See *Hollywood or History? An Inquiry Based Strategy for Using Film to Acknowledge Trauma in Social Studies* [(Yoder & Johnson, 2022] and *Hollywood or History? An Inquiry-Based Strategy for Using Film to teach About Inequality and Inequity Throughout History* [Kaka, 2022]. The first 20 seasons of the show can be found on DVD and some episodes can be found on YouTube. This book is not affiliated with or sanctioned by Disney.

The next steps of designing a *Hollywood or History?* inquiry is to design a good question. In any *Hollywood or History?* lesson, the foundational question that students need to answer is: Is the film material 100% Hollywood (fiction), 100% History (fact), or somewhere in between? (Roberts & Elfer, 2018, p. xi). This book is slightly different in that the lessons featured here cover a wide range of social studies topics and disciplines—not just history. Each of the chapters in this book correspond to one of the "Ten Themes of Social Studies from the National Council for the Social Studies" (NCSS, n.d.). The 10 themes are interdisciplinary, but many of them closely relate to the "big four" social studies disciplines of history, geography, economics,

xvi HOLLYWOOD OR HISTORY?

and civics. Because this book is bigger than just history, sometimes the *Hollywood or History?* strategy is slightly tweaked, but the idea remains the same: How close is *The Simpsons* to real life? For example, one lesson uses "Hollywood or Empathy?" to compare how the characters of Homer and Lisa compare to a self-assessment of empathy. Each chapter features the *Hollywood or History?* graphic organizer developed by Roberts (2014), with some adaptations for grade level and discipline.

To answer any *Hollywood or History?* question, students need to examine sources. In this book, we of course, feature *The Simpsons* as a source. But this needs to be supplemented so students are able to distinguish what is fact and fiction. Authors in this book frequently use primary sources from the Library of Congress (loc.gov) and DocsTeach (docsteach.org) from the National Archives. There are also a wide variety of secondary sources— from textbooks, to news articles, to informational YouTube videos. Within the lesson procedures, the authors detail exactly how to guide students to use these sources to be able to answer the *Hollywood or History?* question. Each lesson also features extension activities if students or teachers want to continue learning and/or apply their learning by taking informed action to better their communities.

LAYOUT OF THE BOOK

Chapter 1

The first chapter of the book focuses on the NCSS theme of *Culture*. Ritu Radhakrishnan created a lesson using "Much Apu About Something" (2016) on cultural differences among South Asian immigrants. There is a lesson on cultural stereotypes and *The Simpsons*, using "Bart vs Australia" (1995) and "The Town" (2016). David A. Johnson offers an interdisciplinary lesson on the economic culture of holidays using "Whacking Day" (1993).

Chapter 2

This chapter centers on the theme of *Time, Continuity, and Change*—the theme most closely related to history. Martin Castro wrote a lesson on the role of monuments in history using "Lisa the Iconoclast" (1996) and Amy Allen asks Hollywood or History? about *The Simpsons'* retelling of Lewis & Clark's voyage in the episode "Margical History Tour" (2004).

Chapter 3

People, Places, and Environments is the theme of Chapter 3. Timothy Monreal uses the episodes "A Tale of Two Springfields" (2000) and "Waverly Hills 9021D'Oh" (2009) to teach about spatial justice. A lesson on "Lisa the Treehugger" (2000) introduces elementary students to environmental activism.

Chapter 4

Chapter 4 focuses on the theme of *Individual Development and Identity* using two lessons around the Simpson children developing their own identities. Lisa becomes a vegetarian in "Lisa the Vegetarian" (1995) and Bart becomes a feminist in "Bart vs. Itchy and Scratchy" (2019).

Chapter 5

The theme of *Individuals, Groups, and Institutions* is the focus of Chapter 5. Jeffrey Koslowski wrote a lesson comparing the law enforcement response to prohibition in Springfield to the real-life Prohibition Era in "Homer vs. the Eighteenth Amendment" (1997). Labor unions are the focus of the other lesson in this chapter, using "The PTA Disbands" (1995).

Chapter 6

This chapter features lessons on the theme of *Power, Authority, and Governance*, the theme most closely aligned to political science. Kymberli Wregglesworth wrote a lesson on finding examples of the "state of nature" concept in the "Das Bus" (1998) episode. This chapter also offers a lesson on how important experience in government is to actually governing, using the episode "Trash of the Titans" (1998) where Homer runs for sanitation commissioner.

Chapter 7

Chapter 7 focuses on the theme of *Production, Distribution, and Contribution*—the theme mostly closely related to economics. Timothy Constant created a lesson on the circular flow model using examples from the "Mr. Plow" (1992) and "Super Franchise Me" (2014) episodes. There is also a lesson on microlending for elementary students, using "Loan-a Lisa" (2010).

Chapter 8

The theme of *Science, Technology, and Society* is interdisciplinary within and across social studies. In this chapter, Erin C. Adams created a lesson on the concept of "technoskepticism" using the recent episode "The Miseducation of Lisa Simpson" (2020). Daniel G. Krutka wrote two lessons for this chapter. The first uses a Treehouse of Horror segment called "House of Whacks" (2001) to illustrate how smart technologies control our lives—something *The Simpsons* predicted more than 20 years ago. Krutka also offers a lesson on media literacy using the episode "The Computer Wore Menace Shoes" (2000).

Chapter 9

Global Connections is the theme of Chapter 9—another interdisciplinary theme that focuses on issues in a global context. The first lesson in this chapter asks students to examine the economic/business concept of outsourcing using the episode "Kiss Kiss and Bang Bangalore" (2006). The second lesson examines the mission of the United Nations and compares that to its depiction in *The Simpsons* episode "Simpson Tide" (1998).

Chapter 10

The final NCSS theme is *Civic Ideals and Practices*. Returning to the theme of immigration, Anthony Salciccioli offers a lesson on what it means to be a naturalized citizen using the episode "Much Apu About Nothing" (1996). The second lesson in this chapter is a lesson on practicing civic ideals through an action project with first grade students. A short clip from "Team Homer" (1996) illustrates the concept of a "public issue."

Chapter 11

The last chapter in this book deviates from the format of a chapter on each of the NCSS themes to instead focus on the show's *Commentary on Public Education*. Over its many episodes, *The Simpsons* has satirized relevant educational issues many times. These types of episodes are great for a *Hollywood or History?* comparison as students can see how accurately the show depicts these issues. Both lessons in this chapter focus on testing. Tiffany Craigie created a lesson that could be used in a college teacher preparation course around the role of aptitude testing using the "Separate

Vocations" (1992) episode. Scott L. Roberts and Kate Van Haren wrote a lesson where secondary students use the lateral reading strategy to identify the pros and cons of standardized testing, using clips from "How the Test Was Won" as sources (2011).

REFERENCES

Gelman, V. (2020, June 26). *Simpsons* will 'no longer' have white actors play non-white characters. *TVLine.* https://tvline.com/2020/06/26/the-simpsons-recast-non-white-characters-actors-voice/

Kaka, S. J. (Ed.). (2022). *Hollywood or history? An inquiry-based strategy for using film to teach about inequality and inequity throughout history.* Information Age.

Learning for Justice. (n.d.). *Social justice standards.* https://www.learningforjustice.org/frameworks/social-justice-standards

National Council for the Social Studies. (n.d.). *National curriculum standards for social studies: Executive summary.* https://www.socialstudies.org/standards/national-curriculum-standards-social-studies-executive-summary

National Council for the Social Studies. (2013). *College, career, and civic life (C3) framework.*

Next Generation Science Standards. (n.d.). *Next generation science standards.* https://www.nextgenscience.org/

Pond, M. (Writer), & Silverman, D. (Director). (1989, December 17). Simpsons roasting on an open fire (Season 1 Episode 1) [TV series episode]. In J. L. Brooks, M. Groening, & S. Simon (Executive Producers), *The Simpsons.* Gracie Films; Twentieth Century Fox Film Corporation.

Roberts, S. L. (2014). Effectively using social studies textbooks in historical inquiry. *Social Studies Research and Practice, 9*(1), 119–128.

Roberts, S. L., & Elfer, C. (Eds.). (2018). *Hollywood or history? An inquiry-based strategy for using film to teach United States history.* Information Age Publishing.

Yoder, P. J., & Johnson, A. P. (Eds.). (2022). *Hollywood or history? An inquiry-based strategy for using film to acknowledge trauma in social studies.* Information Age Publishing.

CHAPTER 1

CULTURE

Culture is often taught as a concept of geography through the idea of "place" and how places have unique cultural characteristics. These cultural characteristics and experiences like traditions, language, clothing, and land use also form the perceptions and worldviews of people in those places (NCGE, 2012). Culture encompasses many social studies disciplines besides geography; culture is bound with history, politics, economics, society, and the environment. NCSS suggests helping students understand how "human beings create, learn, share, and adapt to culture." Studying culture and cultural diversity also helps students appreciate how culture has shaped their lives as well as the lives of others.

In their decades on the air, *The Simpsons* has shared many different cultures with its viewers over the years, but it has not been without controversy. Several of the show's episodes feature the family traveling to different places around the world—so much so that the show now satirizes itself and the trips have become a running joke ("The Simpsons are going to ____!" is a common refrain on the show). However, in depicting the family's adventures experiencing different global cultures, the show has perpetuated harmful stereotypes. This section begins with a lesson by Ritu Radhakrishnan featuring the episode "Much Apu About Something" (Price & Anderson, 2016) from Season 27, an episode that compares the cultural experiences of Apu and his nephew Jay—two South Asian immigrants from different generations. This lesson features the documentary film *The Problem with Apu* (Melamedoff, 2017) written by and starring Hari Kondabolu as a source to compliment this episode. In this film, Kondabolu discussed the poor representation of South Asians in media, how Apu continued a stereotype of Indian males, and how this cultural stereotype impacted him growing up.

Hollywood or History?: An Inquiry-Based Strategy for Using The Simpsons to Teach Social Studies, pp. 1–39
Copyright © 2024 by Information Age Publishing
www.infoagepub.com
All rights of reproduction in any form reserved.

2 HOLLYWOOD OR HISTORY?

As he describes in his film, Kondabolu says that many people dismissed the harmful cultural stereotypes perpetuated by *The Simpsons* because the show "offends everyone equally." The second lesson in this chapter describes two such episodes that did offend people—Australians (Season 6's "Bart vs. Australia" [Oakley et al., 1995] and Bostonians (Season 28's "The Town" [King & Oliver, 2016]. Students can use these episodes to discover the line between stereotype and satire, while also understanding that although these episodes do feature harmful stereotypes of certain groups of white people, white people are represented on television in both positive and stereotypical ways. In the early days of *The Simpsons*, as Kondabolu correctly points out, South Asians were only stereotypically represented on television by Apu.

This chapter also includes an episode that highlights how culture was created (an ultimately critically examined) in Springfield—Season 4's "Whacking Day" episode (Swartzwelder & Lynch, 1993). David A. Johnson's economics lesson has students examining the commercialization of holidays and how cultural celebrations (even fictional ones like Whacking Day) can be economically driven.

Each chapter in this book ends with a "For Further Viewing" section, which guides teachers to episodes that may also fit with the theme but are not highlighted within the lessons. Hopefully these lists inspire you to create your own *Hollywood or History?* lessons. If you're a fan of *The Simpsons*, no doubt you will find your favorite classics in these sections.

REFERENCES

King, D. (Writer), & Oliver, R. (Director). (2016, October 9). The town (Season 28, Episode 3) [TV series episode]. In A. Jean, J. L. Brooks, & M. Groening (Executive Producers), *The Simpsons*. Gracie Films; Twentieth Century Fox Film Corporation.

Melamedoff, M. (Director). (2017). *The problem with Apu* [Film]. Avalon Television.

National Council for Geographic Education. (2012). *Geography for life* (2nd ed.). Washington DC.

Oakley, B. (Writer), Weinstein, J. (Writer), & Archer, W. (Director). (1995, February 19). Bart vs. Australia (Season 6, Episode 16) [TV series episode]. In D. Mirkin, J. L. Brooks, M. Groening, & S. Simon (Executive Producers), *The Simpsons*. Gracie Films; Twentieth Century Fox Film Corporation.

Price, M. (Writer), & Anderson, B. (Director). (2016, January 17). Much Apu about something (Season 27, Episode 12) [TV series episode]. In A. Jean, J. L. Brooks, & M. Groening (Executive Producers), *The Simpsons*. Gracie Films; Twentieth Century Fox Film Corporation.

Swartzwelder, J. (Writer), & Lynch, J. (Director). (1993, April 29). Whacking day (Season 4, Episode 20) [TV series episode]. In A. Jean, M. Reiss, J. L. Brooks, M. Groening, & S. Simon (Executive Producers), *The Simpsons*. Gracie Films; Twentieth Century Fox Film Corporation.

Immigration: South Asian Stories From the Past and Present

Ritu Radhakrishnan

EPISODE:
"Much Apu About Something" (2018, Season 27, Episode 12)

Grade	Subject	Topic
7–12	United States History-Immigrant Stories	Immigration/Stereotypes

Era Under Study	Estimated Time Needed for Lesson
U.S. History 1910–1965	110 minutes (two 55-minute lessons)

State Standards

State	Standards and Descriptions
Illinois	SS.H.1.6-8.LC. Classify series of historical events and developments as examples of change and/or continuity.
	SS.H.2.6-8.MdC. Analyze multiple factors that influenced the perspectives of people during different historical eras (ex: doves, hawks).
	SS.H.4.6-8.LC. Explain multiple causes and effects of historical events.
New York	8.9a. The civil rights movement began in the postwar era in response to long-standing inequalities in American society, and eventually brought about equality under the law, but slower progress on economic improvements.
	8.9b. The civil rights movement prompted renewed efforts for equality by women and other groups.

4 HOLLYWOOD OR HISTORY?

| North Carolina | NCES.8.H.3. Understand the factors that contribute to change and continuity in North Carolina and the United States. |
| | NCES.8.H.3.1. Explain how migration and immigration contributed to the development of North Carolina and the United States from colonization to contemporary times (e.g. westward movement, African slavery, Trail of Tears, the Great Migration and Ellis and Angel Island). |

Common Core Standards

Standard	Description
CCSS.ELA-LITERACY.RH.6-8.1	Cite specific textual evidence to support analysis of primary and secondary sources.
CCSS.ELA-LITERACY.RH.6-8.5	Describe how a text presents information (e.g., sequentially, comparatively, causally).
CCSS.ELA-LITERACY.RH.6-8.6	Identify aspects of a text that reveal an author's point of view or purpose (e.g., loaded language, inclusion or avoidance of particular facts).
CCSS.ELA-LITERACY.RH.6-8.7	Integrate visual information (e.g., in charts, graphs, photographs, videos, or maps) with other information in print and digital texts.

NCSS C3 Framework

Dimension	Description
Developing Questions and Planning Inquiries	D1.1.6-8. Explain how a question represents key ideas in the field.
	D1.4.6-8. Explain how the relationship between supporting questions and compelling questions is mutually reinforcing.
Applying Disciplinary Concepts and Tools (Civics)	D2.Civ.13.6-8. Analyze the purposes, implementation, and consequences of public policies in multiple settings.

Chapter 1: Culture   5

Applying Disciplinary Concepts and Tools (History)	D2.His.3.6-8. Use questions generated about individuals and groups to analyze why they, and the developments they shaped, are seen as historically significant.
	D2.His.5.6-8. Explain how and why perspectives of people have changed over time.
Evaluating Sources and Using Evidence	D3.3.6-8. Identify evidence that draws information from multiple sources to support claims, noting evidentiary limitations.
Communicating Conclusions and Taking Informed Action	D4.2.6-8. Construct explanations using reasoning, correct sequence, examples, and details with relevant information and data, while acknowledging the strengths and weaknesses of the explanations.

NCSS Core Themes and Description

Theme	Description
I. Culture	Through the study of culture and cultural diversity, learners understand how human beings create, learn, share, and adapt to culture, and appreciate the role of culture in shaping their lives and society, as well the lives and societies of others.
II. Time, Continuity, and Change	Studying the past makes it possible for us to understand the human story across time. Historical analysis enables us to identify continuities over time in core institutions, values, ideals, and traditions, as well as processes that lead to change within societies and institutions, and that result in innovation and the development of new ideas, values, and ways of life.
III. People, Places, and Environments	Examining how human beings interact with their environment and the themes of geography reveal myriad views and perspectives of the world. In schools, this theme typically appears in courses dealing with geography and area studies, but it is also important for the study of the geographical dimension of other social studies subjects.
IV. Individual Development and Identity	Personal identity is shaped by family, peers, culture, and institutional influences. Through this theme, students examine the factors that influence an individual's personal identity, development, and actions.

6   HOLLYWOOD OR HISTORY?

X. Civic Ideals and Practices	An understanding of civic ideals and practices is critical to full participation in society and is an essential component of education for citizenship. This theme enables students to learn about the rights and responsibilities of citizens of a democracy, and to appreciate the importance of active citizenship.

Handouts/Materials/Web Links

Handout/Materials:
- Vocabulary Worksheet
- Station 1: Graphic Organizer
- Station 2: Our Stories Cornell Notes Template
- Station 3: The Problem with Apu Graphic Organizer
- Hollywood or History? Graphic Organizer
- South Asian and South Asian American Stories: What Is Missing?

Episode Clips and Video Content:
- "Much Apu About Something," Season 27, Episode 12
    - **Clip 1:** 1:36-1:53
    - **Clip 2:** 5:09-6:06
    - **Clip 3:** 6:06-7:23
    - **Clip 4:** 11:56-13:21
    - **Clip 5:** 13:40-14:09
    - **Clip 6:** 18:35-19:43
- Melamedoff, M. (Director). (2017). *The Problem with Apu* [Film]. Avalon Television.
- PBSNewsHour. (2018, August 15). *'The Problem with Apu' and the American immigrant stories that aren't being told* [Video]. YouTube. https://www.youtube.com/watch?v=sD4sHDRmVz8
- TruTV. (2017, November 3). *The problem with Apu--Kal Penn explains why he can't watch The Simpsons* [Video]. YouTube. https://www.youtube.com/watch?v=bYuaBAvX1rM

Primary Sources:
- Immigration Act of 1917. Pub.L. 64-30, 39 Stat 874 https://www.govinfo.gov/content/pkg/STATUTE-66/pdf/STATUTE-66-PgA72-2.pdf

Chapter 1: Culture   7

- Luce-Celler Act of 1946. Pub. L. No. 79-483, 60 Stat. 416 https://scholarship.tricolib.brynmawr.edu/bit-stream/handle/10066/14442/2014ShahN_thesis. pdf?sequence=1&isAllowed=y
- Civil Rights Act of 1964. Pub.L. 88–352, 78 Stat. 241 https://www.govinfo.gov/content/pkg/STATUTE-78/pdf/STATUTE-78-Pg241.pdf
- Hart-Celler Act/The Immigration and Nationality Act of 1965. Pub. L. 89-236, 79 Stat 911 https://www.govinfo.gov/content/pkg/STATUTE-79/pdf/STATUTE-79-Pg911.pdf
- Parmar, V. (2017). From Bihar to Brooklyn, to Berlin: A quest for sustainability and soul. In R. C. Leong (Ed.), *Asian American matters: A New York anthology* (pp. 167–176). Asian American Research Institute CUNY.

Secondary Sources:
- History.Com Editors. (2021, January 25). *Civil Rights Act.* https://www.history.com/topics/black-history/civil-rights-act
- Immigration and Ethnic History Society. (2019). *The Hart-Celler Act summary.* https://immigrationhistory.org/item/hart-celler-act/
- Immigration and Ethnic History Society. (2019). *Immigration Act of 1917 summary.* https://immigrationhistory.org/item/1917-barred-zone-act/
- Immigration and Ethnic History Society. (2019). *The Luce-Celler Act summary.* https://immigrationhistory.org/item/luce-celler-act/
- Nevis, J. (2017, Nov. 15). Apu was a tool for kids to go after you: Why *The Simpsons* remains problematic. *The Guardian.* https://www.theguardian.com/tv-and-radio/2017/nov/15/problem-with-apu-simpsons-hari-konabolu-documentary
- SAADA. (2021). *Our stories: An introduction to South Asian America.* South Asian American Digital Archive.
    - o   Introduction (pp. 49–50)
    - o   Bhagat Singh Thind (pp. 52–57)
    - o   Civil Rights (pp. 85–88)

Guiding Questions

Primary Question:
- How are South Asians portrayed in United States history and American culture?

8 HOLLYWOOD OR HISTORY?

Secondary Questions:
- How are South Asians portrayed on most television shows or movies?
- How are South Asian Americans portrayed on most television shows or movies?
- What are the roles of South Asian and South Asian Americans in United States history?
- How do these portrayals shape our perceptions about South Asians/South Asian Americans?
- Why do you think South Asians and South Asian Americans are often portrayed this way?
- What are the effects of these portrayals on South Asians and South Asian Americans in our society? Our community?

Important Vocabulary

Civil Rights Act of 1964: This act prohibits discrimination on the basis of race, color, religion, sex, or national origin.

Hart-Celler Act-Immigration and Nationality Act of 1965: This act abolished an earlier system that focused on national origin. A new immigration policy was created to reunite immigrant families and attract skilled labor to the U.S.

Immigration Act (Asiatic Barred Zone)(1917): This act banned immigrants from the Middle East to Southeast Asia. Additionally, the restriction included a literacy test that was intended to hinder immigrants.

Luce-Celler Act (1946): This Act granted naturalization rights to Filipinos and Asian Indians.

Microaggressions: Microaggressions are the everyday, subtle, intentional—and oftentimes unintentional—interactions or behaviors that communicate some sort of bias toward historically marginalized groups.

Naturalization: The act or process of making or becoming a citizen.

South Asian American: Individuals born in the United States of South Asian descent: Bangladesh, Bhutan, India, Nepal, Pakistan, Sri Lanka, and the Maldives

South Asian: Individuals originally born in the South Asian countries of: Bangladesh, Bhutan, India, Nepal, Pakistan, Sri Lanka, and the Maldives.

Stereotypes: A fixed idea, usually developed by preconceived notions, that people have about a group that may not be true or may be incomplete.

Assessment Strategies

Formative Assessments:
- Hollywood or History? Graphic Organizer
- South Asian and South Asian American Stories: What Is Missing?

Summative Assessments:
- Hollywood or History? Graphic Organizer
- South Asian and South Asian American History multimodal product (extension)

Sparking Strategy/Warm-Up

Lesson Introduction

Read this journal entry from Vinit Parmar (2017): "From Bihar to Brooklyn, to Berlin: A quest for sustainability and soul."

> Brown like the color of my skin. I could not wipe it away. Early in my youth, my parents uprooted me from dusty Bihar only to stick me into an uninviting Forest Hills classroom in Queens, New York. Could I scrape off the color? Asked a classmate. No, it would not rub off. From where did I come? India. Why did I smell like this? I don't know. I did not know I was different.... What was worse, being covered in coal-laced grime that killed everything or the desolation of an all-Caucasian school where nothing could survive as I knew it? (Parmar, 2017, p. 167).

Ask students to write a response to the prompt: *How would you respond to the author if this was communicated to you?* (5 min)

Lesson Procedures

Day 1

1. After sharing responses to the warm-up with a shoulder partner, students will move into three teams and receive vocabulary worksheets for five vocabulary words: *microaggressions, naturalizations, South Asian, South Asian American,* and *stereotypes*.
2. Teacher will introduce each vocabulary word and definitions. Students will complete the remainder of the Vocabulary

10   HOLLYWOOD OR HISTORY?

Worksheet as a team. Each team will complete a worksheet for each vocabulary word. (5 min)

3. Vocabulary will be reviewed as a whole class. Students will be invited to share personal connections. (5 min)

4. Students will then view parts of *The Simpsons* episode, "Much Apu about Something". Teacher will present the following clips; then ask students the question following each one: (10 min)

> **Clip 1:** 1:36–1:53
>
> *What do you know about Apu?*
>
> **Clip 2:** 5:09–6:06
>
> *What does Apu and Sanjay's conversation suggest about Indian culture?*
>
> **Clip 3:** 6:06–7:23
>
> *How is Jay different from Apu?*
>
> **Clip 4:** 11:56–13:21
>
> *What stereotypes do you see?*
>
> **Clip 5:** 13:40–14:09
>
> *Why are Apu's and Jay's perspectives so different?*
>
> **Clip 6:** 18:35–19:43
>
> *Why does Apu feel like he belongs?*

5. After clips are played, teams will be assigned a starting station. Each team will have ten minutes at each station. Students will review all the texts/resources at the station. Graphic organizers for each team will be available. Each member of the team should complete a graphic organizer. Students will rotate counterclockwise to the next station after ten minutes, until they have completed all of the stations. (35 min)

Day 2

1. Have students complete a "quick-write" where they write for five minutes about a vocabulary word of their choice from Day 1 and what they learned about that word. (5 min)

2. Students will meet with their teams from Day 1 and complete any missing information. They will discuss the Primary Question and Secondary Questions in their teams based on the information they've learned from their primary and secondary document analysis. After they finish their discussion in their Teams,

students will also complete their Hollywood or History? Graphic Organizer. (25 min)

3. Students will begin a storyboard for their multimodal presentation: South Asian and South Asian American Stories: What is Missing? Students are encouraged to identify connections to the primary sources and what they've learned. Each "idea" box will include a vocabulary word and what they've learned about the vocabulary. Students can also do a historic overview. (20 min)

Differentiation

Scaffolds: Students will be working in blended groups with varying learning preferences and abilities. Each station will include graphic organizers to help make sense of the sources provided. The text in the primary and secondary source articles may be too technical for some students. The teacher may consider chunking strategies or only using specific excerpts and supplement descriptions for students who may struggle with comprehension.

ESL Interventions: Students will work with an aide. Definitions will be translated, and visual images and pronunciation will also be included (collaboration with native speakers).

Extensions:

- "Taking action" is a key component of the NCSS C3 Framework. Allowing students to display their new understanding on a digital platform is a great way for them to educate others about the topic under study in this lesson plan. Students will consider the question: *How can you be an ally?* and create learning materials around this topic and #StopAAPIHate

REFERENCES

Civil Rights Act of 1964. Pub.L. 88–352, 78 Stat. 241

Hart-Celler Act/The Immigration and Nationality Act of 1965. Pub. L. 89-236, 79 Stat 911

History.Com Editors. (2021, January 25). *Civil Rights Act.* https://www.history.com/topics/black-history/civil-rights-act

Immigration Act of 1917. Pub.L. 64-30, 39 Stat 874

Immigration and Ethnic History Society. (2019). *The Hart-Celler Act summary.* https://immigrationhistory.org/item/hart-celler-act/

Immigration and Ethnic History Society. (2019). *Immigration Act of 1917 summary.* https://immigrationhistory.org/item/1917-barred-zone-act/

12 HOLLYWOOD OR HISTORY?

Immigration and Ethnic History Society. (2019). *The Luce-Celler Act summary.* https://immigrationhistory.org/item/luce-celler-act/

Luce-Celler Act of 1946. Pub. L. No. 79-483, 60 Stat. 416

Melamedoff, M. (Director). (2017). *The Problem with Apu* [Film]. Avalon Television.

Nevis, J. (2017, Nov. 15). Apu was a tool for kids to go after you: Why *The Simpsons* remains problematic. *The Guardian.* https://www.theguardian.com/tv-and-radio/2017/nov/15/problem-with-apu-simpsons-hari-konabolu-documentary

Parmar, V. (2017). From Bihar to Brooklyn, to Berlin: A quest for sustainability and soul. In R. C. Leong (Ed.), *Asian American matters: A New York anthology* (pp. 167-276). Asian American and Asian Research Institute, CUNY.

PBSNewsHour. (2018, August 15). *'The Problem with Apu' and the American immigrant stories that aren't being told* [Video]. YouTube. https://www.youtube.com/watch?v=sD4sHDRmVz8

Price, M. (Writer), & Anderson, B. (Director). (2016, January 17). Much Apu about something (Season 27, Episode 12) [TV series episode]. In A. Jean, J. L. Brooks, & M. Groening (Executive Producers), *The Simpsons.* Gracie Films; Twentieth Century Fox Film Corporation.

SAADA. (2021). *Our stories: An introduction to South Asian America.* South Asian American Digital Archive.

TruTV. (2017, November 3). *The problem with Apu--Kal Penn explains why he can't watch The Simpsons* [Video]. YouTube. https://www.youtube.com/watch?v=bYuaBAvX1rM

APPENDIX A

Stations and Document Links

Station A: Primary Sources—Use Graphic Organizer #1-Primary Sources

   i. **Immigration Act (Asiatic Barred Zone) (1917)**

     a. Act: https://www.govinfo.gov/content/pkg/STATUTE-66/pdf/STATUTE-66-PgA72-2.pdf

     b. Summary: https://immigrationhistory.org/item/1917-barred-zone-act/

   ii. **Luce-Celler Act (1946)**

     a. Act: https://scholarship.tricolib.brynmawr.edu/bitstream/handle/10066/14442/2014ShahN_thesis.pdf?sequence=1&isAllowed=y

     b. Summary: https://immigrationhistory.org/item/luce-celler-act/

   iii. **The Civil Rights Act of 1964**

     a. Act: https://www.govinfo.gov/content/pkg/STATUTE-78/pdf/STATUTE-78-Pg241.pdf

     b. Summary: https://www.history.com/topics/black-history/civil-rights-act

Chapter 1: Culture 13

iv. **The Hart-Celler Act/Immigration and Nationality Act of 1965:**
   a. Act: https://www.govinfo.gov/content/pkg/STATUTE-79/pdf/STATUTE-79-Pg911.pdf
   b. Summary: https://immigrationhistory.org/item/hart-celler-act/

Station B: Secondary Source (Our Stories)—Use Graphic Organizer #2-Cornell Notes
   i. Our Stories: Introduction (pp. 49-50)
   ii. Our Stories: Bhagat Singh Thind (pp.52-57)
   iii. Our Stories: Civil Rights (pp. 85-88)

Station C: The Problem with Apu—Use Graphic Organizer #3—The Problem with Apu
   i. Nevis, J. (2017, Nov. 15). Apu was a tool for kids to go after you: Why The Simpsons remains problematic. *The Guardian*. Rertieved from: https://www.theguardian.com/tv-and-radio/2017/nov/15/problem-with-apu-simpsons-hari-konabolu-documentary
   ii. PBSNewsHour. (2018, August 15). *'The Problem with Apu' and the Immigrant Stories That Aren't Being Told* https://www.youtube.com/watch?v=sD4sHDRmVz8
   iii. TruTV. (2017, November 3).*'The Problem with Apu'Kal Penn Explains Why He Can't Watch the Simpsons.* https://www.youtube.com/watch?v=bYuaBAvX1rM

APPENDIX B

Vocabulary Worksheet

Vocabulary Word	What is it? (Definition)

What does this look like? (Draw)	How do you connect to this? (Personal Reflection)

APPENDIX C

Station 1: Graphic Organizer

Act/Law	What Was It? (Use the station sources to help)	What Does It Mean? (Use your own words)	How Did It Affect South Asians? (Draw or write)
Immigration Act (Asiatic Barred Zone) (1917)			
Luce-Celler Act (1946):			

Chapter 1: Culture   15

The Civil Rights Act of 1964			
The Hart-Celler Act/Immigration and Nationality Act of 1965			

APPENDIX D

Station 2: *Our Stories* Cornell Notes Template

Recall *(Use specific quotes and page numbers from the book)*	Notes *(use your own words to describe the information)*
Introduction (pp. 49–51) Bhagat Singh Thind (pp. 52–57) The Civil Rights Movement (pp. 85–88)	

16   HOLLYWOOD OR HISTORY?

Summary
What does this mean for South Asians/South Asian Americans?

APPENDIX E

Station 3: *The Problem with Apu* Graphic Organizer

Media Link	Quotes (Write at least 2 quotes from each media source)	How did this clip highlight stereotypes? Microaggressions?
"The Problem with Apu": Kal Penn Explains Why He Can't Watch the Simpsons *(Watch full clip)*		
"The Problem with Apu" and the Immigrant Stories that Aren't Being Told *(Watch full clip)*		
Apu was a tool for kids to go after you: Why The Simpsons remains problematic. *(Read full article)*		

Why are stereotypes and microaggressions harmful?

Hollywood or History?
"Much Apu About Something" (2016)

"Much Apu About Something" (2016) is an episode from Season 27. The episode follows Apu and his interactions with his nephew, Jay. Apu is a South Asian immigrant and Jay is South Asian American. Students will investigate how both individuals are portrayed and how many of the portrayals reinforce stereotypes. Throughout today's lesson, students will come across a variety of primary and secondary sources which they will use to analyze the various aspects of this film.

Column 1: While evaluating the episode's historical and cultural accuracy, write down bullets listing some of your observations based on how this film represents the following themes (perceptions of immigrants, perceptions of South Asians, perceptions of religion)

Column 2: Provide an example of supporting evidence using outside information obtained while working with various primary or secondary resources in the Stations Activity. This evidence should connect to the observations made in Column 1 to help determine whether this part of the episode was more Hollywood or History.

Column 3: Make your decision; Hollywood, History, or Both? Determine whether or not this specific part of the film was more Hollywood or History. In stations A and B, more primary and secondary sources about Mohenjo Daro are provided. Use this outside information as evidence to support your claim.

Observations from Much Apu about Something:	Evaluating Historical Accuracy Using Evidence	Conclusion: Hollywood or History?
	Primary:	
	Secondary:	

Chapter 1: Culture   19

	Primary:	
	Secondary:	

APPENDIX G

South Asian and South Asian American Stories: What Is Missing?

Idea 1:	Idea 2:	Idea 3:

"A Bootable Offense:" Satire or Stereotype?

Annie McMahon Whitlock

EPISODES:
"Bart vs. Australia" (1995, Season 6, Episode 16)
"The Town" (2016, Season 28, Episode 3)

Grade	Subject	Topic
7–12	Geography, history, social-emotional learning	Cultural and regional stereotypes

Estimated Time Needed for Lesson
110 minutes (two 55-minute class periods)

Learning for Justice Social Justice Standards

Code	Standard
JU.6-8.11	I relate to people as individuals and not representatives of groups, and I can name some common stereotypes I observe people using.
JU.9-12.11	I relate to all people as individuals rather than representatives of groups and can identify stereotypes when I see or hear them.

Common Core Standards

Standard	Description
CCSS.ELA-LITERACY. RI.9-10.2	Determine a central idea of a text and analyze its development over the course of the text, including how it emerges and is shaped and refined by specific details; provide an objective summary of the text.

Chapter 1: Culture   21

| CCSS.ELA-LITERACY. RH.9-10.6 | Compare the point of view of two or more authors for how they treat the same or similar topics, including which details they include and emphasize in their respective accounts. |
| CCSS.ELA-LITERACY. WHST.9-10.1 | Write arguments focused on *discipline-specific content*. |

NCSS C3 Framework

Dimension	Description
Evaluating Sources and Using Evidence	D3.1.9-12. Gather relevant information from multiple sources representing a wide range of views while using the origin, authority, structure, context, and corroborative value of the sources to guide the selection. D3.3.9-12. Identify evidence that draws information directly and substantively from multiple sources to detect inconsistencies in evidence in order to revise or strengthen claims.
Communicating Conclusions and Taking Informed Action	D4.1.9-12. Construct arguments using precise and knowledgeable claims, with evidence from multiple sources, while acknowledging counterclaims and evidentiary weaknesses.

NCSS Core Themes and Description

Theme	Description
I. Culture	Through the study of culture and cultural diversity, learners understand how human beings create, learn, share, and adapt to culture, and appreciate the role of culture in shaping their lives and society, as well the lives and societies of others.
III. People, Places, and Environments	Examining how human beings interact with their environment and the themes of geography reveal myriad views and perspectives of the world.
IV. Individual Development and Identity	Personal identity is shaped by family, peers, culture, and institutional influences. Through this theme, students examine the factors that influence an individual's personal identity, development, and actions.

22 HOLLYWOOD OR HISTORY?

Handouts/Materials/Web Links

Handout/Materials:
- Satire or Stereotype? Graphic Organizer

Episode Clips and Video Content:
- "Bart vs Australia," Season 6, Episode 16
- "The Town," Season 28, Episode 3
  - o **Clip 1:** 7:05 to 9:31
  - o **Clip 2:** 18:07 to 19:51

Secondary Sources:
- Cooks, L. M., & Orbe, M. P. (1993). Beyond the attire: Selective exposure and selective perception in "In Living Color." *Howard Journal of Communications, 4*(3), 217-233.
- Lieu, J. (2016, September 12). A love letter to the glorious "Bart vs Australia" episode of "The Simpsons." *Mashable.com.* https://mashable.com/article/bart-vs-australia-love
- Hawkings, C. J. (2018, April 8). Why "The Simpsons" episode Bart versus Australia is offensive to Australians everywhere. *Medium.com* https://medium.com/wonderpopculture/why-the-simpsons-episode-bart-versus-australia-is-offensive-to-australians-everywhere-482658f0f3aa
- Pan, A. (2020, February 20). Aussies would have a fit over the Simpsons' Australia episode today. *GOAT.com.au.* https://goat.com.au/entertainment/aussies-would-have-a-fit-over-the-simpsons-australia-episode-today/

Guiding Questions

Primary Question:
- How do we know if the media is satirizing a group for comedy or reinforcing harmful stereotypes?

Secondary Questions:
- What cultural and regional stereotypes exist?
- What cultural and regional stereotypes have roots in historical and geographical facts?
- Is it ever a good idea to highlight stereotypes for comedy?
- Does it matter whether creative people are from the culture they're satirizing?

Chapter 1: Culture   23

Important Vocabulary

Parody: An imitation of the style of a particular writer, artist, or genre with deliberate exaggeration for comic effect

Satire: The use of humor, irony, exaggeration, or ridicule to expose and criticize people's stupidity

Stereotype: A widely held, but fixed and oversimplified image or idea of a particular category of people; an expectation that people have that applies to every person of a particular group

Assessment Strategies

Formative Assessments:

- Satire or Stereotype? Graphic Organizer

Summative Assessments:

- Students should write a short essay that answers the following prompt: *Is the episode "Bart vs. Australia" a satire of Australian culture or a harmful stereotype of Australians?*

Sparking Strategy/Warm-Up

Lesson Introduction

Ask the students to close their eyes and imagine an image of a watch. After a few seconds, ask the students whether their mental picture of a watch included something round with numbers and hands. Many of the students will say yes. Now have students look around the room and observe other watches that students may be wearing and/or purposely think about watches that are square, digital, or have no numbers at all. Explain that this is a safe example of a *stereotype*—how the image or a round watch with numbers becomes the "go-to" image for a watch and how that's not actually the complete picture of reality. (5 min)

Adapted from: Kilman, C. (2012). You're not from around here. *Teaching Tolerance*, 42.

Lesson Procedures

Day 1

1. Now that students have a broad understanding of a stereotype, discuss the definition of satire. Have students look at this cartoon and ask: *Who is this cartoon making fun of? What is exaggerated here to make you laugh?* (5 min)

2. After discussing that satire is exaggerating someone's stupidity for laughs (in the case of the "Modern Tan" cartoon, exaggerating the stupidity of people on their phones at the beach by displaying a funny tan line that wouldn't happen in real life), ask the students: *What do you believe is the difference between satire and stereotyping?* (5 min)
3. Before watching "Bart vs. Australia" from 1995, explain that *The Simpsons* is considered a satirical show—often highlighting ridiculous things people do, say, and believe by exaggerating them for laughs. While they watch the episode, have the students use the Satire or Stereotype? Graphic Organizer to note what they believe to be exaggerated comedy, harmful stereotypes of Australians, or what they're not sure could be either. (20 min)
4. Divide the class in half (if the class is large, each half can be further divided into smaller groups). One half of the class reads the article below about why "Bart vs Australia" is a loving satire and one half reads an article about why "Bart vs Australia" is a harmful stereotype. (20 min)

Satire

Lieu, J. (2016, September 12). A love letter to the glorious "Bart vs. Australia" episode of "The Simpsons." Mashable.com

https://mashable.com/article/bart-vs-australia-love

Stereotype

Hawkings, C. J. (2018, April 8). Why "The Simpsons" episode Bart versus Australia is offensive to Australians everywhere. Medium.com

https://medium.com/wonderpopculture/why-the-simpsons-episode-bart-versus-australia-is-offensive-to-australians-everywhere-482658f0f3aa

5. Each half of the class (or each group) should share the main takeaway or argument each author gives for why "Bart vs. Australia" is a satire or stereotype of Australians. (5 min)

Day 2

1. Have students revisit their Satire or Stereotype? Graphic Organizer and add, alter, or annotate anything they wrote the previous day. Ask them: *Did any of the arguments from the two articles make you think differently about any part of this episode?* (5 min)
2. In small groups, have students discuss the question: *The writers of* "Bart vs. Australia" *are not Australian. Does this make a difference in whether the episode is satire or a stereotype?* (10 min)
3. To examine whether authorship of a satire makes a difference, divide the class in small groups. Each group should start by viewing a clip from another *Simpsons* episode from 2016—"The Town"—which is considered a satire of people from Boston. This episode is written by Bostonian Dave King. Then, the groups will read a paragraph from a study about the 1993 television show *In Living Color*, which was created by Keenan Ivory Wayans, who is Black. (20 min)

The Town
Clip 1: 7:05 to 9:31
Clip 2: 18:07 to 19:51

Paragraph referencing *In Living Color*

Hemphill (1990) warned that the "characters [on *In Living Color*] are ultimately dangerous and many [viewers] don't realize the difference between those characters and real life" (p. 38). As discussed within the focus groups, the show is viewed by some African Americans and whites as an inside joke, the meaning of which may elude viewers with little contact with the African American community. Parody has been a successful strategy in other programming efforts by whites, using humor to create awareness of and to stimulate interest in other cultures. However, in the case of African Americans in the media, this is very difficult to accomplish primarily because they have not been portrayed accurately since the inception of television. Parody is only effective when viewers have realistic depictions for comparisons. Many of the focus group participants, both white and African American, had some difficulty differentiating between realistic and parodic depictions.

From: Cooks, L. M., & Orbe, M. P. (1993). Beyond the attire: Selective exposure and selective perception in "In Living Color." *Howard Journal of Communications, 4*(3), 217-233.

4. After watching and reading, each small group should discuss the question: *Does it matter if the creator of the comedy is from the group being satirized? Does it matter that Dave King is from Boston exaggerating or stereotyping Bostonians? Does it matter that Keenan Ivory Wayans is Black and exaggerating or stereotyping Black culture?* After about fifteen minutes, groups should be encouraged to share their ideas in the larger group. (15 min)
5. Using their graphic organizer with evidence from the episode, as well as evidence from the secondary sources, students should write a short essay that answers the following prompt: *Is the episode* "Bart vs. Australia" *a satire of Australian culture or a harmful stereotype of Australians?* to be completed at home. (5 min)

Differentiation

Scaffolds: The two articles about "Bart vs. Australia" may need to be read aloud to some students. The paragraph from the study on *In Living Color* could be annotated so any technical language is explained. Students may need to work through that paragraph in a whole group or several times to understand the main idea of the paragraph.

ESL Interventions: Students should be given the option to watch the clips with their native language subtitles if they are available. ESL learners could

Chapter 1: Culture   27

write their graphic organizer and summative assessment in their native language and have it translated to English.

Extensions:

- Watch an episode of your favorite comedy TV show or rewatch your favorite comedic movie. Make a list of whether any funny parts would be considered satire or stereotypical.
- Connect with a class in Australia to make connections and correct stereotypes. Ask them about their life and culture. This site has ways for teachers to connect their students to cultures from around the world: https://www.weareteachers.com/virtual-pen-pals/

REFERENCES

Cooks, L. M., & Orbe, M. P. (1993). Beyond the attire: Selective exposure and selective perception in "In Living Color." *Howard Journal of Communications, 4*(3), 217-233.

Kilman, C. (2012). You're not from around here. *Teaching Tolerance*, 42.

King, D. (Writer), & Oliver, R. (Director). (2016, October 9). The town (Season 28, Episode 3) [TV series episode]. In A. Jean, J. L. Brooks, & M. Groening (Executive Producers), *The Simpsons*. Gracie Films; Twentieth Century Fox Film Corporation.

Lieu, J. (2016, September 12). A love letter to the glorious "Bart vs Australia" episode of "The Simpsons." *Mashable.com*. https://mashable.com/article/bart-vs-australia-love

Oakley, B. (Writer), Weinstein, J. (Writer), & Archer, W. (Director). (1995, February 19). Bart vs. Australia (Season 6, Episode 16) [TV series episode]. In D. Mirkin, J. L. Brooks, M. Groening, & S. Simon (Executive Producers), *The Simpsons*. Gracie Films; Twentieth Century Fox Film Corporation.

Pan, A. (2020, February 20). Aussies would have a fit over the Simpsons' Australia episode today. GOAT.com.au. https://goat.com.au/entertainment/aussies-would-have-a-fit-over-the-simpsons-australia-episode-today/

Hollywood or History?

Satire or Stereotype?

Take notes on the episode of "Bart vs. Australia" as you watch.

Satire	Stereotype	Not Sure

Whacking Away at Holiday Origins

David A. Johnson

EPISODE:

"Whacking Day" (1993, Season 4, Episode 20)

Grade	Subject	Topic
9–12	Economics	Holiday commercialism

Estimated Time Needed for Lesson
90 minutes (can be split over two days)

State Standards

State	Standards and Descriptions
Kentucky	HS.E.MA.2. Analyze ways in which competition and government regulation influence what is produced and allocated in an economy.
Massachusetts	T2.5. Explain the function of profit in a market economy as an incentive for entrepreneurs to accept the risks of business failure.
	T2.7. Identify factors that cause changes in market supply and demand.
Michigan	1.4.1. Public Policy and the Market – analyze the impact of a change in public policy on consumers, producers, workers, savers, and investors.

Common Core Standards

Standard	Description
CCSS.ELA-LITERACY. RH.11-12.1	Cite specific textual evidence to support analysis of primary and secondary sources, connecting insights gained from specific details to an understanding of the text as a whole.

30 HOLLYWOOD OR HISTORY?

CCSS.ELA-LITERACY. RH.11-12.3	Evaluate various explanations for actions or events and determine which explanation best accords with textual evidence, acknowledging where the text leaves matters uncertain.
CCSS.ELA-LITERACY. RH.11-12.9	Integrate information from diverse sources, both primary and secondary, into a coherent understanding of an idea or event, noting discrepancies among sources.

NCSS C3 Framework

Dimension	Description
Applying Disciplinary Concepts and Tools (Economics)	D2.Eco.3.9-12. Analyze the ways in which incentives influence what is produced and distributed in a market system.
	D2.Eco.5.9-12. Describe the consequences of competition in specific markets.
	D2.Eco.8.9-12. Describe the possible consequence, both intended and unintended, of government policies to improve market outcomes.

NCSS Core Themes and Description

Theme	Description
I. Culture	Through the study of culture and cultural diversity, learners understand how human beings create, learn, share, and adapt to culture, and appreciate the role of culture in shaping their lives and society, as well the lives and societies of others.
II. Time, Continuity, and Change	Through the study of the past and its legacy, learners examine the institutions, values, and beliefs of people in the past, acquire skills in historical inquiry and interpretation, and gain an understanding of how important historical events and developments have shaped the modern world.
V. Individuals, Groups, and Institutions	Institutions such as families and civic, educational, governmental, and religious organizations exert a major influence on people's lives. This theme allows students to understand how institutions are formed, maintained, and changed, and to examine their influence.

Chapter 1: Culture   31

Handouts/Materials/Web Links

Handout/Materials:
- Hollywood or History? Graphic Organizer

Episode Clips and Video Content:
- "Whacking Day," Season 4, Episode 20
  - o **Short Compilation Clip**: https://www.youtube.com/watch?v=vZ-7c7ryljs

Secondary Sources:
- Madowo, L. (2020, June 28). *Could adding a new public holiday boost the economy?* BBC Worklife. https://www.bbc.com/worklife/article/20200629-could-adding-a-new-public-holiday-boost-the-economy
- Organisation for Economic Co-operation and Development. (n.d.) *Holidays are a serious business.* https://www.oecd.org/general/focus/holidaysareaseriousbusiness.htm
- Time and Date. (n.d.). *Fun holidays - Funny, random & weird holidays.* https://www.timeanddate.com/holidays/fun/
- Wikipedia. (n.d.). *Economics of Christmas.* https://en.wikipedia.org/wiki/Economics_of_Christmas

Guiding Questions

Primary Question:
- Why do we celebrate what we celebrate?

Secondary Questions:
- Does what we celebrate affect the local, state, or national economy?
- Does participation or public opinion factor into any economic boosts from a public or religious holiday?

Important Vocabulary

Public Holiday: A holiday generally established by law in the local, state, or national economies.
Public Opinion: Views prevalent among the general public.

32   HOLLYWOOD OR HISTORY?

Assessment Strategies

Formative Assessments:
- At the conclusion of the first day of activities, students should write a brief prediction about what they anticipate might see in Springfield if Whacking Day was no longer a celebration for the town.

Summative Assessments:
- Students will conduct a quick argumentative writing over whether Whacking Day should have been discontinued, utilizing some of the economic examples from some of the readings as the source for their evidence.

Sparking Strategy/Warm-Up

Lesson Introduction

To kick this lesson off, students should spend five minutes on the Strange and Fun Holidays website looking at some of the non-religious holidays from around the United States. Give a few students an opportunity to report on some of the funnier ones they may have come across before asking students: *Can you think of an economic reason one of these holidays may have come into existence? Can you think of how some of these holidays might have come to be?* (10 min)

Lesson Procedures

Day 1

1. Begin by asking students the primary question: *Why do we celebrate what we celebrate?* This is a broad question that asks students to think broadly about holidays and their meaning. Continue by sharing the Wikipedia page "The Economics of Christmas" with students and give them 5-10 minutes to read as much of it as they can. The purpose is not to read and comprehend the entire document, but rather, use it as a jumping-off point for discussion on how a holiday, whether religious or otherwise, can impact economic choices that businesses make. Distribute the Hollywood or History? Graphic Organizer and explain to students that they'll be using this

Chapter 1: Culture   33

throughout the next two class periods to take notes and form their final opinion on whether this adequately portrays the economic concepts they'll be learning more about. Have them record their initial thoughts on "The Economics of Christmas." (10 min)

2. Before playing the clip, ask students to pay attention to some of the economic reasons that "Whacking Day" might have become a holiday in Springfield. Explain that they should take notes both on what they see in the video, and that they'll be given a few minutes after viewing to think of some additional possibilities. They will do this in the center column of their Hollywood or History? Graphic Organizer. (5 min)

3. Show the short compilation clip of the Whacking Day episode from the resource list above. This short is a summary of the entire episode by taking several of the major scenes and splicing them together into a four-minute video. This is an appetizer before having further conversation about the episode in its entirety. (5 min)

4. Using a Think-Pair-Share strategy, have students discuss what they took away from the episode clip for approximately five minutes before leading the class whole group in a discussion over the impact Whacking Day has on Springfield. (15 min)

5. Lead students in a whole group discussion on analyzing the impact of a change in public policy on consumers, producers, workers, savers, and investors, particularly focusing in on examples showcasing how public approval has impacted "what is produced" and how changes in governmental policies have also impacted the economic choices that various stakeholders have made. This is a great time to pull out the "Strange and Fun Holidays" source from the resource list above. *What are the economic consequences/benefits of any of the holidays listed there?* (20 min)

6. To close the first day of the lesson, have students make a prediction about what they anticipate might see in Springfield if Whacking Day was no longer a celebration for the town. (10 min)

Day 2

1. Begin the second day of instruction by asking students to share their predictions from the close of the lesson on Day 1. Continue by showing the Whacking Day episode in its entirety. (25 min)

2. After showing the episode in its entirety, have a brief discussion over whether or not their predictions appeared to be correct or

34   HOLLYWOOD OR HISTORY?

not, and then have students spend 10 minutes reading the article "Holidays are Serious Business." (20 min)
3. Close class with quick argumentative writing over whether Whacking Day should have been discontinued, utilizing some of the economic examples from some of the readings as the source for their evidence. (10 min)

Differentiation

Scaffolds: Students should have extra time to complete the Formative/Summative Assessments, or reduce the amount of writing. Students could also be assigned a scribe or respond orally to the prompts.

ESL Interventions: The episodes of *The Simpsons*, if viewed through Disney+, can be broadcast in a number of languages.

Extensions:
- Have students read the article "Could Adding a New Public Holiday Boost the Economy?" and write a brief proposal for a new holiday that could benefit their local communities.
- Students can make the New Public Holiday campaign larger than the classroom by also creating some promotional materials to underscore why the community should jump on board with their new holiday.

REFERENCES

Madowo, L. (2020, June 28). *Could adding a new public holiday boost the economy?* BBC Worklife. https://www.bbc.com/worklife/article/20200629-could-adding-a-new-public-holiday-boost-the-economy

Organisation for Economic Co-operation and Development. (n.d.) *Holidays are a serious business.* https://www.oecd.org/general/focus/holidaysareaseriousbusiness.htm

Swartzwelder, J. (Writer), & Lynch, J. (Director). (1993, April 29). Whacking day (Season 4, Episode 20) [TV series episode]. In A. Jean, M. Reiss, J. L. Brooks, M. Groening, & S. Simon (Executive Producers), *The Simpsons.* Gracie Films; Twentieth Century Fox Film Corporation.

Time and Date. (n.d.). *Fun holidays - Funny, random & weird holidays.* https://www.timeanddate.com/holidays/fun/

Wikipedia. (n.d.). *Economics of Christmas.* https://en.wikipedia.org/wiki/Economics_of_Christmas

Hollywood or History?

"Whacking Day"

Evaluate each source provided and summarize your observations and analysis in corresponding spaces provided. In the section located at the bottom of the page, explain whether you think the scenes from *The Simpsons* episode "Whacking Day" should be evaluated as accurate accounts of history (in terms of how we celebrate holidays) and economics, pure Hollywood creations, or a mixture of both. Use examples from your sources/documents to explain your answer.

Source	"Whacking Day"

36 HOLLYWOOD OR HISTORY?

What do you think? Hollywood or History?

For Further Viewing

With over 700 episodes to choose from, there are more episodes of *The Simpsons* that could be used to teach the theme of *Culture*. Here are a few other suggestions:

Featuring Apu

There are many episodes that feature Apu, and therefore could be examined for stereotypes of Indian culture. Here are two:

The Two Mrs. Nahasapeemapetilons (1997, Season 9, Episode 7)
This episode focuses on Apu and his arranged wedding to Manjula, which of course takes place in the Simpsons' backyard. (Written by Richard Appel, Directed by Steven Dean Moore)

No Good Read Goes Unpunished (2018, Season 29, Episode 15)
Considered the show's "response" to the Hari Kondabolu documentary, Marge discovers that a book she loved as a kid would be considered racist now. Lisa's character comments "what are you going to do?" a response that showrunner Al Jean later apologized for (Parker, 2018). (Written by Jeff Westbrook, Directed by Mark Kirkland)

Teaching About Cultural Stereotypes

The Simpsons have traveled to many different areas across the world over their decades on the air. Like the lesson using "The Town" and "Bart vs. Australia," any of these episodes could be used to examine the cultural stereotypes that the show has often reinforced.

A Streetcar Named Marge (1992, Season 4, Episode 2)
Marge stars in a play based on *A Streetcar Named Desire*. Roughly 17 minutes into the episode, the play features a song that negatively portrays the city of New Orleans, which angered many residents at the time (Lorando, 1992). (Written by Jeff Martin, Directed by Rich Moore)

Thirty Minutes Over Tokyo (1999, Season 10, Episode 23)
The Simpsons travel to Japan on a discounted vacation but must compete on a Japanese game show to have enough money to travel home. Many Japanese people found this episode offensive to their culture. (Written by Donick Cary and Dan Greaney, Directed by Jim Reardon)

Simpson Safari (2001, Season 12, Episode 17)

The Simpsons win a trip to Africa and travel to an unnamed country there, reinforcing the stereotype that Africa is a monolith of culture. (Written by John Swartzwelder, Directed by Mark Kirkland)

Blame It On Lisa (2002, Season 13, Episode 15)

The family goes to Brazil to find Lisa's pen pal, who has been kidnapped. The Brazilian government condemned this episode as full of harmful and inaccurate stereotypes of Brazil and the tourist board of Rio de Janiero threatened legal action (BBC News, 2002). (Written by Bob Bendetson, Directed by Steven Dean Moore)

The Regina Monologues (2003, Season 15, Episode 4)

Bart comes into some money and takes the family to England, with a special appearance by then Prime Minister Tony Blair—the only head of government to ever guest star on the show. (Written by John Swartzwelder, Directed by Mark Kirkland)

Goo Goo Gai Pan (2005, Season 16, Episode 12)

In this episode, Marge's sister Selma adopts a baby from China and Homer must pretend he is Selma's husband to evade the strict Chinese adoption laws. (Written by Dana Gould, Directed by Lance Kramer)

Little Big Girl (2007, Season 18, Episode 12)

Lamenting the Simpsons lack of cultural heritage, Lisa pretends to have native American ancestry to do well on a school multicultural project. This episode has many cultural stereotypes of Indigenous people, but also addresses the issue of cultural appropriation. (Written by Don Payne, Directed by Raymond S. Persi)

MyPods and Boomsticks (2008, Season 20, Episode 7)

This episode is about Islamophobia and the harmful stereotypes of Muslims that many people in Springfield have once a new family moves in. (Written by Marc Wilmore, Directed by Steven Dean Moore)

Havana Wild Weekend (2016, Season 28, Episode 7)

The family travels to Cuba to secure health care for Grandpa Simpson, but Grandpa rediscovers his youth there and wants to stay. (Written by Deb Lacusta, Dan Castellaneta, and Peter Tilden, Directed by Bob Anderson)

Throw Grampa from the Dane (2018, Season 29, Episode 20)

The Simpsons visit Denmark after they get money for an insurance payment. Marge and Lisa fall in love with Danish culture. (Written by Rob LaZebnik, Directed by Michael Polcino)

Chapter 1: Culture   39

D'Oh Canada (2019, Season 30, Episode 21)
Lisa moves to Canada and enjoys it more than living in America. The rest of the family rescues her by crossing the Detroit River. This episode features many stereotypes of Canadians, and even a few of upstate New Yorkers. (Written by Tim Long and Miranda Thompson, Directed by Matthew Mastuk)

Other Episodes About Culture

The Simpsons also feature episodes about art and music as culture, including any that feature jazz musician Bleeding Gums Murphy.

Moaning Lisa (1990, Season 1, Episode 6)
Lisa is depressed, and she meets jazz musician Bleeding Gums Murphy, who encourages her to channel her sadness into her saxophone playing. (Written by Al Jean and Mike Reiss, Directed by Wes Archer)

Round Springfield (1995, Season 6, Episode 22)
Bleeding Gums Murphy passes away and Lisa sets her sights on honoring his memory by broadcasting his one album to Springfield. Lisa is ultimately successful, and once again channels her grief over his death into her music. (Written by Joshua Sternin and Jeffrey Ventimilia, Directed by Steven Dean Moore)

I'm Just a Girl Who Can't Say D'Oh (2019, Season 30, Episode 20)
This episode is about local theater, as Lisa writes a Hamilton-style play about Jebidiah Springfield. (Written by Jeff Martin and Jenna Martin, Directed by Michael Polcino)

Now Museum, Now You Don't (2020, Season 32, Episode 3)
While Lisa is home sick, she reads a book about western art. The episode is broken into shorter stories about artists Leonardo DaVinci, Henri de Toulouse-Lautrec, Frida Kahlo, and Diego Rivera. (Written by Dan Greaney, Directed by Timothy Bailey)

REFERENCES

BBC News. (2002, April 15). *Simpsons apologise to Rio*. www.bbc.co.uk

Lorando, M. (1992, October 1). 'The Simpsons' takes a shot at Crescent City. *The Times-Picayune*.

Parker, R. (2018, April 13). The Simpsons showrunner vows to find "right" answer to Apu controversy. *Hollywood Reporter*. https://www.hollywoodreporter.com/tv/tv-news/simpsons-showrunner-addresses-apu-controversy-vows-find-right-answer-1102561/

CHAPTER 2

TIME, CONTINUITY, AND CHANGE

History is an account of the past. Seems like a simple statement, but what is considered the past? Is there one account of history or many? How do we make sense of these accounts? This chapter focuses on the NCSS theme most closely associated with the discipline of history: Time, Continuity, and Change. Analyzing multiple accounts of historical events helps us to be able to identify how society has changed and what has continually stayed the same. We learn more about how institutions, people, and ideas have developed over time by examining a wide variety of sources. In many ways, every chapter in this book looks at the themes of social studies through a historical perspective, but in this chapter the authors use *The Simpsons* to examine historical preservation, historical memory, and interpretation.

This chapter begins with a lesson from Martin Castro using the classic Season 7 episode "Lisa the Iconoclast" (Collier & Anderson, 1996), where residents of Springfield are forced to confront an alternative narrative about their beloved founding father Jebediah Springfield. This episode, and Castro's lesson, allows the viewer to examine historical evidence and question the role that monuments play in the heroification of historical figures—even fictional ones. Castro designed a lesson that would be easy to teach in a virtual classroom, complete with digital resources that are ready to use.

Over the years, *The Simpsons* has retold their own versions of historical events using characters from the show "playing roles." These episodes are often broken into smaller segments to show a focused interpretation of a particular event or person. For example, Lisa has played Joan of Arc

---

Hollywood or History?: An Inquiry-Based Strategy for Using The Simpsons to Teach Social Studies, pp. 41–67
Copyright © 2024 by Information Age Publishing
www.infoagepub.com
All rights of reproduction in any form reserved.

41

42 HOLLYWOOD OR HISTORY?

(Season 13, Episode 14), Aunt Selma has played Queen Elizabeth I (Season 20, Episode 20), and Homer has played Henry VIII (Season 15, Episode 11) (for more examples, see the "For Further Viewing" section at the end of this chapter). Amy Allen designed a lesson using a segment about Lewis and Clark (played by Lenny and Carl) from the episode "Margical History Tour" (Kelley & Anderson, 2004) and comparing that interpretation to primary sources from *An Indigenous People's History of the United States for Young People* (Dunbar-Ortiz, 2019).

Of course, the longevity of *The Simpsons* also means the show itself can be a historical source. It also means the show has been said to "predict the future." In the "For Further Viewing" section, check out episodes written more than 20 years ago that are good time capsules of the 1990s era, as well as episodes that have been particularly prophetic in years past.

REFERENCES

Collier, J. (Writer), & Anderson, M. B. (Director). (1996, February 18). Lisa the iconoclast (Season 7, Episode 16) [TV series episode]. In B. Oakley, J. Weinstein, J. L. Brooks, M. Groening, & S. Simon (Executive Producers), *The Simpsons*. Gracie Films; Twentieth Century Fox Film Corporation.

Dunbar-Ortiz, R. (2019). *An Indigenous peoples' history of the United States for young people*. Beacon Press.

Kelley, B. (Writer), & Anderson, M. B. (Director). (2004, February 8). Margical history tour (Season 15, Episode 11) [TV series episode]. In A. Jean, J. L. Brooks, M. Groening, & S. Simon (Executive Producers), *The Simpsons*. Gracie Films; Twentieth Century Fox Film Corporation.

"History Hath a Silver Tongue:" Protecting Our Ideals, or Refusing to Change?

Martin Castro

EPISODE:
"Lisa the Iconoclast" (1996, Season 7, Episode 16)

Grade	Subject	Topic
6–12	United States History	Historiography

Estimated Time Needed for Lesson
240 (four hour-long lessons)

State Standards

State	Standards and Descriptions
California	Chronological and Spatial Thinking 1. Students compare the present with the past, evaluating the consequences of past events and decisions and determining the lessons that were learned. Historical Research, Evidence, and Point of View 1. Students distinguish valid arguments from fallacious arguments in historical interpretations. 2. Students identify bias and prejudice in historical interpretations. 3. Students evaluate major debates among historians concerning alternative interpretations of the past, including an analysis of authors' use of evidence and the distinctions between sound generalizations and misleading oversimplifications.
	Historical Interpretation 3. Students interpret past events and issues within the context in which an event unfolded rather than solely in terms of present-day norms and values.

Massachusetts	3. Organize information and data from multiple primary and secondary sources.
	4. Analyze the purpose and point of view of each source; distinguish opinion from fact.
	5. Evaluate the credibility, accuracy, and relevance of each source.
	6. Argue or explain conclusions, using valid reasoning and evidence.
	7. Determine next steps and take informed action, as appropriate.
New York	Students will be able to understand historical sources, understand the difference between primary and secondary sources, and how to identify and research using reliable sources.

Common Core Standards

Standard	Description
CCSS.ELA-LITERACY.RH.6-8.1	Cite specific textual evidence to support analysis of primary and secondary sources.
CCSS.ELA-LITERACY.RH.9-10.2	Determine the central ideas or information of a primary or secondary source; provide an accurate summary of how key events or ideas developed the course of the text.
CCSS.ELA-LITERACY.RH.11-12.2	Determine the central ideas or information of a primary or secondary source; provide an accurate summary that makes clear the relationships among the key details and ideas.

NCSS C3 Framework

Dimension	Description
Developing Questions and Planning Inquiries	D1.2.9-12. Explain points of agreement and disagreement experts have about interpretations and applications of disciplinary concepts and ideas associated with a compelling question.
Applying Disciplinary Concepts and Tools (History)	D2.His.8.9-12. Analyze how current interpretations of the past are limited by the extent to which available historical sources represent perspectives of people at the time.

Chapter 2: Time, Continuity, and Change 45

Evaluating Sources and Using Evidence	D3.3.9-12. Identify evidence that draws information directly and substantially from multiple sources to detect inconsistencies in evidence in order to revise or strengthen claims.
Communicating Conclusions and Taking Informed Action	D4.2.9-12. Construct explanations using sound reasoning, correct sequence (linear or nonlinear), examples, and details with significant and pertinent information and data, while acknowledging the strengths and weaknesses of the explanation given its purpose (e.g., cause and effect, chronological, procedural, technical).

NCSS Core Themes and Description

Theme	Description
I. Culture	Through the study of culture and cultural diversity, learners understand how human beings create, learn, share, and adapt to culture, and appreciate the role of culture in shaping their lives and society, as well the lives and societies of others.
II. Time, Continuity, and Change	Through the study of the past and its legacy, learners examine the institutions, values, and beliefs of people in the past, acquire skills in historical inquiry and interpretation, and gain an understanding of how important historical events and developments have shaped the modern world
IV. Individual Development and Identity	Personal identity is shaped by family, peers, culture, and institutional influences. Through this theme, students examine the factors that influence an individual's personal identity, development, and actions.
V. Individuals, Groups, and Institutions	Institutions such as families and civic, educational, governmental, and religious organizations exert a major influence on people's lives. This theme allows students to understand how institutions are formed, maintained, and changed, and to examine their influence.

Handouts/Materials/Web Links

Google Sites:

- Martin Castro's Google Site for this lesson: https://sites.google.com/view/hollywood-or-history-mr-martin/home?authuser=0

46   HOLLYWOOD OR HISTORY?

- o This features all the Google Slides, documents, and content mentioned in this chapter, in helpful digital versions that are ready to use
- Simpsons Evidence Google Site: https://sites.google.com/ichs-bronx.org/simpsons-evidence-english/home
- Christopher Columbus Evidence Google Site: https://sites.google.com/ichsbronx.org/columbus-evidence-home/home
  - o This is a collection of the primary and secondary sources listed below

Digital Handouts on Google Slides:
- Organize the Sources Digital Handout: https://docs.google.com/presentation/d/1qRrHToQh4kQw7fzd1KZa5gCfrmyaI0yDPewpnacKuZQ/edit#slide=id.g127124fc485_0_67
- Historical Elements in *The Simpsons* Digital Handout: https://docs.google.com/presentation/d/1hQ16ie7xvR-eTTpvoUYtMzapFcIfqkYDtnChNg-DfZQ/edit#slide=id.g1283fb34002_0_0
- The Purpose of Memorialization Digital Handout: https://docs.google.com/presentation/d/1pEZE6R3twT1LMAvwIuFwH9G0KK0jnDWI8JimH2CPOZg/edit#slide=id.g1283e0a288d_0_0

Handouts:
- Support Your Simpsons Claim
- Columbus Reliable Research
- Hollywood or History? Graphic Organizer

Episode Clips and Video Content:
- "Lisa the Iconoclast," Season 7, Episode 16
  - o **Clip 1:** 0:00–11:00
  - o **Clip 2:** 11:00–end

Primary Sources
- *Columbus reports on his first voyage, 1493* https://www.gilderlehrman.org/history-resources/spotlight-primary-source/columbus-reports-his-first-voyage-1493#:~:text=When%20Columbus%20arrived%20back%20in
- Bartolomé de las Casas (1552). *A Short Account of the Destruction of The Indies.* http://nationalhumanitiescenter.org/pds/amerbegin/contact/text7/casas_destruction.pdf

Secondary Sources:

Chapter 2: Time, Continuity, and Change   47

- CBS Boston News. (2020). Beheaded Christopher Columbus statue in Boston will be removed from North End Park [Review of *Beheaded Christopher Columbus Statue in Boston Will Be Removed From North End Park*]. In *CBS Boston News*. https://www.youtube.com/watch?v=N8ggEA7MR-M
- *History vs. Christopher Columbus - Alex Gendler*. Ted Ed, YouTube. https://youtu.be/GD3dgiDreGc
- Mervosh, S., Romero, S., & Tompkins, L. (2020, June 16). Reconsidering the past, one statue at a time. *The New York Times*. https://www.nytimes.com/2020/06/16/us/protests-statues-reckoning.html
- NBC4 Columbus News. (2020). Christopher Columbus statue removed from city hall [Review of *Christopher Columbus statue removed from city hall*]. In *NBC4 Columbus News*. https://www.youtube.com/watch?v=N8ggEA7MR-M
- Viola, J. M. (2017, October 9). Opinion | Tearing down statues of Columbus also tears down my history. *The New York Times*. https://www.nytimes.com/2017/10/09/opinion/christopher-columbus-day-statue.html
- Zinn, H. (2017). *A people's history of the United States*. Harper, an Imprint of Harper Collins Publishers. (Original work published 1980)

Guiding Questions

Primary Questions:
- How do we learn about the past?
- What makes a historical source reliable?

Secondary Questions:
- Should we question our historical heroes?
- What is the purpose of memorialization?
- What should be the fate of controversial memorials?
- Who decides which memorials are created or accepted?
- What message is it sending if the memorials to Columbus stay in their current locations and are continued to be honored?

Important Vocabulary

Memorial: Something, especially a structure, established to remind people of a person or event.

48 HOLLYWOOD OR HISTORY?

Primary source: Immediate, first-hand accounts of a topic, from people who had a direct connection with it.

Secondary source: Sources that are one step removed from primary sources, though they often quote or otherwise use primary sources, but add a layer of interpretation and analysis.

Assessment Strategies

Formative Assessments:
- Organize the Sources Digital Handout
- The Purpose of Memorialization Digital Handout

Summative Assessments:
- Support Your Simpsons Claim
- Hollywood or History? Graphic Organizer

Sparking Strategy/Warm-Up

Lesson Introduction

Students must review a list of sources (textbooks, old letters, historians, etc.) and decide if they should be considered a primary or secondary source. Students then categorize these using the Organize the Sources Digital Handout. As a class, students will review their choices and discuss any disagreements they may have about their choices. Ask the students: *Which type of source do you believe is more reliable, a primary or a secondary source?* (20 min)

Lesson Procedures

Day 1

1. Students will identify the primary and secondary sources in "Lisa the Iconoclast" that are connected to the question: *How do we learn about the life of Jebediah Springfield?* Have the students watch the first half of the episode, up to the segment where the historian banned Homer and Lisa from the museum. During the clip, students will take notes of the primary and secondary sources they see. (11 min)
    Clip 1: 0:00–11:00

Chapter 2: Time, Continuity, and Change 49

2. Students can create a simple T-chart for their list, or use the Historical Elements in *The Simpsons* Digital Handout (20 min)
3. As a whole class, discuss: *Based on the episode so far, which type of source do you think would give us the most reliable information about Jebediah Springfield?* (10 min)

Day 2

1. To review from Day 1, ask the students to write down their response to these questions: *What do you prefer: a beautiful lie or an ugly truth? What is an example of both of those?* Share their answers as a whole group. Explain during today's lesson, they will determine whether Lisa made the correct choice about Jebediah Springfield. (20 min)
2. Watch the last half of the episode "Lisa the Iconoclast" (or, if time permits, start from the beginning as a review). Explain that they need to keep track of supporting evidence they see for the question: *Do you think Lisa Simpson made the right decision at the end of the episode? (10–25 min)*
3. As a whole group, have students share their responses. To keep the conversation going, ask these sub questions: *Should people always tell the truth despite the consequences? Who do you trust to provide you with the truth? What should we do to our heroes when we discover they are actually villains? How does memorialization affect history? Is history about discovering the truth?* (20 min)

Day 3

1. Ask the students as a whole group: *What do you think is the purpose of memorialization? What is the purpose of creating memorials to people in the past? What is an example you can think of?* (5 min)
2. Individually or in small groups, students should complete The Purpose of Memorialization Digital Handout using a memorial from their local community or the United States. Have some students share what they found. (20 min)
3. Explain that in Days 1 and 2, they found out that Jebediah Springfield may not be all that he seems. To most of Springfield, he is seen as the founding father and hero of the town who inspires so many citizens of Springfield. However, there seems to be unearthed evidence that demonstrates that he is not all he appears to be. In their writing assignment, they must decide on the following: *Should Jebediah Springfield still be honored?*

50 HOLLYWOOD OR HISTORY?

4. Give students the Support Your Simpsons Claim Handout and explain that their position must include supporting evidence and an analysis that explains how the evidence supports your position. Students must choose one of the two positions for this writing assignment (No, Jebediah Springfield should not continue to be honored and Yes, Jebediah Springfield should continue to be honored). Students should use the Simpsons Evidence Google Site to complete their handout. It has a combination of evidence that was used in the episode, along with crafted evidence that could have existed in the episode of *The Simpsons*. (35 min)
5. The handout is a guide to completing the writing assignment, which can be given as homework or given an extra day if not completed on Day 3.

Day 4

1. Begin by playing the video from CBS News Boston about the decapitation of a statue of Columbus. Ask the students as a whole group: *Do you think what they did to the statue in the video is wrong?* (5 min)
2. Explain that in Days 1–3, we learned about a fictional character named Jebediah Springfield who was celebrated as a hero, but it was discovered that he had a problematic past. Today, we are looking at a real-life controversial historical figure who has lots of memorials honoring him throughout the country: Christopher Columbus. Although he, too, was celebrated like Jebediah Springfield, in recent years there has been more information brought to life that has made people want to destroy Columbus statues like we saw in the video during the warm-up.
3. Use the Columbus Evidence Google Site to find information about Columbus that would make someone want to destroy the statues that honor him. Students must read through the various historical sources connected to Columbus to find a specific quote that demonstrates why someone would believe that Columbus does not deserve to be honored. (30 min)
4. After finding quotes, the students should write a response to the following question: *Why do you think some people would want to destroy statues and memorials dedicated to Christopher Columbus?* Students must use a quote, the source of the quote, and an explanation of how this evidence demonstrates their position in their response. This can also be given as homework (15 min)
5. Have students complete the Hollywood or History? Graphic Organizer in small groups to compare the reactions of the towns-

Chapter 2: Time, Continuity, and Change   51

people in Springfield to the reactions of those learning about the destruction of statues of Christopher Columbus, using evidence. As a group, they will determine how close "Lisa the Iconoclast" is to the current debate over memorials. (15 min)

Differentiation

Scaffolds: This lesson is meant to be done with technology in the classroom. This is meant to encourage tech literacy in students but also allows more tech savvy educators the opportunity to use platforms like Nearpod in their classrooms. It also allows students an opportunity to use tech as supports where they may deem necessary. The text in the primary and secondary sources (especially regarding Columbus) may be too advanced in English for students. For this reason, the sources have been translated to ease the cognitive load of having to read an older text in a second language.

ESL Interventions: Throughout the entire lesson, resources, and assignments are translated into English, Spanish, and French. Access these through Martin Castro's Google Site. There are translations for directions during presentations, the evidence websites have the sources in multiple languages, and the episode of the Simpsons that serve as the basis for these lessons has the English, Spanish, and French versions linked.

Extensions:

- Students can give their own answer to the question: *Should statues of Columbus be removed?* They can find their own sources using guidance from the Columbus Reliable Research Handout to support their claim.

REFERENCES

CBS Boston. (2020, June 10). Beheaded Christopher Columbus statue in Boston will be removed from North End Park [Video]. *YouTube.* https://www.youtube.com/watch?v=N8ggEA7MR-M

Collier, J. (Writer), & Anderson, M. B. (Director). (1996, February 18). Lisa the iconoclast (Season 7, Episode 16) [TV series episode]. In B. Oakley, J. Weinstein, J. L. Brooks, M. Groening, & S. Simon (Executive Producers), *The Simpsons.* Gracie Films; Twentieth Century Fox Film Corporation.

de las Casas, B. (1552). *A short account of the destruction of the Indies.* http://nationalhumanitiescenter.org/pds/amerbegin/contact/text7/casas_destruction.pdf

52 HOLLYWOOD OR HISTORY?

Gilder Lehrman Institute of American History (n.d.). *Columbus reports on his first voyage, 1493*. https://www.gilderlehrman.org/history-resources/spotlight-primary-source/columbus-reports-his-first-voyage-1493#:~:text=When%20Columbus%20arrived%20back%20in

Mervosh, S., Romero, S., & Tompkins, L. (2020, June 16). Reconsidering the past, one statue at a time. *The New York Times*. https://www.nytimes.com/2020/06/16/us/protests-statues-reckoning.html

NBC4 Columbus. (2020, July 1). Christopher Columbus statue removed from city hall [Video]. YouTube. https://www.youtube.com/watch?v=N8ggEA7MR-M

TED-Ed. (2014, October 13). *History vs. Christopher Columbus - Alex Gendler* [Video]. YouTube. https://youtu.be/GD3dgiDreGc

Viola, J. M. (2017, October 9). Tearing down statues of Columbus also tears down my history. *The New York Times*. https://www.nytimes.com/2017/10/09/opinion/christopher-columbus-day-statue.html

Zinn, H. (1980). *A people's history of the United States*. Harper.

APPENDIX A

Support Your Simpsons Claim

Directions: Share your opinion about Jebediah Springfield using evidence in order to complete this assignment. Visit this website to find evidence to support your claim (opinion and reason).

Directions	Complete Your Work Here
OPINION AND REASON Choose one of the opinions to focus on to answer this question: Should Jebediah Springfield still be honored? You must also write an explanation of why you Option 1 or Option 2. NOTE: Delete the option you will not use.	Option 1: Jebediah Springfield should not be honored anymore because (write your explanation here) Option 2: Jebediah Springfield should still continue to be honored because (write your explanation here)

Chapter 2: Time, Continuity, and Change   53

EVIDENCE	Source:
Use the Simpsons Evidence Google Site to find evidence that supports your opinion. You must include the name of the source when writing your evidence that supports your opinion.	Quote or summary of information (copy a maximum of 2 sentences):
ANALYSIS Explain how the EVIDENCE connects to your opinion. Explain how the EVIDENCE supports your opinion.	This evidence supports my opinion because

Hollywood or History?

"History Hath a Silver Tongue"

In this inquiry lesson, students are asked to review the reaction of the public when the mythos behind one of their historical heroes is challenged due to previously unknown evidence. In this case, students are comparing reactions of the fictional town of Springfield with real-world reactions upon learning that a nation's hero turns out not to be as heroic as they were once considered. Review the following sources below using *The Simpsons* episode, "Lisa the Iconoclast," as an anchor for how the public may react upon learning that a national hero is not all he seems to be. Read the sources about the actions of Columbus and the public's reactions to Christopher Columbus's life and actions during his discovery and conquest of the Americas. Compare these reactions to how the varied characters on *The Simpsons* reacted to being confronted with the "truth" about Jebediah Springfield, the hero and founder of their beloved town. Are the reactions of the public in *The Simpsons* pure Hollywood creations, or a mixture of both. Use examples from your sources/documents to explain your answer.

Actions of Columbus	Reactions from "Lisa the Iconoclast"	Reactions of the Public
–**Excerpt from Howard Zinn's** *A People's History of the United States* –**Columbus reports on his first voyage, 1493**		–*NY Times* **Article: Reconsidering the Past, One Statue At A Time** –*NY Times* **Article: Tearing Down Statues of Columbus Also Tears Down My History** –**NBC4 News Video: Christopher Columbus Statue Removed From City Hall** –**CBS Boston Video: Beheaded Christopher Columbus Statue in Boston Will Be Removed From North-End Park**

Chapter 2: Time, Continuity, and Change   55

What Do You Think? Hollywood or History?

APPENDIX B

Columbus Reliable Research

Directions: Use the Reliable News Website List to find a reliable answer to this question: Should statues of Columbus be removed?

You must find an answer to this question that you agree with, and you think is a good reason to remove or not remove statues of Columbus.

Use this presentation to know how to search for reliable information using Google and the reliable website list above.

In order to complete this assignment, you must provide all of the following:

A clear answer to this question provided in the article: Should statues of Columbus be removed?	
Name of the reliable news website	
The URL of the article	
The Title of the News Article	
The Author of the News Article	
The Date of the News Article	

Lewis and Clark's Expedition to the West

Amy Allen

EPISODE:
"Margical History Tour" (2004, Season 15, Episode 11)

Grade	Subject	Topic
4–5	United States History	Lewis and Clark

Era Under Study	Estimated Time Needed for Lesson
The New Nation 1783–1815	70–90 minutes

State Standards

State	Standards and Descriptions
California	5.8 Students trace the colonization, immigration, and settlement patterns of the American people from 1789 to the mid-1800s, with emphasis on the role of economic incentives, effects of the physical and political geography, and transportation systems. 3. Demonstrate knowledge of the explorations of the trans-Mississippi West following the Louisiana Purchase (e.g., Meriwether Lewis and William Clark, Zebulon Pike, John Fremont).
Georgia	SS4H3 Explain westward expansion in America. c. Describe territorial expansion with emphasis on the Louisiana Purchase, the Lewis and Clark expedition, and the acquisitions of Texas (the Alamo and independence), Oregon (Oregon Trail), and California (Gold Rush and the development of mining towns)
Texas	(4) History. The student understands political, economic, and social changes that occurred in the United States during the 19th century. The student is expected to: (C) identify significant events and concepts associated with U.S. territorial expansion, including the Louisiana Purchase, the expedition of Lewis and Clark, and Manifest Destiny.

Chapter 2: Time, Continuity, and Change   57

Common Core Standards

Standard	Description
CCSS.ELA-LITERACY. RL.4.7	Make connections between the text of a story or drama and a visual or oral presentation of the text, identifying where each version reflects specific descriptions and directions in the text.
CCSS.ELA-LITERACY. RL.5.3	Compare and contrast two or more characters, settings, or events in a story or drama, drawing on specific details in the text.

NCSS C3 Framework

Dimension	Description
Developing Questions and Planning Inquiries	D1.2.3-5. Identify disciplinary concepts and ideas associated with a compelling question that are open to different interpretations.
Applying Disciplinary Concepts and Tools (History)	D2.His.10.3-5. Compare information provided by different historical sources about the past.
Evaluating Sources and Using Evidence	D3.3.3-5. Identify evidence that draws information from multiple sources in response to compelling questions.
Communicating Conclusions and Taking Informed Action	D4.1.3-5. Construct arguments using claims and evidence from multiple sources.

NCSS Core Themes and Description

Theme	Description
II. Time, Continuity, and Change	Through the study of the past and its legacy, learners examine the institutions, values, and beliefs of people in the past, acquire skills in historical inquiry and interpretation, and gain an understanding of how important historical events and developments have shaped the modern world.

Handouts/Materials/Web Links

Handout/Materials:

- Hollywood or History? Triple Venn Diagram Graphic Organizer
- Summative Writing Assignment Rubric

58   HOLLYWOOD OR HISTORY?

Episode Clips and Video Content:
- "Margical History Tour," Season 15, Episode 11
  - o **Clip:** 7:57-12:40
  - o *Note: Toward the end of the clip, Lewis and Clark reference "mermaid sex." For elementary age students, I recommend pre-watching this clip to determine whether to end the clip before this reference or edit it out while watching.*

Primary Sources:
- Rudersdorf, A. (2015). *The Lewis and Clark Expedition. Digital Public Library of America.* http://dp.la/primary-source-sets/the-lewis-and-clark-expedition.

Secondary Sources:
- Student textbook pages covering Lewis and Clark, Sacagawea, and/or westward expansion
- Dunbar-Ortiz, R. (2019). *An Indigenous peoples' history of the United States for young people.* Beacon Press.

Guiding Questions

Primary Question:
- Were Lewis and Clark successful in their expedition to the west?

Secondary Questions:
- Does the way we tell history matter?
- Whose perspectives are missing from a reading or retelling?

Important Vocabulary

Expansion: The process of becoming greater in size, number, or amount

Indigenous: Also referred to as first peoples, first nations, aboriginal peoples, or native peoples, indigenous describes groups who are culturally and ethnically distinct and are native to a place which has been colonized and settled by a later ethnic group.

Primary source: An artifact, document, diary, manuscript, autobiography, recording, or any other source of information that was created at the time under study. It serves as an original source of information about the topic.

Assessment Strategies

Formative Assessments:
- Hollywood or History? Triple Venn Diagram Graphic Organizer
- Line of contention activity

Summative Assessments:
- Writing activity

Sparking Strategy/Warm-Up

Lesson Introduction

Divide students into small groups. Provide each group with a set of primary source photographs, including images of Lewis, Clark, the Sacagawea dollar, a telescope, Shoshone women, and men from the Discovery Corps building a camp. As students look at the collection of pictures ask them if they know who is in each picture and what event in history they think this group of pictures might represent. After giving groups time to brainstorm and share their prediction with the class, tell students today they will be learning about Lewis and Clark's expedition to the west. These pictures are primary sources from the Lewis and Clark expedition. (10 min)

Lesson Procedures

1. As a whole class, read textbook chapters about the Louisiana Purchase/Lewis and Clark aloud with students, pausing to ask questions designed to help students think about what they are reading and make connections to other historical and/or current events. Ask students: *Whose perspectives are missing from this conversation? If we wanted to know more about Lewis and Clark's Expedition to the West, whose perspective might we want to include?* (5 min)
2. Read aloud an excerpt from *An Indigenous People's History of the United States* (begin at the bottom of page p. 104 and read through p. 107). While reading, the teacher should pause to "think aloud," explicitly asking questions or making statements that model connections (or the lack of connection) between the first and second reading. (5 min)
3. With their initial group and using the Hollywood or History? graphic organizer for the lesson, ask students to complete the

60   HOLLYWOOD OR HISTORY?

top section. *What does their textbook say about Lewis and Clark's Expedition to the West? What does* An Indigenous People's History *say? Which events are the same, and which are different?* Remind students they can use the "Five W's Plus How" to help fill out the Hollywood or History? graphic organizer. (10 min)

4. Tell students that in movies or cartoons, writers and actors will try to portray events that happened throughout history, but they don't always get it right. Explain that today we are going to watch a short clip from the cartoon *The Simpsons* that tells the story of Lewis and Clark's expedition to the west. As you are watching, think about whether this portrayal of history aligns with our textbook, the Indigenous perspective, both, or neither. (5 min)

    Clip: 7:57–12:40

5. Divide students into small groups and ask them to discuss whether this portrayal of history aligns with the perspective presented in the textbook, the Indigenous perspective, both, or neither. Record example of how it aligns with each perspective on the bottom portion of the Hollywood or History? graphic organizer. (10 min)

6. Using their Hollywood or History? graphic organizer as a resource, ask students to evaluate the accuracy of the "Margical History Tour" episode clip. Place signs across the room labeled 0%, 25%, 50%, 75%, and 100%. Each student must physically move to the percentage they think best represents the amount of accurate knowledge in the clip. Once there, have students discuss with other students the parts they felt were accurate/inaccurate, then share with the class. (10 min)

7. Using the attached rubric as a summative assessment guide, ask students to write an appropriate length summary that addresses who Lewis and Clark were, provides reasons why they traveled to the west, and discusses whether this expedition was successful from more than one perspective. (15–30 min)

Differentiation

Scaffolds: A large portion of this lesson places students in small groups. Consider grouping students of varying ability levels together. For students who need additional scaffolding, when completing the Hollywood or History? graphic organizer, you may consider providing a word bank or chart explaining how to use the 5 W's + how as a guide for completing the activity.

ESL Interventions: In addition to the possible suggested scaffolds, teachers may wish to define additional vocabulary and key terms.

Extensions:

- Have students rewrite their textbook chapter to include more of an Indigenous perspective

REFERENCES AND RESOURCES FOR
TEACHERS AND STUDENTS

Blee, L. (2005). Completing Lewis and Clark's westward march. *Oregon Historical Quarterly, 106*(2), 239-245.

Chen, A. (2021, April 23). Guest review: An-Lon Chen's review of WHO WAS SACAGAWEA? by Judith Bloom Fradin and Dennis Brindell Fradin. *American Indians In Children's Literature.* https://americanindiansinchildrensliterature. blogspot.com/2021/04/guest-review-lon-chens-review-of-who.html

Conner, R. (2006). Our people have always been here. In A. M. Josephy Jr. (Ed.), *Lewis and Clark through Indian Eyes: Nine Indian writers on the legacy of the expedition* (pp. 85–123). Vintage Books.

Dunbar-Ortiz, R. (2019). *An Indigenous peoples' history of the United States for young people.* Beacon Press.

Kelley, B. (Writer), & Anderson, M. B. (Director). (2004, February 8). Margical history tour (Season 15, Episode 11) [TV series episode]. In A. Jean, J. L. Brooks, M. Groening, & S. Simon (Executive Producers), *The Simpsons.* Gracie Films; Twentieth Century Fox Film Corporation.

Rudersdorf, A. (2015). *The Lewis and Clark Expedition.* Digital Public Library of America, http://dp.la/primary-source-sets/the-lewis-and-clark-expedition

Schmitke, A., Sabzalian, L., Edmundson, J. (2020). *Teaching critically about Lewis and Clark: Challenging dominant narratives in K-12 curriculum.* Teacher's College Press.

Hollywood or History?

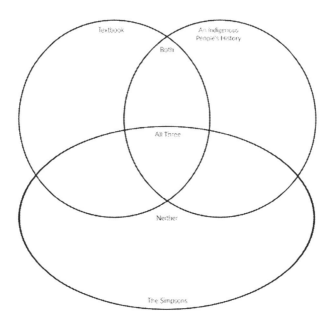

APPENDIX C

Rubric for Writing Assignment

	5-4	3-2	1	0
Lewis and Clark	Provides details about who Lewis and Clark were.	Provides details about Lewis or Clark.	Mentions Lewis and Clark but does not provide any additional details.	No mention of Lewis and Clark.
Expedition to the West	Provides multiple reasons why Lewis and Clark traveled to the West.	Provides two reasons why Lewis and Clark traveled to the West.	Provides one reason why Lewis and Clark traveled to the West.	Provides no reasons why Lewis and Clark traveled to the West.

Chapter 2: Time, Continuity, and Change   63

Success of Expedition	Provides examples of why this expedition was successful or unsuccessful from two perspectives	Provides examples of why this expedition was successful or unsuccessful from one perspective	Provides examples of why this expedition was successful or unsuccessful but does not reference perspective.	Provides no examples of why this expedition was successful or unsuccessful.
Use of Multiple Sources	References all three sources introduced in the lesson (textbook, *Indigenous Peoples Guide*, and Simpsons Episode).	References two of three sources introduced in the lesson (textbook, *Indigenous Peoples Guide*, and Simpsons Episode).	References one of three sources introduced in the lesson (textbook, *Indigenous Peoples Guide*, and Simpsons Episode).	References none of the sources introduced in the lesson (textbook, *Indigenous Peoples Guide*, and Simpsons Episode).
Writing Mechanics	Clearly written with no issues with previously introduced grammar, punctuation, or spelling rules.	Clearly written with few (at most) issues with grammar, punctuation, or spelling.	Issues with grammar, punctuation, or spelling interfere with readability.	

64 HOLLYWOOD OR HISTORY?

For Further Viewing

With over 700 episodes to choose from, there are more episodes of *The Simpsons* that could be used to teach the theme of Time, Continuity, and Change. Here are a few other suggestions:

Hollywood or History?

There are many episodes where *The Simpsons* depict a historical event or historical individual. These are great episodes to use the Hollywood or History? graphic organizer to identify how historically accurate these depictions are.

Treehouse of Horror VIII (1997, Season 9, Episode 4)
In the segment called "Easy-Bake Coven," Marge plays a woman accused of witchcraft in 1649—a nod to the Salem Witch Trials. Because this is a Halloween episode, the twist is that Marge is actually a witch! (Written by Mike Scully, David X. Cohen, and Ned Goldreyer, Directed by Mark Kirkland)

The Wizard of Evergreen Terrace (1998, Season 10, Episode 2)
This episode focuses on Thomas Edison, as Homer is inspired to invent something meaningful, just like Edison. Director Mark Kirkland visited the Thomas Edison National Historical Park in West Orange, New Jersey to make the site as historically accurate as possible in animation (Kirkland, 2007). (Written by John Swartzwelder, Directed by Mark Kirkland)

Tales from the Public Domain (2002, Season 13, Episode 14)
The segment "Hot Child in the City" tells the story of Joan of Arc in the Hundred Years War, where Joan of Arc is "played" by Lisa. (Written by Andrew Kriesberg, Josh Lieb, and Matt Warburton, Directed by Mike B. Anderson)

Helter Shelter (2002, Season 14, Episode 5)
In a parody of the PBS show *The 1900 House*, the Simpsons go on a reality show called "The 1895 Challenge" and are forced to adapt to living in the Victorian era for the purpose of the show. (Written by Brian Pollack and Mert Rich, Directed by Mark Kirkland)

Margical History Tour (2004, Season 15, Episode 11)
In the same episode that featured a parody of the Lewis and Clark expedition (see Amy Allen's lesson in this chapter), Homer plays Henry VIII.

Several female characters of Springfield (including Marge) play his many wives. (Written by Brian Kelley, Directed by Mike B. Anderson)

Treehouse of Horror XV (2004, Season 16, Episode 1)
Lisa and Bart are detectives in Victorian London (the year 1890) to solve a case of a Jack the Ripper-like serial killer named The Muttonchop Murderer in the segment called "Four Beheadings and a Funeral." (Written by Bill Odenkirk, Directed by David Silverman)

The Wettest Stories Ever Told (2006, Season 17, Episode 18)
Although segment "Mayflower Madman" mostly focuses on a love story between Homer and Marge from the 1600s, there are parts of the segment that tell the story of the "first Thanksgiving," including references to colonization of the Wampanoag tribe. (Written by Jeff Westbrook, Directed by Mike B. Anderson)

Love Springfieldian Style (2008, Season 19, Episode 12)-
This episode features three segments related to famous love stories. The first segment tells the story of Bonnie and Clyde (played by Marge and Homer, of course). (Written by Don Payne, Directed by Raymond S. Persi)

4 Great Women and a Manicure (2009, Season 20, Episode 20)-
Selma plays Queen Elizabeth I during the time of the Spanish Armada attack on England in 1588. The episode is four segments featuring smart, powerful women (fictional or historical) and also features a segment where Maggie plays Howard Roark from Ayn Rand's *The Fountainhead*. (Written by Valentina L. Garza, Directed by Raymond S. Persi)

The Color Yellow (2010, Season 21, Episode 13)
Lisa researches one of her ancestors using primary sources and comes to the conclusion that her great-great-great grandaunt helped slaves to freedom on the Underground Railroad. However, other primary sources from Milhouse refute this account. This episode is a great example of source corroboration. (Written by Ian Maxtone-Graham and Billy Kimball, Directed by Raymond S. Persi)

I, Carumbus (2020 Season 32, Episode 2)
The Simpsons visit a museum to learn about Ancient Rome. The entire episode is a fictional story of a poor farmer (played by Homer) joining the Roman Senate. Although none of the characters are real, a Roman history consultant was employed to review the episode for historical accuracy. (Written by Cesar Mazariegos, Directed by Rob Oliver)

66   HOLLYWOOD OR HISTORY?

The Simpsons as a Historical Source

Since the show has been on the air since 1990, a few episodes of *The Simpsons* could be historical artifacts themselves. Here are some suggestions of episodes that truly are "of its time" in the 1990s.

Lisa's Wedding (1995, Season 6, Episode 19)
This episode looks into the future of 2010 (which is of course now the past). While telling the story of Lisa's wedding to Hugh, it gives a glimpse into how the writers imagined the future, which looking back now we can see how their perspective was influenced by 1995—the year it was written. (Written by Greg Daniels, Directed by Jim Reardon)

Two Bad Neighbors (1996, Season 7, Episode 13)
In retirement, former president George H. W. Bush moves to Springfield, across the street from the Simpson family. He clashes with Homer over disciplining Bart, which ignites a prank war between them. This episode is considered a "response" of sorts to critiques the Bushes gave of the show in the early 90s (Chin, 1990; Brooks, 2004). (Written by Ken Keeler, Directed by Wes Archer)

City of New York vs. Homer Simpson (1997, Season 9, Episode 1)
After a drunken night at Moe's Tavern, Homer's designated driver disappears with his car, only to have it turn up in New York City where Homer must retrieve it. This episode could be considered a historical source, as it prominently features the World Trade Center prior to 2001. This episode was taken out of syndication for years after the 9/11 attacks. (Written by Ian Maxtone-Graham, Directed by Jim Reardon)

Bart to the Future (2000, Season 11, Episode 17)
This episode takes place in an unidentified future where Lisa is President of the United States and Bart is her deadbeat brother looking for a job in her administration. Similar to "Lisa's Wedding," this episode's look into the future is heavily influenced by the year 2000 when it was written. It is also considered the episode where the show correctly predicted the presidency of Donald Trump (Salam, 2018). (Written by Dan Greaney, Directed by Michael Mercantel)

Future-Drama (2005, Season 16, Episode 15)
This episode, written in 2005, flashes into the future to look at Bart and Lisa's high school graduation in 2013. Which is now the past. Use this episode with "Lisa's Wedding" and "Bart to the Future" to reflect in

hindsight on what the 2005 writers "got right." (Written by Matt Selman, Directed by Mike B. Anderson)

That 90s Show (2008, Season 19, Episode 11)
In this episode, Homer and Marge are twentysomethings in love in the 1990s and the episode is full of cultural and historical references to the era. One problem—the show debuted in 1989 where it was established that Homer and Marge relationship began in the 1970s and 80s. An example not only of 90s history, but also how the show has played with time in flashbacks and flashforwards over the course of more than 30 years. (Written by Matt Selman, Directed by Mark Kirkland)

REFERENCES

Brooks, J. L. (Producer). (2004). "Bush vs Simpsons." *The Simpsons complete fourth season* [DVD]. Twentieth Century Fox Corporation.

Chin, P. (1990, October 1). In the eye of the storm. *People, 34*(13).

Kirkland, M. (Director). (2007). *The Simpsons complete tenth season* [DVD commentary]. Twentieth Century Fox Corporation.

Salam, M. (2018). "The Simpsons" has predicted a lot. Most of it can be explained. *NY Times*. https://www.nytimes.com/2018/02/02/arts/television/simpsons-prediction-future.html

CHAPTER 3

PEOPLE, PLACES, AND ENVIRONMENTS

In social studies, students learn about people, places, and environments by studying the discipline of geography. Geography is the study of locations and places (two of the five themes of geography). However, it is not just about where places are, but *why* they are there, what certain places are like, and how location influences characteristics of places. In the first lesson by Timothy Monreal, he uses short clips from "A Tale of Two Springfields" (Swartzwelder & Cashman, 2000) and "Waverly Hills, 9021D'Oh" (Burns & Polcino, 2009) to introduce the concept of redlining and spatial injustice to students. Studying structural racism within maps helps students to see how characteristics of places ("New Springfield" and "Waverly Hills") are heavily influenced by their location and the boundaries drawn within and around them.

Although studying geography is very much about maps and representations of places, it's not only about maps. Geography is also about connections—connections between places and connections between people and the places where they live (Gersmehl, 2014). When you broaden the concept of geography to incorporate "connections," you begin to see the integrated nature of the discipline. Students also learn about Human and Environment Interaction (a theme of geography) in science, as they study climate change. Students learn about Movement and Regions (two more themes of geography) in sociology, as they learn about the spread of culture and language in our world and throughout history.

The last lesson in this chapter uses *The Simpsons* to show examples of connections between people and places. The first lesson is for elementary-age students using the episode "Lisa the Tree Hugger" (Selman & Moore,

---

Hollywood or History?: An Inquiry-Based Strategy for Using The Simpsons to Teach Social Studies, pp. 69–88
Copyright © 2024 by Information Age Publishing
www.infoagepub.com
All rights of reproduction in any form reserved.

69

70 HOLLYWOOD OR HISTORY?

2000) to compare Lisa's activism to save a tree in Springfield to other environmental activists featured in picture books. For more episodes of the show that would teach people, places, and environments (as well as other themes of geography), see the "For Further Viewing" section.

REFERENCES

Burns, J. S. (Writer), & Polcino, M. (Director). (2009, May 3). Waverly Hills 9021D'oh (Season 20, Episode 19) [TV series episode]. In A. Jean, J. L. Brooks, M. Groening, & S. Simon (Executive Producers), *The Simpsons*. Gracie Films; Twentieth Century Fox Film Corporation.

Gersmehl, P. (2014). *Teaching geography* (3rd Ed.). The Guilford Press.

Selman, M. (Writer), & Moore, S. D. (Director). (2000, November 19). Lisa the tree hugger (Season 12, Episode 4) [TV series episode]. In M. Scully, J. L. Brooks, M. Groening, & S. Simon (Executive Producers), *The Simpsons*. Gracie Films; Twentieth Century Fox Film Corporation.

Swartzwelder, J. (Writer), & Cashman, S. (Director). (2000, November 5). A tale of two Springfields (Season 12, Episode 2) [TV series episode]. In M. Scully, J. L. Brooks, M. Groening, & S. Simon (Executive Producers), *The Simpsons*. Gracie Films; Twentieth Century Fox Film Corporation.

D'oh! Schools, Race, Segregation ... and Zip Codes?

Timothy Monreal

EPISODE(S):
"A Tale of Two Springfields" (2000, Season 12, Episode 2)
"Waverly Hills, 9021D'Oh" (2009, Season 20, Episode 19)

Grade	Subject	Topic
5–12	United States History	Education

Era Under Study	Estimated Time Needed for Lesson
Post-War United States	105 minutes (Day 1–60 minutes, Day 2–45 minutes)

State Standards

State	Standards and Descriptions
California	Standard 11.11. Students analyze the major social problems and domestic policy issues in contemporary American society.
Georgia	SS5H6. Describe the importance of key people, events, and developments between 1950–1975. a. Analyze the effects of Jim Crow laws and practices.
North Carolina	AH2.H.4.1. Analyze the political issues and conflicts that impacted the United States since Reconstruction and the compromises that resulted (e.g., Populism, Progressivism, working conditions and labor unrest, New Deal, Wilmington Race Riots, Eugenics, Civil Rights Movement, Anti-War protests, Watergate, etc.)
Virginia	VUS.13. The student will apply social science skills to understand the social, political, and cultural movements and changes in the United States during the second half of the 20th century by ... b) evaluating and explaining the impact of the Brown v. Board of Education decision, the roles of Thurgood Marshall and Oliver W. Hill, Sr., and how Virginia responded to the decision; g) evaluating and explaining the changes that occurred in American culture.

72 HOLLYWOOD OR HISTORY?

Common Core Standards

Standard	Description
CCSS.ELA-LITERACY. RH.6-8.1	Cite specific textual evidence to support analysis of primary and secondary sources.
CCSS.ELA-LITERACY. RH.9-10.2	Determine the central ideas or information of a primary or secondary source; provide an accurate summary of how key events or ideas developed the course of the text.
CCSS.ELA-LITERACY. RH.11-12.2	Determine the central ideas or information of a primary or secondary source; provide an accurate summary that makes clear the relationships among the key details and ideas.

NCSS C3 Framework

Dimension	Description
Evaluating Sources and Using Evidence	D3.3.9-12. Identify evidence that draws information directly and substantially from multiple sources to detect inconsistencies in evidence in order to revise or strengthen claims.
Communicating Conclusions and Taking Informed Action	D4.2.9-12. Construct explanations using sound reasoning, correct sequence (linear or nonlinear), examples, and details with significant and pertinent information and data, while acknowledging the strengths and weaknesses of the explanation given its purpose (e.g., cause and effect, chronological, procedural, technical).

NCSS Core Themes and Description

Theme	Description
I. Culture	Through the study of culture and cultural diversity, learners understand how human beings create, learn, share, and adapt to culture, and appreciate the role of culture in shaping their lives and society, as well the lives and societies of others.

II. Time, Continuity, and Change	Through the study of the past and its legacy, learners examine the institutions, values, and beliefs of people in the past, acquire skills in historical inquiry and interpretation, and gain an understanding of how important historical events and developments have shaped the modern world.
IV. Individual Development and Identity	Personal identity is shaped by family, peers, culture, and institutional influences. Through this theme, students examine the factors that influence an individual's personal identity, development, and actions.
V. Individuals, Groups, and Institutions	Institutions such as families and civic, educational, governmental, and religious organizations exert a major influence on people's lives. This theme allows students to understand how institutions are formed, maintained, and changed, and to examine their influence.

Handouts/Materials/Web Links

Handout/Materials:
- Hollywood or History? Graphic Organizer

Episode Clips and Video Content:
- "A Tale of Two Springfields," Season 12, Episode 2
    - **Clip 1:** 6:13-7:52
    - **Clip 2:** 8:05-8:50
    - **Clip 3:** 9:45-10:35
    - **Clip 4:** 13:30-14:30
- "Waverly Hills, 9021D'Oh," Season 20, Episode 19
    - **Clip 1:** 2:30-3:40
    - **Clip 2:** 4:50-8:00

Primary Sources:
- Mapping Inequality: Redlining in New Deal America (n.d.): https://dsl.richmond.edu/panorama/redlining/#loc=5/39.1/-94.58

Secondary Sources:
- Domonoske, C. (2016, October 19). *Interactive redlining map zooms in on America's history of discrimination.* NPR. https://www.npr.org/sections/thetwo-way/2016/10/19/498536077/interactive-redlining-map-zooms-in-on-americas-history-of-discrimination

- Gross, T. (2017). *A "forgotten history" of how the U.S. Government segregated America*. NPR. https://www.npr.org/2017/05/03/526655831/a-forgotten-history-of-how-the-u-s-government-segregated-america
- Guastaferro, L. (2020, November 2). *Why racial inequities in America's schools are rooted in housing policies of the past*. USA TODAY. https://www.usatoday.com/story/opinion/2020/11/02/how-redlining-still-hurts-black-latino-students-public-schools-column/6083342002/
- Popielarz, K., & Monreal, T. (2019). Teaching (for) spatial justice is teaching (for) social justice. *Curriculum in Context, 45*(1), 7–11. https://www.researchgate.net/publication/345178531_Teaching_for_Spatial_Justice_is_Teaching_for_Social_Justice

Guiding Questions

Primary Questions:
- What is spatial segregation and (in)justice?
- How (in)accurate is the depiction of spatial segregation in *The Simpsons*?
- How does redlining continue to impact society today?

Secondary Questions:
- What can be learned from historical housing maps?
- How does geography reproduce injustice?

Important Vocabulary

Race/Racism: Stated succinctly, "race is a concept, a representation or signification of identity that refers to different types of human bodies, to the perceived corporeal and phenotypical markers of difference and the meanings and social practices that are ascribed to these differences" (Omi & Winant, 2015, p. 111). Race is a social and spatial construct, (re)produced in relational ways with corresponding material consequences (e.g., redlining). Racism, then, is any ideology, policy, and/or practice in institutional and interpersonal arenas that normalize unequal, unequitable, and unjust racial practices and outcomes (Omi & Winant, 2015).

Redlining: A process of maintaining racial and spatial segregation by which non-White people could not buy homes in certain neighborhoods.

More specifically, in the late 1930s, the Homeowners' Loan Corporation "graded" neighborhoods into four categories, based in large part on their racial makeup. Neighborhoods with non-White occupants were marked in red (Domonoske, 2016).

Segregation: At a basic level, segregation means separating a person or group of people in a particular way. As a specific example, *de jure* (by law) and *de facto* (by practice) racial segregation has been a prominent feature, even organizing principle, of United States white supremacy. While racial segregation has always been a part of the United States, the Jim Crow Era institutionalized segregation as a system of laws that prohibited African Americans from mixing with whites in all sorts of public settings, from swimming pools, to stores, to restaurants, to even walking past each other on the sidewalk (Cunningham, n.d.).

Spatial (In)justice: Soja (2010) writes in/justice "has a consequential geography" (Soja, 2010, p. 1). Thus, the spatiality of in/justice affects society and social life just as much as social processes shape the geography of in/justice (Soja, 2010, p. 5). In other words, spatial organization and spatial practices bring forth, and seemingly stabilize systems of in/justice (see Popielarz & Monreal, 2019).

Assessment Strategies

Formative Assessments:

- Frayer Models
- Think-Pair-Share
- Hollywood or History? Graphic Organizer

Summative Assessments:

- Answer the *What do you think?* question from the Hollywood or History? graphic organizer

Sparking Strategy/Warm-Up

Lesson Introduction

On the board, the teacher writes one question—*What is segregation?* The teacher then leads a Think-Pair-Share protocol based on this question. After a whole group discussion about segregation, the teacher will lead the class in completing a Frayer Model (see Adolescent Literacy, n.d.) on the word "segregation." Teachers should emphasize there are many ways

76 HOLLYWOOD OR HISTORY?

people and groups segregate/are segregated but importantly, race, racism, and class have been drivers of segregation in the United States. After this discussion and activity, the teacher shares that the class will use clips from *The Simpsons* to investigate geographic and community segregation. More specifically, students will determine the (in)accuracy of the depiction of spatial segregation in *The Simpsons*. (15 min)

Lesson Procedures

Day 1

1. After the Lesson Introduction above, play all the clips from the two episodes of *The Simpsons*, "A Tale of Two Springfields" (Season 12, Episode 2) and "Waverly Hills, 9021D'Oh" (Season 20, Episode 19). As the students watch the clips, they should be taking notes in the middle column of the Hollywood or History? graphic organizer. In particular, students should focus on how and why segregation takes place on the television episodes. (15 min)

2. Explain that the class will now look at how "redlining" was a driver of spatial and racial segregation in the United States. The teacher will also explain that the proceeding secondary and primary sources about redlining will help students investigate the (in)accuracy of *The Simpsons'* depiction of spatial segregation. The class will then read Domonoske's (2016) article "Interactive Redlining Map Zooms in on America's History of Discrimination" while taking notes in the secondary source column of the Hollywood or History? graphic organizer. Teachers can also play portions of Gross' (2017) longer radio show titled "A 'Forgotten History' of How the U.S. Government Segregated America." (15 min)

3. Explain that students will now investigate redlining primary source documents in small groups with the website "Mapping Inequality: Redlining in New Deal America." The teacher explains that students should write down notes about redlining and racial segregation in at least two cities under the primary source column of the Hollywood or History? graphic organizer. (15 min)

Day 2

1. On the board, the teacher writes one question—*What is redlining?* Students will create a Frayer Model (see Adolescent Literacy,

Chapter 3: People, Places, and Environments   77

n.d.) on the word redlining. They can use their Hollywood or History? graphic organizer or any materials from the previous day to aid them. (15 min)

2. After discussing the students' Frayer Models (perhaps with a Think-Pair-Share protocol), tell the class they will read another secondary source to understand the connection between redlining and schooling. Point students to Gustaferro's (2020) article "Why Racial Inequities in America's Schools are Rooted in Housing Policies of the Past" and give each student three sticky notes. As the class reads the article out loud, the teacher stops three times. At each pause, students write a question about the article on a sticky note. At the end of the article, ask students about the questions written down and engage in peer, small group, and/ or whole class discussion. Students can also record notes in the secondary source column of their Hollywood or History? graphic organizer. (15 min)

3. Using their notes, students will draft a paragraph (citing evidence) discussing the (in)accuracy of the depiction of spatial segregation in *The Simpsons*. Space is included on the bottom of Hollywood or History? graphic organizer. (15 min)

Differentiation

Scaffolds: The Hollywood or History? Graphic Organizer, Frayer Models, and Think-Pair-Shares encourages (collaborative) gradual release to guide higher order thinking in a structured, paced way. The secondary source articles may be too technical for some students so the teacher may consider shortening the article and/or only using excerpts for students.

ESL Interventions: The lessons are designed for students to engage and access the texts in multiple ways to facilitate multiple levels of (peer and teacher) support. The use of the Frayer Model helps with important vocabulary. As mentioned previously, the secondary source articles may be too technical for some students, so the teacher may consider amending or supplementing them as they feel necessary.

Extensions:
- Explicitly introduce spatial justice (see Popielarz & Monreal, 2019) with students, and consequently how spatial in/justice impacts their/our lives. This could become the launching point for inquiry into investigations of local issues of spatial in/justice and lead to engaged projects in line with the "taking action" component of the NCSS C3 Framework.

REFERENCES

Adolescent Literacy (n.d.). *Frayer model.* http://www.adlit.org/strategies/22369/

American Panorama. (n.d.). *Mapping inequality: Redlining in New Deal America.* https://dsl.richmond.edu/panorama/redlining/

Burns, J. S. (Writer), & Polcino, M. (Director). (2009, May 3). Waverly Hills 9021D'oh (Season 20, Episode 19) [TV series episode]. In A. Jean, J. L. Brooks, M. Groening, & S. Simon (Executive Producers), *The Simpsons.* Gracie Films; Twentieth Century Fox Film Corporation.

Cunningham, D. (n.d.). *Understanding Jim Crow (setting the setting).* Facing History and Ourselves. https://www.facinghistory.org/resource-library/video/understanding-jim-crow-setting-setting

Domonoske, C. (2016, October 19). *Interactive redlining map zooms in on America's history of discrimination.* NPR. https://www.npr.org/sections/thetwo-way/2016/10/19/498536077/interactive-redlining-map-zooms-in-on-americas-history-of-discrimination

Gross, T. (2017). *A "forgotten history" of how the U.S. Government segregated America.* NPR. https://www.npr.org/2017/05/03/526655831/a-forgotten-history-of-how-the-u-s-government-segregated-america

Guastaferro, L. (2020, November 2). *Why racial inequities in America's schools are rooted in housing policies of the past.* USA TODAY. https://www.usatoday.com/story/opinion/2020/11/02/how-redlining-still-hurts-black-latino-students-public-schools-column/6083342002/

Omi, M., & Winant, H. (2015). *Racial formation in the United States* (3rd ed.). Routledge.

Popielarz, K., & Monreal, T. (2019). Teaching (for) spatial justice is teaching (for) social justice. *Curriculum in Context, 45*(1), 7–11.

Soja, E. W. (2010). *Seeking spatial justice.* University of Minnesota Press.

Swartzwelder, J. (Writer), & Cashman, S. (Director). (2000, November 5). A tale of two Springfields (Season 12, Episode 2) [TV series episode]. In M. Scully, J. L. Brooks, M. Groening, & S. Simon (Executive Producers), *The Simpsons.* Gracie Films; Twentieth Century Fox Film Corporation.

Hollywood or History?

Segregation in *The Simpsons*

Evaluate each source provided and summarize your observations and analysis in corresponding spaces provided. In the section located at the bottom of the page, explain whether you think the clips from either "A Tale of Two Springfields" and "Waverly Hills, 90210D'Oh" are accurate accounts of spatial segregation, pure Hollywood creations, or a mixture of both. Use examples from your sources/documents to explain your answer.

Primary Sources	Secondary Sources	Clips from *The Simpsons*

What Do You Think? Hollywood or History?

"I Don't Eat Anything That Casts a Shadow"

Annie McMahon Whitlock

EPISODE:
"Lisa the Tree Hugger" (2000, Season 12, Episode 4)

Grade	Subject	Topic
3–5	Human Environment Interaction	Environmental activism

Estimated Time Needed for Lesson
50 minutes (could turn into several days if teacher wants to incorporate their own action project)

State Standards

State	Standards and Descriptions
Michigan	4-G5.0.1 Assess the positive and negative consequences of human activities on the physical environment of the United States and identify the causes of those activities.
Nevada	SS.4.24. Examine how and why Nevada's landscape has been impacted by humans.
Oklahoma	4.4.3. Explain how economic activities can threaten the physical environment. A. Identify ways in which humans can change ecosystems, such as clearing forests, draining wetlands, and diverting waterways, by examining present-day issues related to the use of resources.

Chapter 3: People, Places, and Environments　81

Common Core Standards

Standard	Description
CCSS.ELA-LITERACY. RI.3.9	Compare and contrast the most important points and key details presented in two texts on the same topic.
CCSS.ELA-LITERACY. W.4.10	Write routinely over extended time frames (time for research, reflection, and revision) and shorter time frames (a single sitting or a day or two) for a range of discipline-specific tasks, purposes, and audiences.

NCSS C3 FRAMEWORK

Dimension	Description
Evaluating Sources and Using Evidence	D3.1.3-5. Gather relevant information from multiple sources representing while using the origin, structure, and context, to guide the selection.
Communicating Conclusions and Taking Informed Action	D4.6.3-5. Draw on disciplinary concepts to explain the challenges people have faced and opportunities they have created, in addressing local, regional, and global problems at various times.
	D4.7.3-5. Explain different strategies and approaches students and others could take in working alone and together to address local, regional, and global problems, and predict the possible results of their actions.

NCSS Core Themes and Description

Theme	Description
III. People, Places, and Environments	Examining how human beings interact with their environment and the themes of geography reveal myriad views and perspectives of the world.

Handouts/Materials/Web Links

Handout/Materials:

Hollywood or History? Graphic Organizer

82   HOLLYWOOD OR HISTORY?

Episode Clips and Video Content:
Links to Video and Film Clip(s):
- "Lisa the Tree Hugger," Season 12, Episode 4
  - o **Clip**: 10:58 to 15:07

Primary Sources:
- Photos and diary entries from www.juliabutterflyhill.com
- Speeches and articles on Wangari Maathai from www.greenbelt-movement.org/wangari-maathai

Secondary Sources:
- Kostecki-Shaw, J. S. (2015). *Luna and me: The true story of a girl who lived in a tree to save a forest*. Henry Holt and Company.
  - o Read aloud link if you're not able to access the book: https://www.youtube.com/watch?v=4hotZcAMs-k
- Winter, J. (2018). *Wangari's trees of peace: A true story from Africa*. Harcourt.
  - o Read aloud link if you're not able to access the book: https://www.youtube.com/watch?v=yeNljYP1hvk

Guiding Questions

Primary Question:
- What can we do to take care of our environment?

Secondary Questions:
- What have others done to have a positive impact on the environment?
- What environmental issues impact us?

Important Vocabulary

Activist: Someone who takes action to make a change or stop a change in society. Activists can try to make the government change its laws or try to make people change what they do.

Environment: The surroundings or conditions where a person, animal, or plant lives or works.

Assessment Strategies

Formative Assessments:
- Hollywood or History? Graphic Organizer

Summative Assessments:
- Students will write a "bio poem" about Julia Butterfly Hill or Wangari Maathai using information from the sources.
- Optional: Students will create an action plan to address an environmental issue in their school or community.

Sparking Strategy/Warm-Up

Lesson Introduction

In a whole group, ask the students, *What gifts do trees give us?* Record their answers on chart paper. If they don't mention it, guide the students to the idea that trees give us the air we breathe (oxygen). After recording their responses, ask the students to imagine a world without trees. Ask: *How would our lives be different without trees? What would we have to give up?*

Lesson Procedures

1. After the warmup discussion, introduce the vocabulary word "activist." Explain the definition and ask the students if they know of any activists. Explain that they are going to read a book about an environmental activist.
2. Read the book *Luna & Me* (or watch the YouTube video read aloud if the text is not available). Stop periodically to ask questions about Julia's reasons for wanting to stop the tree from getting cut down and the risks she was willing to take.

    A good stopping point is after the page that ends with, "Don't trees have a right to just be?" Ask the students, *Why doesn't Julia want Luna to get cut down?*

    Another good stopping point is after the page that ends with, "In her dream, Luna spoke to her." Ask the students (and/or make a list), *What were the risks of living in the tree?*

    After finishing the book, ask *How was Julia an activist?* (Don't forget to read the Author's Note for more information!

84 HOLLYWOOD OR HISTORY?

3. After reading the book, watch the clip from *The Simpsons*. Explain that the writers of the show were inspired by Julia Butterfly Hill's story and wanted to create something similar for Lisa, the character in the show who typically shows the most activism.

4. In small groups, use the Hollywood or History? Graphic Organizer to compare the real Julia Butterfly Hill to Lisa Simpson. *How were they similar? How were they different?* Make sure to talk about how Lisa abandoned her activism when it became difficult, whereas Julia lived in her tree for two years. However, in the end, the tree was cut down in *The Simpsons* whereas "Luna" stayed put.

5. Next, read the book *Wangari's Trees of Peace: A True Story from Africa* about Wangari Mathai, another activist who planted trees that were already cut down. Using a blank Venn Diagram, compare Mathai to Julia Butterfly Hill. *How were they the same or different? Were there any similarities between Mathai and Lisa Simpson?*

6. After reading about both Julia Butterfly Hill and Wangari Mathai, students should write a "bio poem" about one of the activists, using the format of the bio poem below.

   > *Line 1*: First name of the activist
   >
   > *Line 2*: Title of the activist
   >
   > *Line 3*: Three words that describe the person
   >
   > *Line 4*: Lover of _____ (list 2 things the activist loves)
   >
   > *Line 5*: Who believed _____ (list 1 or more idea)
   >
   > *Line 6*: Who wanted _____ (list 2 things they wanted)
   >
   > *Line 7*: Who used _____ (list 2 methods or things)
   >
   > *Line 8*: Who worked with _____ (list 1 or more people or organizations)
   >
   > *Line 9*: Who said, "___" (give a specific quote)
   >
   > *Line 10*: Last name of the activist

Give the students the primary source photos about both women and encourage them to use one of the photos to illustrate their poem (or as inspiration, such as Matt Selman did when he wrote the episode of *The Simpsons*). Students can create their poem on colorful paper or digitally.

> The bio poem activity comes from *Every Book is a Social Studies Book: How to Meet Standards with Picture Books, K-6* by Andrea Libresco, Jeannette Balantic, and Jonie C. Kipling.

7. If time allows, have students research an environmental issue that exists in their local community and encourage them to become activists around this issue. Although the issue would

Chapter 3: People, Places, and Environments 85

depend on the context, here are some examples of ways other classes have taken action on environmental issues:

> Start a recycling program at the school, or campaign to encourage more recycling.
>
> Work to make your school a "Green Ribbon School" through the U.S. Department of Education (https://www2.ed.gov/programs/green-ribbon-schools/index.html)
>
> Clean up a local park and/or organize a neighborhood clean-up day.

Differentiation

Scaffolds: The bio poem format could be adapted to include more structure to help students fill in the poem, such as suggestions for word choice and quotes for them to choose. The poem can be created in small groups instead of individually.

ESL Interventions: Students should be given the option to watch the clips with their native language subtitles if they are available. ESL learners could write their graphic organizer and summative assessment in their native language and have it translated to English.

Extensions:

- During the lesson, students who are more skilled readers can read a different book about Wangari Mathai (*Wangari Mathaai: The Woman Who Planted Millions of Trees* by Franck Prévot is one example) and/or extend their learning about Julia Butterfly Hill by reading her autobiography *The Legacy of Luna: The Story of a Tree, a Woman, and the Struggle to Save the Redwoods*.
- Learn about environmental activists and create bio poems about them, including activists featured in the book *Old Enough to Save the Planet (Changemakers)* by Loll Kirby.

REFERENCES

Hill, J. (2001). *The legacy of Luna: The story of a tree, a woman, and the struggle to save the redwoods*. HarperCollins.

Kirby, L. (2021). *Old enough to save the planet (changemakers)*. Magic Cat Publishing.

Kostecki-Shaw, J. S. (2015). *Luna and me: The true story of a girl who lived in a tree to save a forest*. Henry Holt and Company.

86   HOLLYWOOD OR HISTORY?

Libresco, A. S., Balantic, J., & Kipling, J. C. (2011). *Every book is a social studies book: How to meet standards with picture books, K-6.* Libraries Unlimited.

Prévot, F. (2015). *Wangari Mathaai: The woman who planted millions of trees.* Charlesbridge.

Selman, M. (Writer), & Moore, S. D. (Director). (2000, November 19). Lisa the tree hugger (Season 12, Episode 4) [TV series episode]. In M. Scully, J. L. Brooks, M. Groening, & S. Simon (Executive Producers), *The Simpsons.* Gracie Films; Twentieth Century Fox Film Corporation.

Winter, J. (2018). *Wangari's trees of peace: A true story from Africa.* Harcourt.

Hollywood or History?

Julia Butterfly Hill

Writers of *The Simpsons* were inspired by Julia Butterfly Hill when they wrote the episode "Lisa the Tree Hugger." Using Hill's own website (the primary source), clips from the episode, and the secondary source (*Luna & Me*). Compare the similarities and differences in Julia's story and Lisa's story.

Julia Butterfly Hill	Lisa Simpson
Hollywood or History? How close is *The Simpsons* to the real story of Julia Butterfly Hill?	

For Further Viewing

With over 700 episodes to choose from, there are more episodes of *The Simpsons* that could be used to teach the theme of People, Places, and Environments. Many of the episodes listed in Chapter 1 on Culture could also be watched to examine how the location and environment shapes the culture of many groups. The episodes suggested below are examples of how people interact with places and have impacts on the environment.

Dude Where's My Ranch? (2003, Season 14, Episode 21)
When the Simpson family takes a vacation to a ranch, Homer and Bart help an Indigenous tribe reclaim their land from a pack of beavers. (Written by Ian Maxtone-Graham, Directed by Chris Clements)

Greatest Story Ever D'Ohd (2010, Season 21, Episode 16)
In this episode, the Simpsons travel to Jerusalem with Ned Flanders and his church group. Ned is furious that Homer doesn't give the place enough respect for its religious significance, but later Homer develops "Jerusalem Syndrome," a condition where people develop religious obsessions after visiting the city; a phenomenon whose existence has been debated (Saner, 2018). (Written by Kevin Curran, Directed by Michael Polcino)

Opposites A-Frack
Lisa discovers the tap water in their home catches fire, and finds it is due to a fracking operation by… who else but Mr. Burns? The episode references the environmental dangers of fracking and the political debates on both sides of the issue. (Written by Valentina L. Garza, Directed by Matthew Nastuk)

REFERENCE

Saner, E. (2018). What is Jerusalem syndrome? *The Guardian*. https://www.theguardian.com/socicty/shortcuts/2018/jan/16/jerusalem-syndrome-psychiatric-condition-oliver-mcafee-british-tourist

CHAPTER 4

INDIVIDUAL DEVELOPMENT AND IDENTITY

Who are we? What do we like? What do we believe in? These are simple questions that are foundational to studying social studies. One's identity is constructed by oneself, but also by society. Parts of one's identity can be visible to others and invisible. It can be based on personal beliefs and formed by the groups we belong to. People have multiple aspects of their identities that form who they are, always intersecting. Since our identities influence how we participate in culture, how we spend money, how we vote, and how we treat others, identity is an important concept in several social studies disciplines.

Despite identity being so important to social studies, understanding identity is rarely mentioned in state standards explicitly. If it is, it's mentioned in early grades such as Kindergarten or first grade. However, identity development continues well beyond early elementary—we are forming our identities well into adulthood! This chapter takes a different approach to designing lessons around standards. Instead of using state standards, this chapter uses Social Justice Standards from Learning for Justice (learningforjustice.org). These standards have an anchor standard and learning outcomes designed specifically around identity. The concept of identity development is also threaded through their standards on diversity, justice, and taking action. Lessons in this chapter also require students to examine their own personal reflection as a primary source and feature a twist on the Hollywood or History? strategy, comparing *The Simpsons* to real-life experiences.

The Simpsons has so many characters and has been around for so long that there are several episodes that speak directly to characters discovering

---

Hollywood or History?: An Inquiry-Based Strategy for Using The Simpsons to Teach Social Studies, pp. 89–107
Copyright © 2024 by Information Age Publishing
www.infoagepub.com
All rights of reproduction in any form reserved.

89

90 HOLLYWOOD OR HISTORY?

who they are and how they belong to society. The first lesson in this chapter is from one of my favorite episodes, "Lisa the Vegetarian" (Cohen & Kirkland, 1995) (at this point, being a fan of *The Simpsons* is part of my identity). In this episode, Lisa is exploring her beliefs on eating animals—which causes conflict with Homer. This lesson uses their disagreement to get students to reflect on and practice their empathetic listening skills. In the second lesson, students explore what it means to be an "ally" for those with marginalized identities. In "Bart vs. Itchy and Scratchy" (Amram & Clements, 2019), Bart becomes a feminist ally, but is it for the wrong reasons? In the "For Further Viewing" section, check out other episodes that could be used for a lesson on identity development.

REFERENCES

Amram, M. (Writer), & Clements, C. (Director). (2019, March 24). Bart vs. Itchy & Scratchy (Season 30, Episode 18) [TV series episode]. In A. Jean, M. Selman., J. L. Brooks, M. Groening, & S. Simon (Executive Producers), *The Simpsons*. Gracie Films; Twentieth Century Fox Film Corporation.

Cohen, D. X. (Writer), & Kirkland, M. (Director). (1995, October 15). Lisa the vegetarian (Season 7, Episode 5) [TV series episode]. In B. Oakley, J. Weinstein, J. L. Brooks, M. Groening, & S. Simon (Executive Producers), *The Simpsons*. Gracie Films; Twentieth Century Fox Film Corporation.

Learning for Justice (n.d.). *Social justice standards*. https://www.learningforjustice. org/frameworks/social-justice-standards

"You Don't Win Friends With Salad"

Annie McMahon Whitlock

EPISODE:
"Lisa the Vegetarian" (1995, Season 12, Episode 5)

Grade	Subject	Topic
6–8th	Social emotional learning	Understanding empathy

Estimated Time Needed for Lesson
90–100 minutes (Day 1–60 minutes, Day 2–40 minutes)

Learning for Justice Social Justice Standards

Code	Standard
DI.6-8.8	I am curious and want to know more about other people's histories and lived experiences, and I ask questions respectfully and listen carefully and non-judgmentally.
DI.6-8.9	I know I am connected to other people and can relate to them even when we are different or when we disagree.
AC.6-8.16	I am concerned about how people (including myself) are treated and feel for people when they are excluded or mistreated because of their identities.

Common Core Standards

Standard	Description
CCSS.ELA.W.6.9	Draw evidence from literary or informational texts to support analysis, reflection, and research

NCSS C3 Framework

Dimension	Description
Applying Disciplinary Concepts and Tools (Anthropology)	Understand and appreciate cultural and social difference, and how human diversity is produced and shaped by local, national, regional, and global patterns.
Applying Disciplinary Concepts and Tools (Civics)	D2.Civ.10.6-8. Explain the relevance of personal interests and perspectives, civic virtues, and democratic principles when people address issues and problems in government and civil society.

NCSS Core Themes and Description

Theme	Description
IV. Individual Development and Identity	Personal identity is shaped by family, peers, culture, and institutional influences. Through this theme, students examine the factors that influence an individual's personal identity, development, and actions.

Handouts/Materials/Web Links

Handout/Materials:
- Are You Empathetic?
- Hollywood or Empathy? Graphic Organizer

Episode Clips and Video Content
- "Lisa the Vegetarian", Season 7, Episode 5
  - o **Clip 1:** 8:30–9:30
  - o **Clip 2:** 12:30–end of the episode

Secondary Sources:
- Someone Else's Shoes scenarios from Learning for Justice. https://www.learningforjustice.org/sites/default/files/general/someone%20else's%20shoes.pdf

Chapter 4: Individual Development and Identity   93

Guiding Questions

Primary Question:
- What does empathy mean?

Secondary Questions:
- How empathetic am I?
- How can people better show empathy toward others?

Important Vocabulary

Empathy: The understanding of or the ability to identify with another person's feelings or experiences.
Vegetarian: The practice of eating foods that come from plants rather than animals.

Assessment Strategies

Formative Assessments:
- Are You Empathetic?

Summative Assessments:
- Hollywood or Empathy? Graphic Organizer

Sparking Strategy/Warm-Up

Lesson Introduction

Have the students turn to a partner and discuss the questions: *Have you ever been in an argument with a friend or family member where you wished someone understood how you felt? How does it make you feel to be misunderstood?* After a few minutes of discussion in pairs, come back to the whole class and take volunteers of students who can share how being misunderstood makes them feel in just one word. Create a list of these feelings words as students share. (10 min)

Lesson Procedures

This lesson was adapted from a Learning for Justice (learningforjustice.org) lesson called "Developing Empathy."

94 HOLLYWOOD OR HISTORY?

Day 1

1. Explain to students that when we try to relate to what another person is going through or feeling, we're being "empathetic." This is sometimes called "putting yourself in someone else's shoes." Refer to the word list the class made in the lesson introduction about feeling misunderstood. Explain that we are not being empathetic to others, it can make people feel these negative feelings. (5 min)
2. Hand out the Are You Empathetic? reflection and have students answer the five "yes" or "no" questions about their own levels of empathy toward others. Students should do this individually—responding "yes" to a statement that describes something they do and "no" if they don't do it. (5 min)
3. Explain that if students answered mostly "yes," then they probably do a good job of showing empathy toward other people. The statements they answered "no" to are things they could work on to be more empathetic. (5 min)
4. On the bottom half of the Are You Empathetic? Reflection sheet, have students answer the reflection questions either with a partner or a small group. If time allows, have students share some of the answers to the questions, particularly the question: *What are things you can do to show people you're being empathetic?* (15 min)
5. Explain to the class that you're going to play for them a clip from an episode of *The Simpsons* called "Lisa the Vegetarian." Set up the clip by explaining that Lisa and her dad Homer have different opinions on Lisa's desire to be a vegetarian and they both hurt each other's feelings (you may have to explain the concept of a vegetarian if students don't know). As they watch the clip, students should listen for how Lisa and Homer would be feeling. (15 min)
6. For the summative assessment, have students fill out the Hollywood or Empathy? Graphic Organizer comparing how Homer and Lisa acted with the definition of empathy. (5 min and/or assigned for homework)

Day 2

1. To begin, review their Are You Empathetic? formative assessment from Day 1 and their responses to the question *What are things you can do to show people you're being empathetic?* from Step 4 above. These answers could include making eye contact, asking

Chapter 4: Individual Development and Identity   95

questions, or not interrupting. Explain that they will each get to practice their empathetic listening skills. (10 min)

2. Students should pair up and each take a different character scenario from the Someone Else's Shoes handout from Learning for Justice. Each partner reads their scenario as the other partner practices empathetic listening. The reader may have to improvise a little and expand on the story within the card. Get creative! After the scenario is read, the listener should identify how they think their partner is feeling (as their character). The reader should give the listener specific ways that they demonstrated empathetic listening. Then they should switch roles. (20–30 min)

Differentiation

Scaffolds: Some students may need more practice with identifying feelings within themselves and identifying others' feelings. This "Empathy with Moby" video (https://www.youtube.com/watch?v=cMDrR2cUSGU) shows more simplistic examples of empathy than the "Lisa the Vegetarian" episode.

ESL Interventions: Students should be given the option to watch the clips with their native language subtitles if they are available. ESL learners could write their graphic organizer and summative assessment in their native language and have it translated to English.

Extensions:

- Write and perform a skit where people are showing empathy toward each other and perform it for a class of younger students to teach them about empathy.
- Keep a journal of ways you practiced empathetic listening with others outside of class.

REFERENCES

Art and Graphic Design. (2020, July 24). *Empathy with Moby* [BrainPOP Jr. Video]. You Tube. https://www.youtube.com/watch?v=cMDrR2cUSGU&t=22s

Cohen, D. X. (Writer), & Kirkland, M. (Director). (1995, October 15). Lisa the vegetarian (Season 7, Episode 5) [TV series episode]. In B. Oakley, J. Weinstein, J. L. Brooks, M. Groening, & S. Simon (Executive Producers), *The Simpsons*. Gracie Films; Twentieth Century Fox Film Corporation.

96 HOLLYWOOD OR HISTORY?

Learning for Justice. (n.d.) *Developing empathy*. https://www.learningforjustice.org/classroom-resources/lessons/developing-empathy

APPENDIX A

Are You Empathetic?

Read each item below and circle "yes" if the statement describes you and circle "no" if it does not.

1.	I often think about other people's feelings.	**YES**	**NO**
2.	I don't make fun of other people because I can imagine what it feels like to be in their shoes.	**YES**	**NO**
3.	I listen to others about what they're going through.	**YES**	**NO**
4.	I try to understand other people's point of view	**YES**	**NO**
5.	I am aware that not everyone reacts to situations the same way I do.	**YES**	**NO**

How do you notice how someone else is feeling?

How can you try to understand how others feel?

What are things you can do to show people you're being empathetic?

This lesson was adapted from a Learning for Justice (learningforjustice.org) lesson called "Developing Empathy."

Hollywood or Empathy?

As you watch the clips from "Lisa the Vegetarian," write down how you think both Lisa and Homer are feeling about their disagreement.

Homer	Lisa

After watching the end of the clips, write down ways that Homer and Lisa show empathy to each other. How do they compare to the definition of empathy? Are they showing empathetic listening?

Homer showing empathy to Lisa	Lisa showing empathy to Homer
How did they do?	

"Ruthless Bader Ginsburgs"

Annie McMahon Whitlock

EPISODE:
"Bart vs. Itchy & Scratchy" (2019, Season 30, Episode 18)

Grade	Subject	Topic
12th	Sociology	Allyship and performative activism

Estimated Time Needed for Lesson
100 minutes (2 class periods)

Learning for Justice Social Justice Standards

Code	Standard
JU.9-12.12	I can recognize, describe, and distinguish unfairness and injustice at different levels of society.
AC.9-12.17	I take responsibility for standing up to exclusion, prejudice and injustice.
AC.9-12.20	I will join with diverse people to plan and carry out collective action against exclusion, prejudice, and discrimination, and we will be thoughtful and creative in our actions in order to achieve our goals.

Common Core Standards

Standard	Description
CCSS.ELA.W.6.9	Draw evidence from literary or informational texts to support analysis, reflection, and research

NCSS C3 Framework

Dimension	Description
Applying Disciplinary Concepts and Tools (Civics)	D2.Civ.10.9-12. Analyze the impact and the appropriate roles of personal interests and perspectives on the application of civic virtues, democratic principles, constitutional rights, and human rights.
Evaluating Sources and Using Evidence	D3.1.9-12. Gather relevant information from multiple sources representing a wide range of views while using the origin, authority, structure, context, and corroborative value of the sources to guide the selection.

NCSS Core Themes and Description

Theme	Description
IV. Individual Development and Identity	Personal identity is shaped by family, peers, culture, and institutional influences. Through this theme, students examine the factors that influence an individual's personal identity, development, and actions.
V. Individuals, Groups, and Institutions	Institutions such as families and civic, educational, governmental, and religious organizations exert a major influence on people's lives. This theme allows students to understand how institutions are formed, maintained, and changed, and to examine their influence.

Handouts/Materials/Web Links

Handout/Materials:
- Hollywood or Allyship? Graphic Organizer

Episode Clips and Video Content:
- "Bart vs. Itchy & Scratchy," Season 30, Episode 18
  - o **Clip 1:** 1:34–2:42
  - o **Clip 2:** 6:18–11:40
  - o **Clip 3:** 12:40–14:40
  - o **Clip 4:** 14:40–16:10

100 HOLLYWOOD OR HISTORY?

Secondary Sources:
- Above the Noise. (n.d.). *Can performative activism actually make a difference?* PBS Learning Media. https://wgvu.pbslearningmedia. org/resource/can-performative-activism-actually-make-a-differen/ above-the-noise-video/
- Sebastian, H. (2017). How to tell if you're being a good ally. *Teen Vogue.* https://www.teenvogue.com/story/how-to-tell-if-youre-being-a-good-ally

Guiding Questions

Primary Question:
- What makes a good ally?

Secondary Questions:
- Am I a good ally?
- What is performative activism?

Important Vocabulary

Ally: Someone that aligns with and supports a cause with another individual or group of people.
Performative Activism: Activism done to increase one's social capital rather than because of one's devotion to the cause.

Assessment Strategies

Formative Assessments:
- Read the article "How to Tell If You're Being a Good Ally" and write a paragraph answering the following reflection questions: *When have I been a good ally towards others? What are ways I can be a better ally?*

Summative Assessments:
- Hollywood or Allyship? Graphic Organizer

Sparking Strategy/Warm-Up

Lesson Introduction

Individually, students should do a quick-write to answer the following prompts. Set a timer for five minutes and encourage the students to write whatever comes to mind for the entire time.

Chapter 4: Individual Development and Identity 101

- *What causes or issues do you care about?*
- *What actions have you taken online and/or in your community to advocate for or spread the word about these cause(s)?*

Ask students who are willing to share some of their writing. Explain that this lesson is about identifying when and how we can take action to support our identities and the identities of others. (10 min)

This activity was created by PBS Learning Media (KQED Media—Above the Noise)

Lesson Procedures

Day 1

1. Begin the lesson by starting the video "Can Performative Activism Actually Make a Difference?" Stop the video at 1:08 and ask the students to define the term "performative activism" in their own words to a partner or small group. (5 min)
2. In a whole group, ask the class to provide examples of performative activism they have seen—these can be from the Above the Noise video or from their personal experiences. (5 min)
3. Next, have the class jigsaw the article "How to Tell If You're Being a Good Ally." Read the introduction together, then divide the class into three groups. Each group takes a section of the article that begins with the heading "A good ally…" These groups are the "expert groups." The groups should read their section together, identify any words they don't know, and come up with a summary of the main idea of that section. (20 min)
4. Next, have one person from each expert group join another group—these become their "jigsaw groups." The jigsaw groups should have people from each of the three sections of the article. In the jigsaw groups, everyone from each of the expert groups should share their group's summary. After everyone has shared ways to be a good ally, the jigsaw groups should come up with examples they have seen in their lives or in the media of good allyship. If time, have the jigsaw groups share these examples with the whole class. (20 min)
5. Assign the entire article for homework to read and to answer the following questions in a written paragraph: *When have I been a good ally towards others? What are ways I can be a better ally?*

Day 2

1. Start Day 2 by reviewing the article "How to Tell If You're Being a Good Ally." Using the Hollywood or Allyship? Graphic

102   HOLLYWOOD OR HISTORY?

Organizer, on the left side of the "Ally" section, have the students write down the three ways the article says to be a good ally. Add any other ways you discussed as a class in Day 1. On the left side of the "Performative Activism" section, write down the definition of performative activism that you came up with in Day 1. (5 min)

2. Explain that they are going to practice identifying performative activism and allyship using the "Bart vs. Itchy and Scratchy" episode of *The Simpsons*. However, it's not going to be as "black or white" as they think. Start with the first clip, which is more obvious, to do together:

    Clip 1: 1:34–2:42

    After watching this clip, ask the students: *How is Krusty the Clown showing an example of performative activism?*

3. On the right side of the "Peformative Activism" section of their graphic organizer, students should write that Krusty is making a female reboot of Itchy and Scratchy to look good and make money, rather than from a real belief about gender equality or feminism. (5 min)

4. Give some context to the next set of clips by explaining that Bart and his friends at first agree to boycott the female reboot, but then Bart sees some of it and laughs. He then must face his friends when they find out he actually likes the female reboot. Explain that as they watch the next clips, they should write down ways they see Bart being an ally to the feminist protest group "Bossy Riot" and write it in the right side of the "Ally" section of their graphic organizer. Have students share after Clip 2 and before Clip 3. (10 min)

    Clip 2: 6:18–11:40
    Clip 3: 12:40–14:40

5. Give some context to the next set of clips by explaining that Bart's sister Lisa is upset about him joining Bossy Riot because she believes it is only performative activism. As they watch this clip, they should fill out the right side of the "Performative Activism" section of their graphic organizer using Lisa's evidence. (5 min)

    Clip 4: 14:40–16:10

    After watching this clip, ask the students: *How is Bart showing performative activism? Why does he accuse Lisa of the same thing?*

Chapter 4: Individual Development and Identity   103

6. To wrap up the lesson, go back to the Above the Noise video "Can Performative Activism Actually Make a Difference?" This time, start the video at the 4:00 mark and play until the end. In this section, host Myles Bess explains that performative activism may be helpful, and he gives data as examples. After watching this clip, fill out the bottom of the Hollywood or Allyship? Graphic Organizer by answering the question—*Was Bart a good ally to the Bossy Riot group, why or why not?* Use examples from the Above the Noise video and the article from Day 1 to defend your answer. (20-25 min)

Differentiation

Scaffolds: The "How to Tell If You're Being a Good Ally" article may need to be read aloud to some students. Written reflections could also be recorded as oral responses.

ESL Interventions: In addition to the scaffolds above, students should be given the option to watch the clips with their native language subtitles if they are available. ESL learners could write their formative and summative assessment in their native language and have it translated to English.

Extensions:

- Identify examples of sexism you see among individuals and institutions in their beliefs, behaviors, language, and policies. Make a plan to address the issue you care the most about. For more guidance on this, see the Learning for Justice lesson "Sexism: From Identification to Activism." https://www.learningforjustice.org/classroom-resources/lessons/sexism-from-identification-to-activism
- Create an infographic showing people how to be a good ally. Use this one from Amnesty International as inspiration. https://amnestyusa.tumblr.com/post/153528354956/whether-youre-in-standing-rock-or-your-hometown

REFERENCES

Above the Noise. (n.d.). *Can performative activism actually make a difference?* PBS Learning Media. https://wgvu.pbslearningmedia.org/resource/can-performative-activism-actually-make-a-differen/above-the-noise-video/

104 HOLLYWOOD OR HISTORY?

Amnesty International. (n.d.). *10 tips for showing up in solidarity.* https://amnestyusa.tumblr.com/post/153528354956/whether-youre-in-standing-rock-or-your-hometown

Amram, M. (Writer), & Clements, C. (Director). (2019, March 24). Bart vs. Itchy & Scratchy (Season 30, Episode 18) [TV series episode]. In A. Jean, M. Selman., J. L. Brooks, M. Groening, & S. Simon (Executive Producers), *The Simpsons.* Gracie Films; Twentieth Century Fox Film Corporation.

Learning for Justice. (n.d.). *Sexism: From identification to activism.* https://www.learningforjustice.org/classroom-resources/lessons/sexism-from-identification-to-activism

Sebastian, H. (2017). How to tell if you're being a good ally. *Teen Vogue.* https://www.teenvogue.com/story/how-to-tell-if-youre-being-a-good-ally

Hollywood or Allyship?

As you watch the clips from "Bart vs Itchy and Scratchy," write down examples of allyship and performative activism that you see. After watching all the clips, identify whether Bart was a good ally to the Bossy Riot group, using evidence from the episode and the Above the Noise video.

Definition of a good ally	*Examples from Bart vs Itchy and Scratchy*

Definition of performative activism	*Examples from Bart vs Itchy and Scratchy*
Was Bart a good ally to the Bossy Riot group? Why or why not?	

For Further Viewing

With over 700 episodes to choose from, there are more episodes of *The Simpsons* that could be used to teach the theme of Individual Identity and Development.

Forming Identity at School

The Simpsons has always compared Bart, the proud underachiever, to Lisa—the wise-beyond-her-years overachiever. These two episodes feature Bart and Lisa coming to terms with their identities at school:

Bart the Genius (1990, Season 1, Episode 2)
The second episode of the series focuses on Bart's identity as an "underachiever" in school. When he cheats on an IQ test and others think he is a genius, he struggles with where he fits in. (Written by Jon Vitti, Directed by David Silverman)

Stealing First Base (2010, Season 21, Episode 15)
In a subplot of this episode, Lisa struggles with the fact that she only becomes popular after people think she failed a test. Michelle Obama (played by Angela Bassett) comes to Springfield Elementary to encourage students to embrace their identities as "overachievers." (Written by John Frink, Directed by Steven Dean Moore)

Who Is Seymour Skinner?

Springfield Elementary School principal Seymour Skinner is one of the show's many secondary characters whose identity has been formed through many episodes over the years. These are two landmark episodes of *The Simpsons* for different reasons, but they both feature Principal Skinner and who he is (or isn't) as a character.

Sweet Seymour Skinner's Baadasssss Song (1994, Season 5, Episode 19)
The 100th episode of the series also focuses on Bart's identity as a school troublemaker and rival to Principal Skinner. When Skinner gets fired after one of Bart's stunts, Bart is unhappy at school without him. This episode also comments on Principal Skinner's development as a person outside of his job. (Written by Bill Oakley and Josh Weinstein, Directed by Bob Anderson)

The Principal and the Pauper (1997, Season 9, Episode 2)
This episode reveals the mistaken identity of Principal Skinner—turns out his name is Armin Tamzarian and he took over the life of the real Seymour Skinner after he died in Vietnam. When it turns out the real Skinner isn't dead and returns to Springfield to take his life back, the town doesn't know what to think. This episode is widely considered the worst episode of *The Simpsons* (Sloane, 2004; Turner, 2004) because of the contradiction to the Skinner character's established identity. Harry Shearer, the voice of Skinner, called it "so wrong" (Wilonsky, 2001). (Written by Ken Keeler, Directed by Steven Dean Moore)

Gender Identity

There are a few episodes that briefly touch on issues of gender stereotypes, toxic masculinity, sexuality, sexism, and feminism. These two episodes go deeper into these issues and could provide a rich discussion for students.

Homer's Phobia (1997, Season 8, Episode 15)
Bart begins to hang out with a gay owner of a nostalgia shop after they bond over their love of toys. Even though Homer likes John the shop owner (played by John Waters), he is afraid John will "turn Bart gay." This episode won a GLAAD media award in 1998. (Written by Ron Hague, Directed by Mike B. Anderson)

Girls Just Wanna Have Sums (2006, Season 17, Episode 19)
This episode focuses on the gender stereotype that boys are better at math than girls. Springfield Elementary is segregated by gender and Lisa learns that the all-female classes have lower expectations in math than the boys. This episode also addresses sexism displayed by Principal Skinner, Homer, and Bart. (Written by Matt Selman, Directed by Nancy Kruse)

REFERENCES

Sloane, R. (2004). Who wants candy? Disenchantment in The Simpsons. In J. Alberti (Ed.), *Leaving Springfield: The Simpsons and the possibility of oppositional culture* (pp. 165). Wayne State University Press.

Turner, C. (2004). *Planet Simpson: How a cartoon masterpiece defined a generation*. Random House Canada.

Wilonsky, R. (2001). Shearer delight. *East Bay Express*. https://eastbayexpress.com/shearer-delight-1

CHAPTER 5

INDIVIDUALS, GROUPS, AND INSTITUTIONS

The previous chapter focused on identity—how people develop their own identities and show up for others who have marginalized identities. This chapter focuses on what outside sources influence our identities. The NCSS Theme of Individuals, Groups, and Institutions refers to the "formal and informal political, economic, and social organizations that help us carry out, organize, and manage our daily affairs" (NCSS, n.d., para 1). All episodes of *The Simpsons* focus on one influential group—family—and many episodes also focus on the community of Springfield and its influence on various characters. However, in this chapter we focus on more formal institutions in our society and examine them from a historical and contemporary lens—the government and labor unions.

In "Homer vs. the Eighteenth Amendment" (Swartzwelder & Anderson, 1997), Springfield decides to enforce a long-standing law requiring prohibition in the town. This change in law enforcement has a large influence on the town, as some residents seek out speakeasies like Moe's "Pet Shop." The law also turns Homer to a life of crime as he becomes the "Beer Baron," supplying Springfield with illegal drinks. Jeffrey Koslowski created a lesson where students compare *The Simpsons* to the real Prohibition Era, examining the influence of the 18th amendment of the U.S. Constitution on women, local businesses, and law enforcement.

The other lesson in this chapter focuses on the institution of labor unions and the labor movement of the late 19th century. The classic episode "The PTA Disbands" (Crittenden & Scott, 1995) is used to compare the teachers' demands and their strike at Springfield Elementary to laborers and the Haymarket Riot. In the "For Further Viewing" section, check out other

---

Hollywood or History?: An Inquiry-Based Strategy for Using The Simpsons to Teach Social Studies, pp. 109–129
Copyright © 2024 by Information Age Publishing
www.infoagepub.com
All rights of reproduction in any form reserved.

109

episodes that could be used for a lesson on other institutions that influence society, such as religion (there are many options in *The Simpsons*!) and higher education.

REFERENCES

Crittenden, J. (Writer), & Scott, S. O., III., (Director). (1995, April 16). The PTA disbands (Season 6, Episode 21) [TV series episode]. In D. Mirkin, J. L. Brooks, M. Groening, & S. Simon (Executive Producers), *The Simpsons*. Gracie Films; Twentieth Century Fox Film Corporation.

National Council for the Social Studies (n.d.). *National curriculum standards for social studies: Executive summary.* https://www.socialstudies.org/standards/national-curriculum-standards-social-studies-executive-summary

Swartzwelder, J. (Writer), & Anderson, B. (Director). (1997, March 16). Homer vs. the eighteenth amendment (Season 8, Episode 18) [TV series episode]. In B. Oakley, J. Weinstein, J. L. Brooks, M. Groening, & S. Simon (Executive Producers), *The Simpsons*. Gracie Films; Twentieth Century Fox Film Corporation.

"The Cause of, and Solution to, All of Life's Problems:" *The Simpsons* and Prohibition

Jeffrey Koslowski

EPISODE:
"Homer vs. The Eighteenth Amendment" (1997, Season 8, Episode 18)

Grade	Subject	Topic
9–12	United States History	Prohibition, Roaring '20s

Era Under Study	Estimated Time Needed for Lesson
Roaring '20s	70 minutes (could be spread over two days if necessary)

State Standards

State	Standards and Descriptions
California	Standard 11.5.3—Examine the passage of the 18th amendment to the constitution and the Volstead Act (Prohibition).
Michigan	7.1.1—The Twenties—Explain and evaluate the significance of the social, cultural, and political changes and tensions in the "Roaring Twenties"
New York	11.5 b—Students will trace the temperance and prohibition movements leading to the ratification of the 18th amendment (1919).

Common Core Standards

Standard	Description
CCSS.ELA-LITERACY. RH.9-12.1	Cite specific textual evidence to support analysis of primary and secondary sources.

112 HOLLYWOOD OR HISTORY?

CCSS.ELA-LITERACY. RH.9-12.2	Determine the central ideas or information of a primary or secondary source; provide an accurate summary of how key events or ideas developed the course of the text.
CCSS.ELA-LITERACY. RH.11-12.2	Determine the central ideas or information of a primary or secondary source; provide an accurate summary that makes clear the relationships among the key details and ideas.

NCSS C3 Framework

Dimension	Description
Developing Questions and Planning Inquiries	D1.1.9-12. Explain how a question is an enduring issue in the field.
Applying Disciplinary Concepts and Tools (History)	D2.His.14.9-12. Analyze multiple and complex causes and effects of events in the past.
Evaluating Sources and Using Evidence	D3.3.9-12. Identify evidence that draws information directly and substantively from multiple sources to detect inconsistencies in evidence in order to revise or strengthen claims.
Communicating Conclusions and Taking Informed Action	D4.6.9-12. Use disciplinary and interdisciplinary lenses to understand the characteristics and causes of local, regional, and global problems; instances of such problems in multiple contexts; and challenges and opportunities faced by those trying to address these problems over time and place.

NCSS Core Themes and Description

Theme	Description
I. Culture	Through the study of culture and cultural diversity, learners understand how human beings create, learn, share, and adapt to culture, and appreciate the role of culture in shaping their lives and society, as well the lives and societies of others.
II. Time, Continuity, and Change	Through the study of the past and its legacy, learners examine the institutions, values, and beliefs of people in the past, acquire skills in historical inquiry and interpretation, and gain an understanding of how important historical events and developments have shaped the modern world.

V. Individuals, Groups, and Institutions	Institutions such as families and civic, educational, governmental, and religious organizations exert a major influence on people's lives. This theme allows students to understand how institutions are formed, maintained, and changed, and to examine their influence.
VI. Power, Authority, and Governance	One essential component of education for citizenship is an understanding of the historical development and contemporary forms of power, authority, and governance. Through this theme, learners become familiar with the purposes and functions of government, the scope and limits of authority, and the differences between democratic and non-democratic political systems.
VII. Production, Distribution, and Consumption	This theme provides for the study of how people organize for the production, distribution, and consumption of goods and services, and prepares students for the study of domestic and global economic issues.

Handouts/Materials/Web Links

Handout/Materials:
- Hollywood or History? Graphic Organizer

Episode Clips and Video Content:

- "Homer vs. The Eighteenth Amendment," Season 8, Episode 18

Primary Sources:
- For Group A: Gender
  - o Digital Public Library of America. (n.d.). *A 1901 photograph of Carrie (Carry) Nation with a hatchet and a Bible.* https://dp.la/primary-source-sets/women-and-the-temperance-movement/sources/1785
  - o Benjamin Rush's Temperance Thermometer (Smithsonian Magazine): Gambino, M. (2015). This chart from 1790 lays out the many dangers of alcoholism. *Smithsonian Magazine.* https://www.smithsonianmag.com/history/chart-1790-lays-out-many-dangers-alcoholism-180954777/
- For Group B: Speakeasies
  - o Lardner, R. & Bayes, N. (1919). *Prohibition blues* [Song audio recording]. Library of Congress. https://www.loc.gov/item/jukebox-707519/

114   HOLLYWOOD OR HISTORY?

    o   Harlan, J. (2020, January 1). 100 years ago, the booziest January suddenly dried up. *New York Times*. https://www.nytimes.com/2020/01/01/us/100-years-ago-the-booziest-january-suddenly-dried-up.html

- For Group C: Law Enforcement
  - o Library of Congress. (1924). *Coast Guard Cutter, USS Seneca chasing and capturing a "rum runner" 1924: Armed CG men aiming at rum runner.* https://www.loc.gov/item/2006675958/
  - o Library of Congress. (1924). *Prohibition unit (cow shoes), 6/28/24.* https://www.loc.gov/item/2016849213/

Secondary Sources:
- For Group A: Gender
  - o Rorabaugh, W. J. (2018). *Prohibition: A very short introduction.* Oxford University Press.
    - ■ Page 2 references the heavy Christian influence. Note how two of the more prominent people pushing for Prohibition were Maude Flanders and Helen Lovejoy
  - o Burton, T. I. (2016). The feminist history of prohibition. *JSTOR Daily.* https://daily.jstor.org/feminist-history-prohibition/
- For Group B: Speakeasies
  - o The Mob Museum. (n.d.). *Bootleggers and bathtub gin.* Prohibition: An Interactive History. https://prohibition.the-mobmuseum.org/the-history/the-prohibition-underworld/bootleggers-and-bathtub-gin/
  - o The Mob Museum. (n.d.). *The speakeasies of the 1920's.* Prohibition: An Interactive History. https://prohibition.the-mobmuseum.org/the-history/the-prohibition-underworld/the-speakeasies-of-the-1920s/
- For Group C: Law Enforcement
  - o Okrent, D. (2010). *Last call: The rise and fall of prohibition.* Scribner.

Guiding Questions

Primary Question:
- How was violence a factor in Springfield's desire for prohibition?
- What role did women play in the Prohibition movement?
- How did speakeasies oppose and represent the Prohibition era?

Chapter 5: Individuals, Groups, and Institutions 115

- How was law enforcement an agent to both support and oppose prohibition?

Secondary Questions:
- What is a primary/secondary source?
- How important is it for a movie, TV show, or modern form of entertainment to be historically accurate?

Important Vocabulary

Bootlegger: A person who makes, distributes, or sells goods illegally.
Hooch: A colloquial term for an alcoholic distilled beverage.
Prohibition: The forbidding law of the manufacture, transportation, and sale of alcoholic liquors except for medicinal and sacramental purposes.
Speakeasy: A place where alcoholic beverages are illegally sold.

Assessment Strategies

Formative Assessments:
- Hollywood or History? Graphic Organizer

Summative Assessments:
- Hollywood or History? Graphic Organizer (bottom paragraph)

Sparking Strategy/Warm-Up

Lesson Introduction

Ask students to write down anything they might already know about the Prohibition movement. If electronic or virtual, students can contribute to a Jamboard screen. Have students share what they know in the whole group. (5 min)

Lesson Procedures

1. Begin with a discussion about morals. *What does it mean to have morals? How do they dictate your lives, if at all? Should others abide by your morals?* Allude to the Prohibition movement having roots in other movements to help fix perceived moral lessons. (5 min)

116 HOLLYWOOD OR HISTORY?

2. Explain that the students will be watching an episode from *The Simpsons* called "Homer vs. The Eighteenth Amendment" that closely mirrors what really happened during Prohibition in the United States. Introduce the Hollywood or History? Graphic Organizer handout and work with students to detail how they can use the outline to record information during the film clip and document analysis in which they will take part. (5 min)
3. Break the students into three groups to have them analyze what they will see in the episode. The groups should each focus on A. Gender (specifically the role of women) B. The Speakeasy (aka Moe's Tavern/Pet Shop) and C. Law Enforcement.
4. Play the episode in its entirety. If you choose, pause the episode at various times including: the women of Springfield demanding Prohibition to Mayor Quimby, scenes involving Moe's Tavern and its evolving role, and scenes where the police act to both enforce the law and at times let it be broken. (25 min)
5. After the episode has completed, distribute relevant primary and secondary sources to the groups. Have the students analyze the material and compare/contrast them with the scenes from the show. (15 min)
6. After examining the sources, students should draft their own individual statements regarding their material and if *The Simpsons* did the Prohibition Era historical justice. (10 min)
7. In a nod to one of the last scenes of the episode, representatives from each group will stand in an imaginary space in the classroom to represent the catapult. The students will retell a particular scene, character, or event from the episode. After the retelling, they will state how accurate or inaccurate they believe this scene was, according to the sources they were given. The student will then compare/contrast it with one or more of their primary or secondary sources to determine how accurate they felt it was. Create a line graph on a board and students can place a mark where they felt the accuracy was (for example, a spot on the far left would mean 100% fiction based on the sources while a spot on the far right would be 100% accurate. A spot in the middle would be 50% accurate, 50% fiction). (10-15 min)

Differentiation

Scaffolds: Groups could be made of mixed ability with specific tasks assigned to students for structure. Sources from books are already shortened down into relevant paragraphs only.

ESL Interventions: Many episodes of *The Simpsons* are available in other languages. Students with ESL intervention should be told of this assignment ahead of time to see if they could potentially watch it early in a language with which they are more comfortable.

Extensions:

- Have students from each group form into new groups of three with one person from each of the original groups represented. Students can then share their sources with one another to make an overall analysis of the episode as a whole using the same rating system as before (100% fiction, 100% accurate, or somewhere in between).
- Students can create a mock indexing of events from the scenes of the episodes for future students to look up.

REFERENCES

Burton, T. I. (2016). The feminist history of prohibition. *JSTOR Daily.* https://daily.jstor.org/feminist-history-prohibition/

Digital Public Library of America. (n.d.). *A 1901 photograph of Carrie (Carry) Nation with a hatchet and a Bible.* https://dp.la/primary-source-sets/women-and-the-temperance-movement/sources/1785

Federal Bureau of Investigation. (2020, January 24). *The Bureau and the great experiment: How prohibition fueled bootleggers, mobsters, and corruption.* https://www.fbi.gov/news/stories/the-bureau-and-the-great-experiment-012420

Gambino, M. (2015). This chart from 1790 lays out the many dangers of alcoholism. *Smithsonian Magazine.* https://www.smithsonianmag.com/history/chart-1790-lays-out-many-dangers-alcoholism-180954777/

Harlan, J. (2020, January 1). 100 years ago, the booziest January suddenly dried up. *New York Times.* https://www.nytimes.com/2020/01/01/us/100-years-ago-the-booziest-january-suddenly-dried-up.html

Lardner, R. & Bayes, N. (1919). *Prohibition blues* [Song audio recording]. Library of Congress. https://www.loc.gov/item/jukebox-707519/

Library of Congress. (1924). *Coast Guard Cutter, USS Seneca chasing and capturing a "rum runner" 1924: Armed CG men aiming at rum runner.* https://www.loc.gov/item/2006675958/

Library of Congress. (1924). *Prohibition unit (cow shoes), 6/28/24.* https://www.loc.gov/item/2016849213/

Okrent, D. (2010). *Last call: The rise and fall of prohibition.* Scribner.

Rorabaugh, W. J. (2018). *Prohibition: A very short introduction.* Oxford University Press.

The Mob Museum. (n.d.). *Bootleggers and bathtub gin.* Prohibition: An Interactive History. https://prohibition.themobmuseum.org/the-history/the-prohibition-underworld/bootleggers-and-bathtub-gin/

118   HOLLYWOOD OR HISTORY?

The Mob Museum. (n.d.). *The speakeasies of the 1920's.* Prohibition: An Interactive History. https://prohibition.themobmuseum.org/the-history/the-prohibition-underworld/the-speakeasies-of-the-1920s/

Swartzwelder, J. (Writer), & Anderson, B. (Director). (1997, March 16). Homer vs. the eighteenth amendment (Season 8, Episode 18) [TV series episode]. In B. Oakley, J. Weinstein, J. L. Brooks, M. Groening, & S. Simon (Executive Producers), *The Simpsons.* Gracie Films; Twentieth Century Fox Film Corporation.

Hollywood or History?

Prohibition Era

As you examine your group's primary and secondary sources, take notes on the far left and far right columns of the table below. While you watch the "Homer vs. The Eighteenth Amendment" episode, take notes in the middle column to compare them. After your group has examined the evidence related to your topic (Gender, Speakeasies, or Law Enforcement), individually answer the question Hollywood or History? Was this episode historically accurate?

Primary Sources	"Homer vs. The Eighteenth Amendment"	Secondary Sources
What do you think? Hollywood or History?		

The Influence of Teachers' Unions Purple Monkey Dishwasher

Annie McMahon Whitlock

EPISODE:
"The PTA Disbands" (1995, Season 6, Episode 21)

Grade	Subject	Topic
9–12	United States History/Civics	Labor unions

Era Under Study	Estimated Time Needed for Lesson
Labor Movement/Progressive Era	75 minutes

State Standards

State	Standards and Descriptions
Arizona	HS.H3.1. Analyze how societies, leaders, institutions, and organizations respond to societal needs and changes.
Illinois	SS.H.7.9-12. Identify the role of individuals, groups, and institutions in people's struggle for safety, freedom, equality, and justice.
Michigan	C-4.3.1. Identify and explain personal rights, political rights, and economic rights as well as how these rights might conflict.

Common Core Standards

Standard	Description
CCSS.ELA-LITERACY. RH.11-12.1	Cite specific textual evidence to support analysis of primary and secondary sources, connecting insights gained from specific details to an understanding of the text as a whole.

Chapter 5: Individuals, Groups, and Institutions   121

CCSS.ELA-LITERACY. RH.11-12.9	Integrate information from diverse sources, both primary and secondary, into a coherent understanding of an idea or event, noting discrepancies among sources.

NCSS C3 Framework

Dimension	Description
Applying Disciplinary Concepts and Tools (Civics)	D2.Civ.5.9-12. Evaluate citizens' and institutions' effectiveness in addressing social and political problems at the local, state, tribal, national, and/or international level.
Applying Disciplinary Concepts and Tools (History)	D2.His.9.9-12. Analyze the relationship between historical sources and the secondary interpretations made from them.

NCSS Core Themes and Description

Theme	Description
V. Individuals, Groups, and Institutions	Institutions such as families and civic, educational, governmental, and religious organizations exert a major influence on people's lives. This theme allows students to understand how institutions are formed, maintained, and changed, and to examine their influence.
VI. Power, Authority, and Governance	One essential component of education for citizenship is an understanding of the historical development and contemporary forms of power, authority, and governance. Through this theme, learners become familiar with the purposes and functions of government, the scope and limits of authority, and the differences between democratic and non-democratic political systems.

Handouts/Materials/Web Links

Handout/Materials:

- Hollywood or History? Graphic Organizer

122 HOLLYWOOD OR HISTORY?

Episode Clips and Video Content:
- "The PTA Disbands," Season 6, Episode 21
  - o **Clip 1:** 3:50–7:30
  - o **Clip 2:** 10:08–11:08
  - o **Clip 3:** 13:25–15:12
  - o **Clip 4:** 19:55–21:10
- "The Haymarket Square Riot and the Fight for Workers' Rights" History4Humans: https://www.youtube.com/watch?v=wHRL4hlYJvg

Primary Sources:
- American Federation of Labor. (n.d.). Trade unions foster education and uproot ignorance… *Library of Congress.* https://www.loc.gov/resource/rbpe.20900700/
- Horydczak, T. (1920). Pittsburgh Plate Glass Co. factory no. 12, Clarksburg, West Virginia. Pittsburgh Plate Glass Co. factory interior VII. *Library of Congress.* https://www.loc.gov/resource/thc.5a38937/

Secondary Sources:
- History.com Editors. (2020). Sit-down strike begins in Flint. *History.com* https://www.history.com/this-day-in-history/sit-down-strike-begins-in-flint
- History For Humans (2021, August 26). The Haymarket Square riots and the fight for workers' rights [Video]. *YouTube.* https://www.youtube.com/watch?v=wHRL4hlYJvg
- U-S-History.com. (n.d.) *Fair Labor Standards Act.* http://www.u-s-history.com/pages/h1701.html
- U-S-History.com (n.d.). *Mother Jones.* http://www.u-s-history.com/pages/h1635.html
- Smith, M., & Davey, M. (2019, October 31). Chicago teachers' strike, longest in decades, ends. *New York Times.* https://www.nytimes.com/2019/10/31/us/chicago-cps-teachers-strike.html

Guiding Questions

Primary Question:
- How do labor unions use collective power to ensure the rights of workers?

Chapter 5: Individuals, Groups, and Institutions   123

Secondary Questions:
- Was there a need for organized labor?
- What rights do workers have today that we can attribute to the collective action of labor unions in the past?

Important Vocabulary

Labor Union: An organized association of workers formed to protect and further their rights and interests.
Scab: A replacement worker hired by managers to try to break a strike.
Strike: A refusal to work by a mass of employees until demands are met.

Assessment Strategies

Formative Assessments:
- Hollywood or History? Graphic Organizer

Summative Assessments:
- Students should make a "broadside" (poster) encouraging people to join the Knights of Labor or the Springfield Elementary teachers. The broadside should list a specific issue the group was fighting for and why it would improve their quality of life to join.

Sparking Strategy/Warm-Up

Lesson Introduction

Ask students if they have a part-time job or have ever been employed. For those that have, ask them: *Are you allowed to take breaks? Do you earn minimum wage? How long are your shifts?* Explain that there was a time when workers in the United States did not get to rest at work, they were paid terribly, often worked in unsafe conditions, and feared losing their jobs if they complained. Labor unions worked as a group to ensure workers had rights to proper conditions at their jobs. (5 min)

Lesson Procedures

1. Start the lesson by projecting the image of the Pittsburgh Plate Glass Factory worker. With the person next to them or in a small

124   HOLLYWOOD OR HISTORY?

group, have them discuss what they notice about the man's working conditions from the photograph. After a few minutes, debrief as a whole class. Some students may notice that the man appears to be in loose fitting street clothes, he's not wearing gloves or a helmet, and his face is not covered. Students may notice that the machine could be dangerous with its moving parts, and some may infer that since he is shaping glass, it could be hot to touch. (10 min)

2. Begin showing the video "The Haymarket Square Riot and the Fight for Workers' Rights," stopping at the 7:30 mark. Individually, students should answer the questions in the top left box of the Hollywood or History? Graphic Organizer: *Why was there a need for organized labor in the late 19th century? Who was Mother Jones? How was she influential?* Students should share out their answers. (15 min)

3. Play the rest of the video and tell students to pay attention to how the workers protested for their rights in Haymarket Square and what happened to the labor movement after that. As they watch, they should fill out the bottom left box of the Hollywood or History Graphic Organizer and answer the question: *What happened at Haymarket Square? What are scabs and how did their presence lead to violence among the workers?* (10 min)

4. Explain that teachers are often unionized laborers, and many belong to local Education Associations or the National Education Association (NEA) or American Federation of Teachers (AFT). Teachers fought for (and continue to advocate for) better working conditions for themselves, but also for their students. Explain that they will be watching an episode of *The Simpsons* that shows how the teachers at Springfield Elementary fought for their rights as workers. (5 min)

5. Show the first two clips from "The PTA Disbands" and have students fill out the top right box about the conditions the teachers were fighting for. After the clip, the students should note the similarities between the 19th century labor movement and the Springfield Elementary teachers in the top middle box. (10 min)
   Clip 1: 3:50-7:30
   Clip 2: 10:08-11:08

6. Show the last two clips from "The PTA Disbands" and have students answer the questions about the process and outcome of the Springfield Elementary teacher's strike in the bottom right box:

Chapter 5: Individuals, Groups, and Institutions   125

How did Mrs. Krabappel lead the strike? Who were the scabs at Springfield Elementary and how did they influence the outcome of the strike? (10 min)

> **Clip 3:** 13:25-15:12
> **Clip 4:** 19:55-21:10

7. In small groups, hand out a one-pager about Mother Jones and the Fair Labor Standards Act for students to reference as they discuss the similarities and differences between the Chicago laborers, Mother Jones, and the influence of the Haymarket Riot and the strike at Springfield Elementary. They should make their notes about whether *The Simpsons* is more Hollywood or History in the bottom middle box. (15 min)
8. For the summative assessment, students should make a "broadside" (poster) encouraging people to join the Knights of Labor or the Springfield Elementary teachers. The broadside should list a specific issue the group was fighting for and why it would improve their quality of life to join. Show the students the "Trade Unions" broadside from the Library of Congress as an example. This could be done in class on a separate day or assigned for homework.

Differentiation

Scaffolds: The background information on Mother Jones and the Fair Labor Standards Act could be shortened to just the essential paragraphs, annotated, or adapted to aid in comprehension.

ESL Interventions: Episodes of *The Simpsons* are available in other languages. The History4 Humans YouTube video is not. Students should be able to access the captioning for the video and/or be able to watch it in smaller chunks with someone to help summarize.

Extensions:

- Read about the GM Sit-Down Strike in Flint, Michigan from 1936 and discuss: *How are sit-down strikes potentially more impactful than refusing to come in to work?* https://www.history.com/this-day-in-history/sit-down-strike-begins-in-flint
- Students can learn more about teachers' strikes by reading about the Chicago Teachers' Union strike of 2019 in this *New York Times* article: https://www.nytimes.com/2019/10/31/us/chicago-cps-teachers-strike.html

126 HOLLYWOOD OR HISTORY?

- Conduct a labor negotiation simulation, such as this one from PBS Classroom: https://www.pbs.org/newshour/classroom/2020/09/negotiation-labormanagement-simulation/

REFERENCES

American Federation of Labor. (n.d.). Trade unions foster education and uproot ignorance ... *Library of Congress.* https://www.loc.gov/resource/rbpe.20900700/

Crittenden, J. (Writer), & Scott, S. O., III., (Director). (1995, April 16). The PTA disbands (Season 6, Episode 21) [TV series episode]. In D. Mirkin, J. L. Brooks, M. Groening, & S. Simon (Executive Producers), *The Simpsons.* Gracie Films; Twentieth Century Fox Film Corporation.

History.com Editors. (2020). Sit-down strike begins in Flint. *History.com* https://www.history.com/this-day-in-history/sit-down-strike-begins-in-flint

History For Humans (2021, August 26). The Haymarket Square riots and the fight for workers' rights [Video]. *YouTube.* https://www.youtube.com/watch?v=wHRL4hlYJvg

Horydczak, T. (1920). Pittsburgh Plate Glass Co. factory no. 12, Clarksburg, West Virginia. Pittsburgh Plate Glass Co. factory interior VII. *Library of Congress.* https://www.loc.gov/resource/thc.5a38937/

PBS Newshour Classroom (2022, September 1). Lesson plan: For Labor Day, explore this labor/management 'negotiation' scenario. *Lesson Plans.* https://www.pbs.org/newshour/classroom/2022/09/negotiation-labormanagement-simulation/

Smith, M., & Davey, M. (2019, October 31). Chicago teachers' strike, longest in decades, ends. *New York Times.* https://www.nytimes.com/2019/10/31/us/chicago-cps-teachers-strike.html

U-S-History.com. (n.d.) *Fair Labor Standards Act.* http://www.u-s-history.com/pages/h1701.html

U-S-History.com (n.d.). *Mother Jones.* http://www.u-s-history.com/pages/h1635.html

Hollywood or History?

Compare the fight of labor unions in the late 19th century to the fight for better working conditions for the Springfield Elementary teachers in *The Simpsons*. How were their approaches the same or different?

Labor Movement	Hollywood or History?	Springfield Elementary Teachers
Why was there a need for organized labor in the late 19th century?		*What were the demands of the teachers?*
Who was Mother Jones?		*How did Mrs. Krabappel lead the strike?*
How was she influential?		
What happened at Haymarket Square?		*Who were the scabs at Springfield Elementary and how did they influence the outcome of the strike?*
What are scabs and how did their presence lead to violence among the workers?		*What was the outcome of the teachers' strike?*

128 HOLLYWOOD OR HISTORY?

For Further Viewing

With over 700 episodes to choose from, there are more episodes of *The Simpsons* that could be used to teach the theme of Individuals, Groups, and Institutions.

Labor Unions

"The PTA Disbands" is not the only episode to deal with labor unions. Here are two others:

Last Exit to Springfield (1993, Season 4, Episode 17)
Considered one of the best episodes of *The Simpsons* (*Entertainment Weekly*, 2003), Homer unionizes the nuclear power plant in order to get better dental insurance from Mr. Burns. (Written by Jay Kogen and Wallace Wolodarsky, Directed by Mark Kirkland)

Labor Pains (2013, Season 25, Episode 5)
At a football game for the Springfield Atoms, Lisa discovers that the cheerleaders are poorly paid and helps them to organize a union. (Written by Don Payne and Mitchell H. Glazer, Directed by Matthew Faughnan)

Higher Education/School

There are many episodes that satirize the institution of schooling on *The Simpsons*—both public elementary and secondary school and higher education. Chapter 11 of this book features lesson plans with two episodes on public education, but here are two others:

Homer Goes to College (1993, Season 5, Episode 3)
After a meltdown at the nuclear plant that is Homer's fault, he is required to go back to college at Springfield University to take a course to get his degree. He protests against the stuffy higher ed administration—except they're not very oppressive after all. (Written by Conan O'Brien, Directed by Jim Reardon)

Team Homer (1996, Season 7, Episode 12)
In the subplot of this episode, Principal Skinner introduces school uniforms at Springfield Elementary which causes a revolt among the students. (Written by Mike Scully, Directed by Mark Kirland)

Chapter 5: Individuals, Groups, and Institutions   129

Religion

Over the years, *The Simpsons* has aired several episodes about the institution of religion. The show regularly features the Simpson family and other characters in church and discussing their faith. The three episodes listed below are classics, but books such as *The Gospel According to The Simpsons* (Pinsky, 2007) go into more depth about religion on *The Simpsons*.

Like Father, Like Clown (1991, Season 3, Episode 6)
This episode establishes that Krusty the Clown is Jewish and that his father is a rabbi who disowned him for becoming a clown. Bart and Lisa help Krusty reunite with his father and embrace his Jewish faith. This episode featured actual Bible and Torah verses heavily researched by Jewish rabbi consultants (Pinsky, 2007). (Written by Jay Kogen and Wallace Wolodarsky, Directed by Jeffrey Lynch and Brad Bird)

Homer the Heretic (1992, Season 4, Episode 3)
Homer denounces his Christian faith after he has a comfortable Sunday morning at home instead of at church. God speaks to Homer in a dream and gives him a blessing to worship in his own way, despite Marge trying to convince him to come back to organized religion. After Homer is saved from a house fire by members of the congregation, he agrees to come back. (Written by George Meyer, Directed by Jim Reardon)

She of Little Faith (2001, Season 13, Episode 6)
In this episode, it's Lisa who leaves the Christian faith after she is disappointed with the commercialism of the church. She converts to Buddhism and Marge tries to get her to come back to Christianity. However, in the end they agree to respect one another's religious faiths. (Written by Bill Freiberger, Directed by Steven Dean Moore)

REFERENCES

Entertainment Weekly. (2003, January 31). The family dynamic. *Entertainment Weekly*. https://web.archive.org/web/20141018160211/http://www.ew.com/ew/article/0,,417748~3~0~25bestand1,00.html

Pinsky, M. I. (2007). *The gospel according to The Simpsons, bigger and possibly even better edition* (2nd Ed.). Westminster John Knox Press

CHAPTER 6

POWER, AUTHORITY, AND GOVERNANCE

This NCSS theme is the one most closely related to the discipline of civics and political science. Studying the concepts of power, authority, and governance leads to understanding the purpose and function of government and political systems in the United States and around the world. Understanding how power and authority interact in government can help citizens be better able to navigate these systems to enact social change.

In this chapter, two classic episodes from Season 9 are featured—"Das Bus" (Cohen & Michels, 1998) and "Trash of the Titans" (Maxtone-Graham & Reardon, 1998). Both of these episodes feature citizens working within power and authoritative structures to enact change and build a better society, albeit with not ideal results. "Das Bus" is a parody of *Lord of the Flies*, where the students of Springfield Elementary are stranded on a deserted island and learn to work together and govern themselves as a society until they are rescued by "let's say ... Moe." Kymberli Wregglesworth uses "Das Bus" in a lesson on the philosophies and foundations of government from Thomas Hobbes and John Locke. In her lesson, students experience a simulation similar to the "stranded on a deserted island" concept to practice what they have learned about these philosophers.

The episode "Trash of the Titans" focuses on formalized government structures as Homer has an issue with garbage pickup and decides to run for Sanitation Commissioner of Springfield. When he wins, he realizes that he actually has to work to enact the change that he wants. Even though it originally aired in 1998, Homer's campaign as the government outsider who wins an election off outrageous promises he can not keep, and whose

---

Hollywood or History?: An Inquiry-Based Strategy for Using The Simpsons to Teach Social Studies, pp. 131–153

Copyright © 2024 by Information Age Publishing
www.infoagepub.com
All rights of reproduction in any form reserved.

HOLLYWOOD OR HISTORY?

ineptitude at governing causes the town to literally become a trash dump is eerily similar to different television celebrity's run for office (Kurp, 2016). This lesson asks students to examine what makes a "good" candidate and whether experience in government is necessary to govern effectively.

In *The Simpsons*, power and authority in the city of Springfield is primarily shown through the character of the corrupt Mayor Quimby. However, there are frequent town meetings over the course of the show, and decisions are often made by the citizenry of Springfield, no matter how ridiculous those decisions may be! The "For Further Viewing" section features episodes about local, state, and national government—even though we still have no idea what state Springfield is in.

REFERENCES

Cohen, D. X. (Writer), & Michels, P. (Director). (1998, February 15). Das bus (Season 9, Episode 15) [TV series episode]. In M. Scully, J. L. Brooks, M. Groening, & S. Simon (Executive Producers), *The Simpsons*. Gracie Films; Twentieth Century Fox Film Corporation.

Kurp, J. (2016, October 13). A "Simpsons" episode about garbage predicted the rise of Donald Trump. *Uproxx*. https://uproxx.com/media/simpsons-donald-trump-hillary-clinton/

Maxtone-Graham, I. (Writer), & Reardon, J. (Director). (1998, April 26). Trash of the titans (Season 9, Episode 22) [TV series episode]. In M. Scully, J. L. Brooks, M. Groening, & S. Simon (Executive Producers), *The Simpsons*. Gracie Films; Twentieth Century Fox Film Corporation.

Chapter 6: Power, Authority, and Governance   133

The Simpsons State of Nature

Kymberli Wregglesworth

EPISODE(S):
"Das Bus" (1998, Season 9, Episode 14)

Grade	Subject	Topic
9–12	Civics	Philosophical Foundations of Civic Society and Government

Era Under Study	Estimated Time Needed for Lesson
Foundations of Government	150 minutes (split over two class periods)

State Standards

State	Standards and Descriptions
Massachusetts	WHI.T6.1. Identify the origins and the ideals of the European Enlightenment, such as happiness, reason, progress, liberty, and natural rights, and how intellectuals of the movement (e.g., Denis Diderot, Emmanuel Kant, John Locke, Charles de Montesquieu, Jean-Jacques Rousseau, Mary Wollstonecraft, Cesare Beccaria, Voltaire, or social satirists such as Molière and William Hogarth) exemplified these ideals in their work and challenged existing political, economic, social, and religious structures.
	T1.3. Define and provide examples of different forms of government, including direct democracy, representative democracy, republic, monarchy, oligarchy, and autocracy.
Michigan	C1.1.1. Describe, compare, and contrast political philosophers' views on purposes of government(s) including but not limited to Aristotle, Locke, Hobbes, Montesquieu, and Rousseau.
	C1.1.2. Identify, provide examples of, and distinguish among different systems of government by analyzing similarities and differences in sovereignty, power, legitimacy, and authority.

Virginia	CE.2a.1.b. Limited government: Government is not all-powerful and may do only those things the people have given it the power to do.
	CE.2a.1.d. Democracy: In a democratic system of government, the people rule.
	WHII.5c.4.a. Thomas Hobbes' Leviathan: Humans exist in a primitive "state of nature" and consent to government for self-protection.
	WHII5c.4.b. John Locke's Two Treatises of Government: People are sovereign and consent to government for protection of natural rights to life, liberty, and property.

Common Core Standards

Standard	Description
CCSS.ELA-LITERACY. RH.9-10.2	Determine the central ideas or information of a primary or secondary source; provide an accurate summary of how key events or ideas developed the course of the text.
CCSS.ELA-LITERACY. RH.11-12.2	Determine the central ideas or information of a primary or secondary source; provide an accurate summary that makes clear the relationships among the key details and ideas.
CCSS.ELA-LITERACY. RH.11-12.7	Integrate and evaluate multiple sources of information presented in diverse formats and media (e.g., visually, quantitatively, as well as in words) in order to address a question or solve a problem.

NCSS C3 Framework

Dimension	Description
Developing Questions and Planning Inquiries	D1.2.9-12. Explain points of agreement and disagreement experts have about interpretations and applications of disciplinary concepts and ideas associated with a compelling question.
Applying Disciplinary Concepts and Tools (Civics)	D2.Civ.1.9-12. Distinguish the powers and responsibilities of local, state, tribal, national, and international civic and political institutions.
Evaluating Sources and Using Evidence	D3.3.9-12. Identify evidence that draws information directly and substantially from multiple sources to detect inconsistencies in evidence in order to revise or strengthen claims.

Chapter 6: Power, Authority, and Governance   135

Communicating Conclusions and Taking Informed Action	D4.2.9-12. Construct explanations using sound reasoning, correct sequence (linear or nonlinear), examples, and details with significant and pertinent information and data, while acknowledging the strengths and weaknesses of the explanation given its purpose (e.g., cause and effect, chronological, procedural, technical).

NCSS Core Themes and Description

Theme	Description
I. Culture	Through the study of culture and cultural diversity, learners understand how human beings create, learn, share, and adapt to culture, and appreciate the role of culture in shaping their lives and society, as well the lives and societies of others.
II. Time, Continuity, and Change	Through the study of the past and its legacy, learners examine the institutions, values, and beliefs of people in the past, acquire skills in historical inquiry and interpretation, and gain an understanding of how important historical events and developments have shaped the modern world.
V. Individuals, Groups, and Institutions	Institutions such as families and civic, educational, governmental, and religious organizations exert a major influence on people's lives. This theme allows students to understand how institutions are formed, maintained, and changed, and to examine their influence.
VI. Power, Authority, and Governance	One essential component of education for citizenship is an understanding of the historical development and contemporary forms of power, authority, and governance. Through this theme, learners become familiar with the purposes and functions of government, the scope and limits of authority, and the differences between democratic and non-democratic political systems.
X. Civic Ideals and Practices	An understanding of civic ideals and practices is critical to full participation in society and is an essential component of education for citizenship. This theme enables students to learn about the rights and responsibilities of citizens of a democracy, and to appreciate the importance of active citizenship.

136 HOLLYWOOD OR HISTORY?

Handouts/Materials/Web Links

Handout/Materials:
- Hollywood or History? Graphic Organizer

Episode Clips and Video Content:
- "Das Bus," Season 9, Episode 14

Primary Sources:
- Hobbes, T. (1651/2002). *Leviathan*. Project Gutenberg. https://www.gutenberg.org/files/3207/3207-h/3207-h.htm
- Locke, J. (1690/2003). *Second treatise of government*. Project Gutenberg. https://www.gutenberg.org/files/7370/7370-h/7370-h.htm

Secondary Sources:
- Antonini, D. (2018, October 3). Social contract theory. *1000 word philosophy: An introductory anthology*. https://1000wordphilosophy.com/2018/10/03/social-contract-theory/

Guiding Questions

Primary Question:
- What type of government best balances the protection of natural rights with law and order?

Secondary Questions:
- How much power should a government/ruler have?
- Who should choose the government? How should it be chosen?

Important Vocabulary

Consent of the Governed: The authority of a government depends on the consent of the people being ruled, as expressed by votes in an election.

Democracy: Literally, rule by the people; direct participation of citizens in democratic decision making.

Dictatorship: Form of government in which one person or a small group possesses absolute power without effective constitutional limitations.

Monarchy: A political system based upon the undivided sovereignty or rule of a single person which is inherited from parent to child.

Natural Rights: Rights that people acquire inherently, from God or nature, including rights such as life, liberty, and property.

Republic: Form of government in which a state is ruled by representatives of the citizen body.

Social Contract: In political philosophy, an actual or hypothetical compact, or agreement, between the ruled or between the ruled and their rulers, defining the rights and duties of each.

State of Nature: In political theory, the real or hypothetical condition of human beings before or without political association.

Theocracy: Government by divine guidance or by officials who are regarded as divinely guided; in many theocracies, government leaders are members of the clergy, and the state's legal system is based on religious law.

Assessment Strategies

Formative Assessments:

- After watching "Das Bus" and learning about the concepts of *state of nature* and *social contract*, write two paragraphs explaining how the deserted island in "Das Bus" was an example of the two concepts.

Summative Assessments:

- If students should write an essay in which they defend a modern type of government (monarchy, democracy, republic, theocracy, dictatorship, etc.) as being the best type of government to balance protecting natural rights and ensuring everyone's survival. This essay should be based on their "Under the Dome" discussion with their small group.

Sparking Strategy/Warm-Up

Lesson Introduction

Ask students: *What would life be like without any rules or laws to govern your behavior?* Introduce the concept of *state of nature* to describe the situation of life before government and laws and *social contract* to describe the agreement between the ruled and their rulers. (10 min)

138 HOLLYWOOD OR HISTORY?

Lesson Procedures

Day 1

1. As a whole group, watch the episode, "Das Bus." Discuss the following questions related to the episode and take notes on the discussion in the "Das Bus" column of the Hollywood or History? Graphic Organizer. Ask students to give specific examples from the episode. *When does the state of nature begin? How do you know? Who takes charge to start a "government? Do the others consent to that government? How do you know? Is the government successful? What rights do the kids have once they arrive on the island? Does the government they create protect their natural rights? What are some examples of the strong dominating the weak? How are these examples of Hobbes's belief about the state of nature? What example is there of a social contract?* (40 min)

2. Read together the 1000-Word Philosophy article on Social Contract Theory. Discuss with students the concepts of *state of nature* and *social contract*. Use the excerpts from Hobbes's *Leviathan* and Locke's *Second Treatise of Government* to further develop student understanding of these concepts. Students should take notes in the "State of Nature/Social Contract" column in their graphic organizer. Ask students: *How was the episode "Das Bus" an example of the two concepts?* Students should then independently write two paragraphs explaining how the deserted island in "Das Bus" were examples of the two concepts in the space at the bottom of the graphic organizer. (30 min)

Day 2

1. Read the scenario description below to students. Give them time to ask questions (you can answer however you like, as long as you don't contradict the information provided):

    > *Imagine that five minutes before the school day ends, all of the adults in school disappear. Every student who has come to school today is still here, but everyone who is not a student is mysteriously gone. Additionally, a dome-shaped forcefield has appeared around the school. You can see out, and people on the outside can see in, but no one can figure out how to get through the dome. Cell phones, landline phones, and the Internet have stopped working because of the dome. Everything that was in the school this morning is still there (except the adults, of course). Every*

day exactly enough food for all the students to survive mysteriously appears in the cafeteria. If one person takes more than their share, though, another person will have to go without. The electricity continues to work, as do the water and sewer. Your goal is for everyone to survive until the dome disappears, or the people on the outside figure out how to get through to save you. (10 min)

2. Divide students into small groups (3–5 students depending on class size). Have them do a deeper dive into what life under the dome would be like with only a group of teens. They should discuss the questions on the Under the Dome handout. Once small group discussion is complete, student groups will share their ideas to the full class. (20 min)

3. Review the different types of government: *Monarchy*, *Democracy*, *Republic*, *Theocracy*, *Dictatorship*. Students should consider their group discussions and identify which type of government their group chose. (20 min)

4. Have students complete the summative assessment where they write an essay in which they defend a modern type of government (monarchy, democracy, republic, theocracy, dictatorship, etc.) as being the best type of government to balance protecting natural rights and ensuring everyone's survival. This essay should be based on their Under the Dome discussion with their small group. (20 min)

Differentiation

Scaffolds: There should be extra time for students to complete the Formative/Summative Assessments or reduce the amount of writing. Students could also be assigned a scribe or respond orally to the prompts.

ESL Interventions: The episodes of *The Simpsons*, if viewed through Disney+, can be broadcast in a number of languages.

Extensions:
- Read excerpts, or watch clips, from *Lord of the Flies* by William Golding. Discuss how the book/movie is an example of the state of nature, and how it is similar to the episode of *The Simpsons*
- Have students identify additional books, movies, television shows that might be examples of people living in the state of nature (*Mad Max*, *Avatar*, *The Purge*, etc.) Discuss how/why they are

140 HOLLYWOOD OR HISTORY?

examples and how they can help us to understand the idea of the state of nature.

- Students can read about the controversy surrounding vaccine mandates at AllSides (https://www.allsides.com/news/2021-10-15-0700/vaccine-mandates). Based on their research, discuss: *How is the government trying to balance protection of natural rights with protecting the health and safety of the greater public?*

REFERENCES

Allsides.com. (2021, October 14). *Vaccine mandates.* https://www.allsides.com/news/2021-10-15-0700/vaccine-mandates

Antonini, D. (2018, October 3). Social contract theory. *1000 word philosophy: An introductory anthology.* https://1000wordphilosophy.com/2018/10/03/social-contract-theory/

Cohen, D. X. (Writer), & Michels, P. (Director). (1998, February 15). Das bus (Season 9, Episode 15) [TV series episode]. In M. Scully, J. L. Brooks, M. Groening, & S. Simon (Executive Producers), *The Simpsons.* Gracie Films; Twentieth Century Fox Film Corporation.

Golding, W. (1954). *Lord of the flies.* Berkley Publishing Group.

Hobbes, T. (1651/2002). *Leviathan.* Project Gutenberg. https://www.gutenberg.org/files/3207/3207-h/3207-h.htm

Locke, J. (1690/2003). *Second treatise of government.* Project Gutenberg. https://www.gutenberg.org/files/7370/7370-h/7370-h.htm

APPENDIX A

Under the Dome

Imagine that five minutes before the school day ends, all of the adults in school disappear. Every student who has come to school today is still here, but everyone who is not a student is mysteriously gone. Additionally, a dome-shaped forcefield has appeared around the school. You can see out, and people on the outside can see in, but no one can figure out how to get through the dome. Cell phones, landline phones, and the Internet have stopped working because of the dome. Everything that was in the school this morning is still there (except the adults, of course). Every day exactly enough food for all the students to survive mysteriously appears in the cafeteria. If one person takes more than their share, though, another person will have to go without. The electricity continues to work, as do the water and sewer. Your goal is for everyone to survive until the dome disappears, or the people on the outside figure out how to get through to save you. In your group, discuss the following questions:

What would your life under the dome be like without any rules, laws, or people in charge?

- What might happen if you weren't rescued in a few days?
- What rights would you have in this situation?
- What would you do if your rights were violated?
- How would your group maintain order?
- Who will be in charge? How will you decide who will be in charge? How will you know if there needs to be a change in leadership?
- What are some advantages/disadvantages of creating rules, order, and choosing a leader(s)?
- What types of rules would you need to create? (Make a list of at least 5).
- Who will enforce the rules you create? How will they be enforced?
- What resources do you have (aside from the mysteriously appearing food) and how will you distribute and monitor the supplies?

Hollywood or History?

State of Nature and Social Contract

The episode contains elements of both the concept of "state of nature" and "social contract." These are two of the basic concepts of governmental philosophy. Students will use primary and secondary source materials to gain a deeper understanding of these concepts.

Read the sources provided and record your ideas about the two concepts in the corresponding space below. Then, analyze the episode of *The Simpsons* and connect the scenes to the concepts of "state of nature" and "social contract." You will extend this thinking into the next step, by showing how the hypothetical "under the dome" scenario further develops these ideas.

Primary Sources	Secondary Sources	The Simpsons "Das Bus" and "under the dome" hypothetical scenario

"Can't Someone Else Do It?" Experience in Governing

Annie McMahon Whitlock

EPISODE(S):
"Trash of the Titans" (1998, Season 9, Episode 22)

Grade	Subject	Topic
11–12th	Civics	The American Presidency

Era Under Study	Estimated Time Needed for Lesson
2008–present	90 minutes—could be broken up into two days

State Standards

State	Standards and Descriptions
Michigan	C-6.3.1. Explain the personal dispositions that contribute to knowledgeable and engaged participation in civic communities.
North Carolina	FP.C&G.4.3. Analyze the roles of citizens of North Carolina and the United States in terms of responsibilities, participation, civic life and criteria for membership or admission.
Texas	HS.9.A. Identify different methods of filling public offices, including elected and appointed offices, at the local, state, and national levels.

Common Core Standards

Standard	Description
CCSS.ELA-LITERACY. W.11-12.1	Write arguments to support claims in an analysis of substantive topics or texts, using valid reasoning and relevant and sufficient evidence.
CCSS.ELA-LITERACY. RH.11-12.7	Integrate and evaluate multiple sources of information presented in diverse formats and media (e.g., visually, quantitatively, as well as in words) in order to address a question or solve a problem.

NCSS C3 Framework

Dimension	Description
Applying Disciplinary Concepts and Tools (Civics)	D2.Civ.2.9-12. Analyze the role of citizens in the U.S. political system, with attention to various theories of democracy, changes in Americans' participation over time, and alternative models from other countries, past and present.
	D2.Civ.10.9-12. Analyze the impact and the appropriate roles of personal interests and perspectives on the application of civic virtues, democratic principles, constitutional rights, and human rights.
Communicating Conclusions and Taking Informed Action	D4.1.9-12. Construct arguments using precise and knowledgeable claims, with evidence from multiple sources, while acknowledging counterclaims and evidentiary weaknesses.

NCSS Core Themes and Description

Theme	Description
V. Individuals, Groups, and Institutions	Institutions such as families and civic, educational, governmental, and religious organizations exert a major influence on people's lives. This theme allows students to understand how institutions are formed, maintained, and changed, and to examine their influence.
VI. Power, Authority, and Governance	One essential component of education for citizenship is an understanding of the historical development and contemporary forms of power, authority, and governance. Through this theme, learners become familiar with the purposes and functions of government, the scope and limits of authority, and the differences between democratic and non-democratic political systems.
X. Civic Ideals and Practices	An understanding of civic ideals and practices is critical to full participation in society and is an essential component of education for citizenship. This theme enables students to learn about the rights and responsibilities of citizens of a democracy, and to appreciate the importance of active citizenship.

Chapter 6: Power, Authority, and Governance   145

Handouts/Materials/Web Links

Handout/Materials:
- Hollywood or History? Graphic Organizer

Episode Clips and Video Content:
- "Trash of the Titans," Season 9, Episode 22
    - o **Clip 1:** 7:01-8:15
    - o **Clip 2:** 8:34-11:10
    - o **Clip 3:** 12:04-14:35
    - o **Clip 4:** 17:29-21:33
- C-SPAN Classroom. (2019, May 19). Video clip: Is experience important for candidates running for president? [Video]. *C-SPAN Classroom.* https://www.c-span.org/classroom/document/?9522

Secondary Sources:
- Balz, D. (2019, May 18). Nos. 44 and 45 broke the mold. What does that mean for the future of the presidency? *The Washington Post.* https://www.washingtonpost.com/politics/nos-44-and-45-broke-the-mold-what-does-that-mean-for-the-future-of-the-presidency/2019/05/18/97d64320-77e9-11e9-bd25-c989555e7766_story.html

Guiding Questions

Primary Question:
- Does experience (or lack of) make a difference when choosing elected officials?

Secondary Questions:
- What makes an elected official "good?"
- Does a candidate's lack of experience in government make our country more democratic?

Important Vocabulary

Notoriety: The state or quality of being famous or well-known, especially for a negative reason

146 HOLLYWOOD OR HISTORY?

Provocative: Causing annoyance, anger, or another strong reaction, especially deliberately

Sanitation Commissioner: A government official in a city that manages the city's waste collection, recycling, and disposal

Assessment Strategies

Formative Assessments:
- Hollywood or History? Graphic Organizer

Summative Assessments:
- Write an essay that answers the primary question: *Does a candidate's experience (or lack of) make a difference when choosing elected officials?* Use examples from the Washington Post article, "Trash of the Titans," or other historical examples to make your argument.

Sparking Strategy/Warm-Up

Lesson Introduction

Start by posing this question to the whole class: *What makes an elected official "good?"* The students can think about the U.S. presidency or other governmental roles (governor, mayor, etc.). Ask the students to quick-write as many descriptive words as possible in two minutes, then ask for volunteers to share with the class to make a whole-group list. Ask any students to explain answers that are not completely clear. (10 min)

Lesson Procedures

Day 1

1. If any student mentions "experience in leadership" or "experience in government" as something that makes a "good" elected official, ask the class: *Why might experience in government be a good thing for elected officials?* If nobody has mentioned it, ask the class: *Why didn't anyone mention experience in government as important? Is it important?* Make sure that regardless of whether "experience" makes the list that eventually the teacher guides the students to thinking about this question: *Does a candidate's experience in government make a difference when choosing elected officials?* (10 min)

Chapter 6: Power, Authority, and Governance   147

2. Show the clip from C-SPAN from 2019 on presidential experience. Explain that Michael Smerconish, the talking head in this clip, is talking about the diverse set of Democratic candidates for president in the 2020 election and how experience in government may be irrelevant to people when choosing their leaders. Teachers may have to stop the video and explain who some of the people are that he's referring to, such as "Mayor Pete" and "AOC." (5 min)

3. Hand out the full *Washington Post* article from 2019 about the elections of Barack Obama and Donald Trump. Give students time to read the article, highlighting important quotes that show the argument the author is making about how a candidate's lack of experience in government might be a good thing. Or at least a lack of experience might be what people *want* in their elected leaders. Students can work individually or read the article together in small groups. This can also be assigned for homework if short on time. (20 min)

4. Have volunteer students share the main points from the *Post* article. Students should collectively write these down in the Hollywood or History? Graphic Organizer in the far left column. (10 min)

Day 2

1. If doing this on a following day, ask students to review reasons why a candidate's lack of experience might be a good quality to have, or at least a desired quality. Then ask the students: *Do you agree with this argument?* (10 min)

2. Explain that they will now see the other side of this argument, using a fictional character of Homer Simpson. Explain that many people saw connections between Homer's campaign and eventual election for sanitation commissioner and Donald Trump's presidential campaign and eventual election. They were both government "outsiders" who used their lack of experience as a badge of honor. After each clip, stop and have students write down examples of why Homer's tenure as sanitation commissioner is an argument against an outsider candidate.

    Clip 1: 7:01–8:15

    This clip gives context to Homer wanting to run for sanitation commissioner (he is upset about the trash pickup). There is a line at the end about registering as a sex offender that a teacher may want to cut out of the clip.

148 HOLLYWOOD OR HISTORY?

Clip 2: 8:34–11:10
First ask the students: *How does Homer gain notoriety?* (The U2 concert) *How is his lack of experience a bad thing?* (Students should note that Homer has no plan for how he is going to govern as sanitation commissioner).

Clip 3: 12:04–14:35
Ask the students: *What is Homer's provocative statement?* ("Can't someone else do it?") *How is his lack of experience a bad thing?* (Students should note that Homer's plans are unrealistic and not possible, and that his debate is mostly digs on the other candidate)

Clip 4: 17:29–21:33
How is Homer's lack of experience problematic once he's elected? (He can't budget his department, he fills Springfield with garbage, ultimately costing the town an expensive move). At this point, the students will be ready for the summative assessment, but you may need to review the arguments against a candidate with no experience. (25 min)

3. Have students examine the pros and cons to a candidate with no experience in government from their Hollywood or History? Graphic Organizer. They should write an essay answering the primary question from this lesson: *Does a candidate's experience (or lack of) make a difference when choosing elected officials?* They should give their opinion on what they prefer in a candidate but using evidence from the *Washington Post* article or "Trash of the Titans." (10 min, with option to complete at home)

Differentiation

Scaffolds: The *Washington Post* article can be read to students or select passages from the article can be given to students instead of reading the entire article. Students may need to be given a structured outline on how to organize their essay for their summative assessment.

ESL Interventions: In addition to the scaffolds above, students can view clips of *The Simpsons* in other languages. If possible, students should be able to write their summative assessment in their native language.

Extensions:

- Students can research candidates for an upcoming election, including local elections. They could make a list of how much governing experience each candidate has relative to the position they are running for. Their information could be turned into a pamphlet or Google Doc to give out to voters to help them make decisions.
- In groups, students can select a president from the past to research and then find out how much governing experience they had before becoming president. Then give a presentation about the qualities that made that president a good leader and whether they think their experience made a difference.
- Students can research positions within their city or county government (such as sanitation commissioner) and find out what kind of experience would be necessary to do those jobs effectively. If students are old enough or eligible, they should consider running for office!

REFERENCES

Balz, D. (2019, May 18). Nos. 44 and 45 broke the mold. What does that mean for the future of the presidency? *The Washington Post*. https://www.washingtonpost.com/politics/nos-44-and-45-broke-the-mold-what-does-that-mean-for-the-future-of-the-presidency/2019/05/18/97d64320-77e9-11e9-bd25-c989555e7766_story.html

C-SPAN Classroom. (2019, May 19). Video clip: Is experience important for candidates running for president? [Video]. *C-SPAN Classroom*. https://www.c-span.org/classroom/document/?9522

Maxtone-Graham, I. (Writer), & Reardon, J. (Director). (1998, April 26). Trash of the titans (Season 9, Episode 22) [TV series episode]. In M. Scully, J. L. Brooks, M. Groening, & S. Simon (Executive Producers), *The Simpsons*. Gracie Films; Twentieth Century Fox Film Corporation.

Hollywood or History?

Does a candidate's experience in government make a difference when choosing elected officials? Is it better or worse to have a candidate with very little or no previous experience in government? Compare the elections of Barack Obama and Donald Trump, as described in the *Washington Post* article to the election of Homer Simpson for Sanitation Commissioner of Springfield. After reading and watching both sources, write an essay on your opinion of whether a candidate's experience in government makes a difference to voters, or to their ability to govern.

A Candidate's Lack of Experience is a Good Thing	A Candidate's Lack of Experience is a Bad Thing
Washington Post article from 2019	*Homer Simpson in "Trash of the Titans"*

Chapter 6: Power, Authority, and Governance 151

For Further Viewing

With over 700 episodes to choose from, there are more episodes of *The Simpsons* that could be used to teach the theme of Power, Authority, and Governance.

Power and Authority

Students can study the concept of power and authority without studying traditional government roles. In *The Simpsons*, the character of Nelson Muntz (the bully) is a good example of someone with power at Springfield Elementary, with no legitimized authority. Nelson's bullying has been a feature in many episodes, including "Das Bus." Here are two more:

Bart the General (1990, Season 1, Episode 5)
This is the first episode of the series to feature Nelson. This is a great example of the power Nelson holds over students, and what happens when Bart challenges that power. (Written by John Swartzwelder, Directed by David Silverman)

Bart Star (1997, Season 9, Episode 6)
Nelson is the star quarterback of the pee wee football team, mostly by bullying everyone on the field. A great example of his power in bullying his teammates, but also some legitimized authority as leader of the team. (Written by Donic Cary, Directed by Dominic Polcino)

Governing

Local Springfield government appears in many episodes, not just "Trash of the Titans." Mayor "Diamond" Joe Quimby is a satire of a Kennedy family politician and is often portrayed as corrupt or indifferent to his constituents. Here are two episodes where Mayor Quimby is featured, both from Season 10:

Mayored to the Mob (1998, Season 10, Episode 9)
Homer becomes Mayor Quimby's bodyguard and gets an up-close look at the corruption from the mayor's office, including that Mayor Quimby takes bribes from the local mobster, Fat Tony. (Written by Ron Hauge, Directed by Swinton O. Scott III)

152 HOLLYWOOD OR HISTORY?

They Saved Lisa's Brain (1998, Season 10, Episode 22)
Although this episode features Mayor Quimby, he disappears early on, leaving the governance of Springfield to the local Mensa chapter. They find it very difficult to govern the town as a group. (Written by Matt Selman, Directed by Pete Michels)

Fictional Political Candidates

The Simpsons has many episodes that feature fictional candidates for elected offices at the local, state (yes, even though the state is never mentioned!), and national level. Any of these episodes could be used to explore how the various candidates depicted exhibit power, authority, and ability to govern:

2 Cars in Every Garage and 3 Eyes on Every Fish (1990, Season 2, Episode 4)
This is the episode that introduces Blinky, the three-eyed fish that Bart finds in the water by the nuclear plant. Mr. Burns runs for governor of the show's unnamed state so that he can avoid his plant getting shut down for environmental concerns. (Written by Sam Simon and John Swartzwelder, Directed by Wesley Archer)

Mr. Lisa Goes to Washington (1991, Season 3, Episode 2)
Lisa wins an essay contest about "what makes America great" and the Simpsons win a trip to Washington, D.C. where Lisa witnesses a fictional congressman Bobby Arnold take a bribe. She takes back her patriotic essay, but in the end, she helps bring the congressman to justice. (Written by George Meyer, Directed by Wes Archer)

Sideshow Bob Roberts (1994, Season 6, Episode 5)
The villainous Sideshow Bob, in prison for multiple crimes, is released and runs for mayor of Springfield against Mayor Quimby. He wins in a landslide, but only because he committed election fraud. (Written by Bill Oakley and Josh Weinstein, Directed by Mark Kirkland)

E Pluribus Wiggum (2008, Season 19, Episode 10)
Springfield moves up its election day and suddenly becomes the first presidential primary of election season. When Ralph Wiggum wins the Springfield primary, he needs to prove his candidacy. (Written by Michael Price, Directed by Michael Polcino)

The Old Blue Mayor She Ain't What She Used to Be (2017, Season 29, Episode 6)
Marge runs against Mayor Quimby and wins but struggles to govern while balancing competing interests. (Written by Tom Gammill and Max Pross, Directed by Matthew Nastuk)

Commentary on Real Political Candidates

Sometimes, *The Simpsons* reference actual U.S. elections, blurring the line between real life and the world of Springfield. The show often plays with reality and fantasy in their Halloween episodes, called "Treehouse of Horror." Since these often air right around Election Day in November, these horror stories have featured several presidential candidates over the years:

Treehouse of Horror VII (1996, Season 8, Episode 1)
The segment "Citizen Kang" features aliens Kang and Kodos taking over the forms of Bill Clinton and Bob Dole to take over the 1996 election. It's the source of the famous line, "Don't blame me, I voted for Kodos!" ("Citizen Kang" written by David X. Cohen, Directed by Mike B. Anderson)

Treehouse of Horror XIX (2008, Season 20, Episode 4)
Although more for fun than for educational purposes, the opening of this episode features Homer attempting to vote for Barack Obama in the 2008 election, but a crazy voting machine won't let him. (Written by Matt Warburton, Directed by Bob Anderson)

Treehouse of Horror XXXI (2020, Season 32, Episode 4)
In another segment that's more fun than educational ("2020 Election"), Homer can't decide who to vote for president in 2020. When he finally decides, he realizes he dreamt the whole thing and the country is in chaos. (Written by Julia Prescott, Directed by Steve Dean Moore)

CHAPTER 7

PRODUCTION, DISTRIBUTION, AND CONSUMPTION

This theme most corresponds with the social studies discipline of economics. Economics is about choices—choices about what we produce, how we distribute what we produce, and what we consume. In *The Simpsons*, a central focus of the show has been the family's lack of monetary resources. The first episode of the show, which aired in 1989, featured Homer taking on a second job as a mall Santa to afford Christmas presents for his family (Pond & Silverman, 1989). Homer and Marge take on several jobs over the years of the show, which shows how they make decisions about their scarce family resources. Of course, Homer's main job is his work as a nuclear safety inspector at the Springfield Nuclear Power Plant, run by the evil Mr. Burns. In the show, Mr. Burns is an example of the evils of capitalism, as he is the epitome of the 1%—a man who literally blocked out the sun for profit.

In this chapter, Timothy Constant uses two episodes to explain to high school students the circular flow model. One of them, the classic "Mr. Plow" episode (Vitti & Reardon, 1992), features Homer making an investment of his money into a plow truck to go into business plowing snow. The other, "Super Franchise Me" (Odenkirk & Kirkland, 2014), shows Marge making an investment into a sandwich business. This episode is a great example of several economic concepts, including supply, demand, and competition in a market.

The Simpsons also featured an episode about microfinance in "Loan-a Lisa" (Garza & Faughnan, 2010). In this episode, Lisa invests a small amount of money into a business that Nelson wants to start, showing that small interactions to empower small businesses can have a major impact.

Hollywood or History?: An Inquiry-Based Strategy for Using The Simpsons to Teach Social Studies, pp. 155–184
Copyright © 2024 by Information Age Publishing
www.infoagepub.com
All rights of reproduction in any form reserved.

155

156 HOLLYWOOD OR HISTORY?

The other lesson in this chapter is for elementary students to see how microfinance works in real life and gives a different look at the capitalist market concepts often taught at the elementary level.

Whether its family resources, the nuclear plant, or any other side jobs that the Simpsons take on over the years, economic choices feature heavily in plot points of many episodes. In the "For Further Viewing" section, there are more episodes listed about the investments in businesses that the family takes on and Mr. Burns' sketchy business practices.

REFERENCES

Garza, V. L. (Writer), & Faughnan, M. (Director). (2010, October 3). Loan-a Lisa (Season 22, Episode 2) [TV series episode]. In A. Jean, M. Scully, J. L. Brooks, M. Groening, & S. Simon (Executive Producers), *The Simpsons*. Gracie Films; Twentieth Century Fox Film Corporation.

Odenkirk, B. (Writer), & Kirkland, M. (Director). (2014, October 12). Super franchise me. (Season 26, Episode 3) [TV series episode]. In A. Jean, M. Scully, J. L. Brooks, M. Groening, & S. Simon (Executive Producers), *The Simpsons*. Gracie Films; Twentieth Century Fox Film Corporation.

Pond, M. (Writer), & Silverman, D. (Director). (1989, December 17). Simpsons roasting on an open fire (Season 1, Episode 1) [TV series episode]. In J. L. Brooks, M. Groening, & S. Simon (Executive Producers), *The Simpsons*. Gracie Films; Twentieth Century Fox Film Corporation.

Vitti, J. (Writer), & Reardon, J. (Director). (1992, November 19). Mr. Plow (Season 4, Episode 9) [TV series episode]. In A. Jean, M. Reiss, M. Scully, J. L. Brooks, M. Groening, & S. Simon (Executive Producers), *The Simpsons*. Gracie Films; Twentieth Century Fox Film Corporation.

Chapter 7: Production, Distribution, and Consumption   157

Is Competition Always Good?

Timothy Constant

EPISODE(S):
"Mr. Plow" (1992, Season 4, Episode 9)
"Super Franchise Me" (2014, Season 26, Episode 3)

Grade	Subject	Topic
9–12	Economics	Circular Flow Model

Estimated Time Needed for Lesson
180 minutes (three 60-minute lessons)

State Standards

State	Standards and Descriptions
Michigan	1.1.2. Entrepreneurship—analyze the risks and rewards of entrepreneurship and associate the functions of entrepreneurs with alleviating problems associated with scarcity.
	1.2.2. Market structures—identify the characteristics of perfect competition, monopolistic competition, oligopoly, and monopoly market structures.
	1.3.2. Price, equilibrium, elasticity, and incentives-analyze how prices change through the interaction of buyers and sellers in a market, including the role of supply, demand, equilibrium, and elasticity, and explain how incentives (monetary and non-monetary) affect choices of households and economic organizations.
	2.1.1. Circular low and the national economy—using the concept of circular flow, analyze the roles and relationship between households, business firms, and government in the economy of the United States.
	4.1.2. Buying goods and services—describe factors that consumers may consider when purchasing a good or service, including the costs, benefits, and the role of government in obtaining the information.

New York	12.E2a. Given that the resources of individuals (and societies) are limited, decisions as to what goods and services will be produced and to whom to sell one's resources are driven by numerous factors, including a desire to derive the maximum benefit from and thus the most efficient allocation of those resources.
	12.E2b. The choices of buyers and sellers in the marketplace determine supply and demand, market prices, allocation of scarce resources, and the goods and services that are produced. In a perfect world, consumers influence product availability and price through their purchasing power in the product market. Product market supply and demand determine product availability and pricing.
	12.E2c. Businesses choose what to supply in the product market, based on product market prices, available technology, and prices of factors of production. The prices of those factors are determined based on supply and demand in the factor market. The supply and demand of each factor market is directly related to employment. Debates surround various ways to minimize unemployment (frictional, structural, cyclical).
Ohio	EFL.9-12.4. Different economic systems (traditional, market, command, and mixed) utilize different methods to allocate resources.
	EFL.9-12.5. Markets exist when consumers and producers interact. When supply or demand changes, market prices adjust. Those adjustments send signals and provide incentives to consumers and producers to change their own decisions.
	EFL.9-12.6. Competition among sellers lowers costs and prices and encourages producers to produce mor of what consumers are willing and able to buy. Competition among buyers increases prices and allocates goods and services to those people who are willing and able to pay the most for them.
	EFL.9-12.4.7. A nation's overall level of economic well-being is determined by the interaction of spending and production decisions made by all households, firms, government agencies and others in the economy. Economic well-being can be assessed by analyzing economic indicators gathered by the government.

Common Core Standards

Standard	Description
CCSS.ELA-LITERACY. RH.9-10.1	Cite specific textual evidence to support analysis of primary and secondary sources.
CCSS.ELA-LITERACY. RH.9-10.2	Determine the central ideas or information of primary or secondary sources; provide an accurate summary of how key events develop over the course of the text.

NCSS C3 Framework

Dimension	Description
Developing Questions and Planning Inquiries	D1.1.9-12. Explain how a question reflects an enduring issue in the field.
Applying Disciplinary Concepts and Tools (Economics)	D2.Eco.1.9-12. Analyze how incentives influence choices that may result in policies with a range of costs and benefits for different groups.
	D2.Eco.3.9-12. Analyze the ways incentives influence what is produced and distributed in a market system.
	D2.Eco.4.9-12. Evaluate the extent to which competition among sellers and buyers exists in specific markets.
	D2.Eco.5.9-12. Describe the consequences of competition in specific markets.
Evaluating Sources and Using Evidence	D3.1.9-12. Gather relevant information from multiple sources representing a wide range of views while using the origin, authority, structure, context, and corroborative value of the sources to guide the selection.
Communicating Conclusions and Taking Informed Action	D4.4.9-12. Construct explanations using sound reasoning, correct sequence, examples, and details with significant and pertinent information and data.

NCSS Core Themes and Description

Theme	Description
VII. Production, Distribution, and Consumption	This theme provides for the study of how people organize for the production, distribution, and consumption of goods and services, and prepares students for the study of domestic and global economic issues.

Handouts/Materials/Web Links

Handout/Materials:
- 3-2-1 Exit Ticket
- Circular Flow Model Graphic Organizer
- Hollywood or History? Is Competition Always Good?

Episode Clips and Video Content:
- "Mr. Plow," Season 4, Episode 9
  - o **Clip 1:** 2:33–3:20
  - o **Clip 2:** 6:17–6:40
  - o **Clip 3:** 8:45–10:22
  - o **Clip 4:** 10:38–11:00
  - o **Clip 5:** 11:11–11:22
  - o **Clip 6:** 12:41–13:20
  - o **Clip 7:** 15:02–15:32
  - o **Clip 8:** 16:08–17:52
  - o **Clip 9:** 18:45–20:48
- "Super Franchise Me," Season 26, Episode 3
  - o **Clip 1:** 1:58–3:40
  - o **Clip 2:** 4:49–5:34
  - o **Clip 3:** 5:36–7:04
  - o **Clip 4:** 9:24–10:50
  - o **Clip 5:** 11:42–13:02
  - o **Clip 6:** 13:30–14:30
  - o **Clip 7:** 16:47–17:09
  - o **Clip 8:** 17:34–17:54

Chapter 7: Production, Distribution, and Consumption   161

- Federal Reserve Bank of St. Louis. (n.d.). *Circular flow – The economic lowdown video series.* https://www.stlouisfed.org/education/economic-lowdown-video-series/episode-6-circular-flow

Secondary Sources:
- Federal Reserve Bank of Atlanta. (n.d.). *The circular flow model infographic.* https://www.atlantafed.org/education/classroom-economist/infographics/circular-flow
- Federal Reserve Bank of St. Louis. (n.d.). *Glossary of economics and personal finance terms.* https://www.stlouisfed.org/education/glossary
- Mentimeter Word Cloud Generator:—https://www.mentimeter.com/features/word-cloud

Guiding Questions

Primary Question:
- Is competition always good?

Secondary Questions:
- What drives demand for a product or service?
- What are the benefits and challenges with competition?
- What is the relationship between households and businesses?

Important Vocabulary

Circular Flow Model: A graphical representation of the relationship between businesses and households as they interact with the product and resource markets.

Competition: Sellers working to attract the business of others by offering the best deal for prospective buyers. Competition acts as a control on self-interest.

Demand: The desire and ability to own something.

Entrepreneurs: Individuals willing to take risks in order to develop new products or services and start new businesses.

Factor/Resource Markets: Where businesses acquire the resources (land, labor, capital, and entrepreneurship) needed to make a product or provide a service.

Goods: Tangible/physical items for purchase.

162 HOLLYWOOD OR HISTORY?

Market Economy: A type of economy system based on individual choice and voluntary exchange.

Need: A product or service that is essential.

Product Markets: Where businesses have an opportunity to sell their goods and services to households.

Services: Work performed for other for a fee.

Supply: The quantity of goods and services producers are willing and able to offer for sale at each possible price during a period of time.

Want: A product or service that is desired but not a necessity.

Assessment Strategies

Formative Assessments:
- Mentimeter Word Cloud
- 3-2-1 Exit Ticket
- Circular Flow Model Graphic Organizer
- Developing an Argument Small Group Activity

Summative Assessments:
- Students will select one of the two business opportunities (Mr. Plow or Mother Hubbard's Sandwich Cupboard) and serve as a business consultant to this business. Students will develop a written argument that Homer or Marge should remain in business and that the competition they face is good for their business. Explain changes they should make to their business strategy and why. Students will develop a claim and support their claim with evidence from the relevant episode and specific references to components of the Circular Flow Model.

Sparking Strategy/Warm-Up

Lesson Introduction

Ask students to identify their favorite restaurant. Ask them, *What are the qualities that make it their favorite restaurant?* Students will go to Mentimeter and enter words to describe the qualities of their favorite restaurant (https://www.mentimeter.com/features/word-cloud). Review the Word Cloud created by Mentimeter with the class and ask students to identify any words that stand out to them and if they see any common qualities. Explain to students that these qualities are important to them because it satisfies their

Chapter 7: Production, Distribution, and Consumption   163

wants and needs which is an important economic concept which drives the demand for a product and/or service. (10 min)

Lesson Procedures

Day 1

1. Ask students to take a blank piece of paper and fold it in half vertically. Students will then draw along the crease and then a horizontal line close to the top of the paper to create a T-chart. Students will label the left column with the name of their favorite restaurant. The right column will be labeled "Competition." Using the results of the Mentimeter, students will list under their favorite restaurant the characteristics that make the restaurant their favorite. Under the Competition column, students will list characteristics identified in the Mentimeter that their favorite restaurant does not have but should. (5 min)
2. Students will pair with a partner and share their T-chart. With a partner, students will discuss their lists and write a narrative at the bottom as to why it is important to identify these competitive differences. Students will also draft an argument for why this competition is good for their favorite restaurant and why it may be bad. (15 min)
3. Once the partners have identified the pros and cons of competition, the teacher will ask for volunteers to share their thoughts to the whole class. (10 min)
4. Students will write on the 3-2-1 Exit Ticket handout three things they learned from Day 1, two things they found interesting, and one question they have. (5 min)

Day 2

1. Post the questions from the 3-2-1 activity around the classroom. Give students sticky notes and have students complete a gallery walk and read the questions submitted from the Day 1 exit ticket. If students believe they have an answer to the question, have them write the answer on a sticky note and place the answer on the question posted on the wall. (10 min)
2. Show students the video *Circular Flow – The Economic Lowdown Video Series* from the Federal Reserve Bank of St. Louis. After the video, show students the infographic of the Circular Flow Model from the Federal Reserve Bank of Atlanta. Define each part of

164 HOLLYWOOD OR HISTORY?

the Circular Flow Model using the infographic. Also explain that these and other economic definitions are available through the Federal Reserve Bank of St. Louis Glossary of Economics and Personal Finance Terms at: https://www.stlouisfed.org/education/glossary:

a. Explain that the market economy of the United States is dependent on the interaction between buyers (households) and sellers (businesses). A market economy is based on individual choice and voluntary exchange.
b. Explain that the choice of households is based on their wants and needs. Define wants and needs for students. These wants and needs drives demand for goods and services and the demand influences supply. Define goods, services, demand, and supply.
c. Explain that businesses represented in the Circular Flow Model are in competition with each other to provide products and services for households who in turn spend money for those goods and services which is revenue to the businesses. (15 min)

3. Students will watch clips from *The Simpsons* "Mr. Plow" episode. Explain that the episode shows the interaction between businesses and households and how competition influences business decisions. As students watch the clips, they will fill in a blank Circular Flow Model graphic organizer with specific content from the episode. (15 min)

Clip 1: 2:33–3:20—Shows an example of the need to create an entrepreneurial opportunity

Clip 2: 6:17–6:40—Money making opportunity using the plow truck

Clip 3: 8:45–10:22—Homer buys advertising time late at night because it is affordable and plows a convenience store so it can remain open. The time is affordable because few people are watching television at the time. It is not at peak viewing hours.

Clip 4: 10:38–11:00—Homer plows the street so there can be school

Clip 5: 11:11–11:22—Homer is rewarded by the mayor with a key to the city

Chapter 7: Production, Distribution, and Consumption   165

Clip 6: 12:41–13:20—Plow King becomes Mr. Plow's competition

Clip 7: 15:02–15:32—Details about competition. Plow King is faster, more responsive, and has a larger truck. Plow King has better advertising.

Clip 8: 16:08–17:52—Homer pays for a new advertisement. Homer tricks Plow King to get a competitive advantage over him since he is taking business away from Mr. Plow.

Clip 9: 18:45–20:48—Homer saves Barney and they decide to partner in the business of snow removal.

4. Discuss as a whole class what information they filled in on their Circular Flow Model from the "Mr. Plow" episode. (10 min)
5. Students will make changes to their Circular Flow Model based on information stated by fellow students during the whole group discussion.

Day 3

1. Provide students a blank copy of the Circular Flow Model to label from memory. (5 min)
2. Students will watch clips from the "Super Franchise Me" episode. As students watch the clips, they will fill in a blank Circular Flow Model graphic organizer with specific content from the episode. (15 min)

Clip 1: 1:58–3:40—Marge takes advantage of a mistake by Homer which will turn into a business opportunity.

Clip 2: 4:49–5:34—Marge approached with a franchise opportunity based on the popularity of her sandwiches.

Clip 3: 5:36–7:04—Marge starts her franchise

Clip 4: 9:24–10:50—Marge is concerned about the lack of customers. The supply costs of franchises are high. She is having issues with an employee.

Clip 5: 11:42–13:02—Due to a labor shortage, the family has to work in the business.

166 HOLLYWOOD OR HISTORY?

Clip 6: 13:30–14:30—Marge refers to her pursuing the "American Dream" but an express version of the franchise opens across the street and takes business away from her location.

Clip 7: 16:47–17:09—The competition advertises on television. The advertising shows the poor quality of the sandwiches and their use of social media.

Clip 8: 17:34–17:54—Marge speaks to corporate about the competition across the street.

3. Discuss as a whole class what information they filled in on their Circular Flow Model from the "Super Franchise Me" episode. Explain to students that both episodes provide valuable information about what it means to be an entrepreneur, about business competition, and about supply and demand. Define entrepreneur, supply, and demand for the students. (10 min)
4. After watching both episodes, students will practice synthesizing the information by answering the following questions in small groups (arrange groups of no more than four to five students per group): (10 min)

    What did the two episodes have in common regarding starting a business?

    What drove the demand for goods and services in the episodes?

    What were the benefits and challenges of competition?

    What did you learn about the interactions between households and businesses?

5. After small group discussion, small groups will be tasked with developing an argument using the Hollywood or History? graphic organizer.

Differentiation

Scaffolds: Work with students individually if needed. Provide context and explanations for all materials and assignments. Facilitate the movement

Chapter 7: Production, Distribution, and Consumption   167

of the gallery walk and monitor the selection of small groups to provide proper balance and diversification of students.

ESL Interventions: Provide students with a vocabulary list of terms used in the lesson. Carefully craft definitions using simplified wording and a photo/picture representation of the vocabulary words. Provide more white space on handouts. Focus more on the visual and kinesthetic aspects of the lesson. Ask students to identify words in their home language connected to the lesson vocabulary. Show videos multiple times if needed to improve comprehension.

Extensions:
- Arrange to take students on a field trip to one of the 12 Federal Reserve Bank locations or one of their satellite branch locations. If you are unable to arrange for a field trip, some branches have a Speakers Bureau, and you can arrange for one of their speakers to visit your classroom or school. The Cleveland and Chicago banks have the Money Museum for students to visit:
  - o Federal Reserve Bank of Cleveland, Money Museum: https://www.clevelandfed.org/learningcenter/about.aspx
  - o Federal Reserve Bank of Chicago, Money Museum: https://www.chicagofed.org/education/money-museum/index

REFERENCES

Federal Reserve Bank of Atlanta. (n.d.). *The circular flow model infographic.* https://www.atlantafed.org/education/classroom-economist/infographics/circular-flow

Federal Reserve Bank of Chicago (2022). *Chicago Fed's Money Museum.* https://www.chicagofed.org/education/money-museum/index

Federal Reserve Bank of Cleveland. (2022). *Money museum.* https://www.clevelandfed.org/en/learningcenter/about.aspx

Federal Reserve Bank of St. Louis. (n.d.). *Circular flow – The economic lowdown video series.* https://www.stlouisfed.org/education/economic-lowdown-video-series/episode-6-circular-flow

Federal Reserve Bank of St. Louis. (n.d.). *Glossary of economics and personal finance terms.* https://www.stlouisfed.org/education/glossary

Morton, J. S., Shug, M. C., & Wentworth, D. R. (1995). *Economics: A multimedia program student handbook.* McDougal Littell.

Odenkirk, B. (Writer), & Kirkland, M. (Director). (2014, October 12). Super franchise me. (Season 26, Episode 3) [TV series episode]. In A. Jean, M. Scully, J. L. Brooks, M. Groening, & S. Simon (Executive Producers), *The Simpsons.* Gracie Films; Twentieth Century Fox Film Corporation.

Vitti, J. (Writer), & Reardon, J. (Director). (1992, November 19). Mr. Plow (Season 4, Episode 9) [TV series episode]. In A. Jean, M. Reiss, M. Scully, J. L. Brooks, M. Groening, & S. Simon (Executive Producers), *The Simpsons*. Gracie Films; Twentieth Century Fox Film Corporation.

APPENDIX A

Circular Flow Model Blank Handout

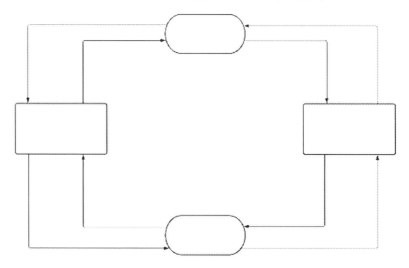

Chapter 7: Production, Distribution, and Consumption   169

Hollywood or History?

Is Competition Always Good?

Sitcoms often reference and connect to various subjects within social studies including economics. In this inquiry task, students will investigate, using the Hollywood or History analysis model, the validity of the economic concept of competition as portrayed in two episodes of *The Simpsons*.

Evaluate specific clips from *The Simpsons* using primary and secondary sources and summarize your observations and analysis in the corresponding spaces. In the section located at the bottom of the organizer, argue whether you think the scenes from "Mr. Plow" (Season 4, Episode 9) and "Super Franchise Me" (Season 26, Episode 3) are accurate accounts of how competition historically responds to changing societal conditions, is pure Hollywood creation, or a mixture of both. Use examples from your sources/documents to support your argument.

Primary Source	Clips from *The Simpsons*	Secondary Source
What Do You Think? Hollywood or History?		

"No More PB or J for Me!" Microlending on *The Simpsons*

Annie McMahon Whitlock

EPISODE(S):

"Loan-a Lisa" (2010, Season 22, Episode 2)

Grade	Subject	Topic
4th	Economics	Microfinance loans

Estimated Time Needed for Lesson
180 minutes (three 60-minute lessons)

State Standards

State	Standards and Descriptions
California	3.5 Students demonstrate basic economic reasoning skills and an understanding of the economy of the local region. 3. Understand that individual economic choices involve trade-offs and the evaluation of benefits and costs. 4. Discuss the relationship of students' "work" in school and their personal human capital.
Georgia	SS4E1. Use the basic economic concepts of trade, opportunity cost, specialization, voluntary exchange, productivity, and price incentives to illustrate historical events. a. Describe opportunity cost and its relationship to decision-making across time (e.g., decisions to settle in the west). SS5E3. Describe how consumers and producers interact in the U. S. economy. a. Describe how competition, markets, and prices influence consumer behavior. b. Describe how people earn income by selling their labor to businesses. c. Describe how entrepreneurs take risks to develop new goods and services to start a business.

Chapter 7: Production, Distribution, and Consumption   171

| Michigan | 4- E1.0.2. Describe some characteristics of a market economy. |
| | 4- E1.0.3. Describe how positive and negative incentives influence behavior in a market economy. |

Common Core Standards

Standard	Description
CCSS.ELA-LITERACY. RL.4.3	Describe in depth a character, setting, or event in a story or drama, drawing on specific details in the text.
CCSS.ELA-LITERACY. RL.5.3	Compare and contrast two or more characters, settings, or events in a story or drama, drawing on specific details in the text.

NCSS C3 Framework

Dimension	Description
Applying Disciplinary Concepts and Tools (Economics)	D2.Eco.4.3-5. Explain why individuals and businesses specialize and trade.
	D2.Eco.8.3-5. Identify examples of external benefits and costs.
Communicating Conclusions and Taking Informed Action	D4.1.3-5. Construct arguments using claims and evidence from multiple sources.

NCSS Core Themes and Description

Theme	Description
VII. Production, Distribution, and Consumption	This theme provides for the study of how people organize for the production, distribution, and consumption of goods and services, and prepares students for the study of domestic and global economic issues.
X. Civic Ideals and Practices	An understanding of civic ideals and practices is critical to full participation in society and is an essential component of education for citizenship. This theme enables students to learn about the rights and responsibilities of citizens of a democracy, and to appreciate the importance of active citizenship.

172 HOLLYWOOD OR HISTORY?

Handouts/Materials/Web Links

Handout/Materials:
- Microfinance Vocabulary
- Hollywood or History? Graphic Organizer

Episode Clips and Video Content:
- "Loan-a Lisa," Season 22, Episode 2
    - o **Clip 1:** 7:13–7:52
    - o **Clip 2:** 9:20–10:33 (optional)
    - o **Clip 3:** 10:33–11:31
    - o **Clip 4:** 12:35–13:05
- Opportunity International. (2009, May 1). *The life story of Kojo of One Hen* [Video]. YouTube. https://www.youtube.com/watch?v=Mi-DD9aJyQ0
- TGC. (2010, April 4). *Pennies a day* [Video]. YouTube. https://www.youtube.com/watch?v=veaVikY3u98

Primary Sources:
- Microfinance Profiles Handouts

Secondary Sources:
- Smith Millway, K. (2008). *One hen: How one small loan made a big difference*. Kids Can Press.
    - o https://www.amazon.com/One-Hen-Small-Difference-CitizenKid/dp/1894786092/ref=sr_1_1?crid=1TU38RUAO ZVUQ&keywords=one+hen+how+one+small+loan+ma de+a+difference&qid=1659217351&sprefix=one+hen%2 Caps%2C268&sr=8-1

Guiding Questions

Primary Question:
- How can entrepreneurs help the community?

Secondary Questions:
- How do loans help people start a business?
- What is microfinance?

Important Vocabulary

Borrow: With permission, taking and using someone's money, which you will return to them later.

Entrepreneur: Someone who takes the risk of running a business.

Interest: Extra money that a person who borrows money must pay back in addition to the money they borrowed.

Lend: To let someone use your money, which they will return to you later.

Loan: Money that someone borrows (usually from a bank) and has to pay back later.

Microfinance: Small loans made to people who may not have resources to obtain a large loan from a bank to start a business.

Opportunity Cost: The next best alternative that must be given up when a choice is made; not all alternatives, just the next best choice (e.g., when you want a bicycle and a video game, but you only have enough to buy one; what you decide not to buy is your opportunity cost).

Assessment Strategies

Formative Assessments:
- Microfinance Vocabulary Handout

Summative Assessments:
- Hollywood or History? Graphic Organizer

This lesson is adapted from One Hen, Inc. in consultation with Dr. Annie McMahon Whitlock.

Sparking Strategy/Warm-Up

Lesson Introduction

Show students a map of Africa and ask them to identify the country of Ghana on the map. Together, do a Google Image search of Ghana and find images of what life is like there. Ask the students: *What do you think it would be like to live in Ghana?* If time permits, look up facts about Ghana, such as the population, the climate, and the major cities. (10 min)

Lesson Procedures

Day 1

1. Explain to the students that they will be reading about Kojo, a boy who lives in Ghana in the book *One Hen*. Explain that

174 HOLLYWOOD OR HISTORY?

although Kojo is fictional, he is based on a true story from a real person named Kwabena Darko. Stop at various points in the story to ask the students questions:

- After each page 1–11, stop and ask the students if they hear any problems Kojo has or any solutions he has figured out.
- On page 12, after the line that says: "Or maybe he can pay for something he's been dreaming of: fees and a uniform so he can go back to school" ask: *What do you think Kojo should do with the money he has made? What do you think Kojo's mother will say he should do with the money he has made?* Explain to the students that every day we all have choices about what to do with our time and our money. We can't always have everything we wish to buy to spend time on because we have limited time and money, but we need to make choices that will benefit us or others. This is called "opportunity cost."
- After page 15, ask the students: *What was Kojo's goal on this page? How did he achieve his goal? What choices did he have to make to achieve it?*
- At the end of pages 19, 20, 23, and 27, ask the students who is benefitting from Kojo's business at the end of each page. (40 min)

2. Show the video the Life of Kojo of One Hen and/or read p. 28 of One Hen. Ask the students: *What are ways that businesses like Kojo help people? When have you seen examples of businesses giving to help others?* (10 min)

Day 2

1. To start the lesson, hand out the Microfinance Vocabulary worksheet. In small groups, students discuss each of the vocabulary words and talk about what they think the definitions might be. Have them agree on an answer as a group and write it in the column "What I Think It Means." (15 min)
2. Show the "Pennies a Day" YouTube video. Before starting the video, explain that they should be able to fill in a lot of the last column of their handout "What It Means" by watching the video. Teachers could choose to stop the video whenever a definition is given or play it through first and then discuss. (10-15 min)
3. Introduce microfinance by explaining to the students that microfinance is small loans made to people who are called to start or grow a small business. Sometimes microfinance loans are given

Chapter 7: Production, Distribution, and Consumption   175

to those people who are unable to get a large loan from a bank. These microfinance loans can be given for other things such as roofing a house or paying for school fees. Microfinance banks such as Opportunity International usually lend to small groups of people. Each person gets an individual loan. However, if one member of the group cannot pay back his or her loan, then no one in the group will be able to get another loan. Each person pays back a small portion of his or her loan every week. The groups meet once a week to collect the money for the payments. That's when they discuss how their businesses are doing and learn more about how to run their businesses well. Explain that many of the clients of microfinance banks are women who are very poor, yet extremely hardworking. (5 min)

4. In the whole group, ask the students: *Why do people need loans?* Write down their answers on a flip chart. Push them to think of reasons why others need loans that go beyond starting a business: home loans, college loans, car loans, etc. Share personal experiences of when you have borrowed money and paid it back with interest. (15 min)

5. Ask the students: *Why might some people not be able to borrow enough money to start a business?* Explain to the students that some banks, like those in Kojo's village, may not have access to a lot of money to lend. Some banks will not lend to people in poverty because they are afraid they will not be able to pay back the loan. Stop to point out any vocabulary words in the discussion. (5 min)

6. Explain to the students that there are statements people make about others in poverty that are not true: 1) poor people are lazy, 2) poor people are not smart, 3) poor people do not pay back their loans. Ask the students how they feel about these statements. Guide them to realize that many people in poverty work hard to make money for their families and must come up with creative ways to save money. Also, people are more likely to pay back microfinance loans than other kinds of loans. (5 min)

Day 3

1. In small groups, give each group one of the Microfinance Profiles to read. Have them fill in any definitions they find and add them to their Microfinance Vocabulary Handout. (15 min)

2. Explain that they will be watching an episode of *The Simpsons* where Nelson is an inspiring entrepreneur and Lisa gives him

176 HOLLYWOOD OR HISTORY?

a small loan to help him. Watch the episode together, stopping after each clip to write if necessary.

Clip 1: 7:13–7:52

Clip 2: 9:20–10:33

(Although this clip does have an appearance from Mohammed Yunus, Nobel Prize winner and founder of Grameen Bank and the concept of microfinance, it also has the word "Assy" written on Nelson's mom's stomach. This clip isn't necessary to understand the concepts, so choose at your own risk)

Clip 3: 10:33–11:31

Clip 4: 12:35–13:05

3. In small groups, have the students compare the person in their Microfinance Profile to Nelson in the "Loan-a Lisa" episode using the Hollywood or History? Graphic Organizer. (15 min)

4. For the summative assessment, students should write a paragraph about how accurate *The Simpsons* is to real-life entrepreneurs. Students should use as many vocabulary words as they can from their Microfinance Vocabulary Handout in the paragraph. (10 min or assigned as homework)

Differentiation

Scaffolds: The reading of the *One Hen* book could be spread out over several days as opposed to all being done in Day 1. The Microfinance Profiles may have to be annotated or shortened for some students. The Microfinance Vocabulary sheet can be filled out with pictures or drawings instead of words. The paragraph of the summative assessment could be given orally.

ESL Interventions: Microfinance Profiles could be translated, annotated, or shortened for students. The Microfinance Vocabulary sheet can be filled out with pictures or drawings instead of words. The paragraph of the summative assessment could be given orally or in their native language.

Extensions:

- Donate to an entrepreneur from Kiva, an organization that highlights entrepreneurs that need help (www.kiva.org)
- Conduct a market simulation where students start a business that helps their community, using a small loan given by their teacher. One Hen is also an organization that has more lesson plans on

how to do this. Visit their website (onehen.org) or check out these articles on one classroom's experience for ideas:

- o Whitlock, A. M. (2019). Elementary school entrepreneurs. *Interdisciplinary Journal of Project-Based Learning, 13*(1). https://doi.org/10.7771/1541-5015.1780

- o Whitlock, A. M. (2017). Teaching about social business: The intersection of economics instruction and civic engagement. *Journal of Social Studies Research, 41(3)*, 235-242.

- o Whitlock, A. M. (2015). Economics through inquiry: Creating social businesses in fifth grade. *The Social Studies, 106*(3), 117–125.

- o Whitlock, A. M., & Fox, K. (2014). One Hen: Using children's literature in project-based learning. *Social Studies and the Young Learner, 26*(4), 26–29.

REFERENCES

Garza, V. L. (Writer), & Faughnan, M. (Director). (2010, October 3). Loan-a Lisa (Season 22, Episode 2) [TV series episode]. In A. Jean, M. Scully, J. L. Brooks, M. Groening, & S. Simon (Executive Producers), *The Simpsons*. Gracie Films; Twentieth Century Fox Film Corporation.

One Hen, Inc. (n.d). Program overview. https://www.onehen.org/program-overview/

Opportunity International. (2009, May 1). *The life story of Kojo of One Hen* [Video]. YouTube. https://www.youtube.com/watch?v=Mi-DD9aJyQ0

Smith Millway, K. (2008). *One hen: How one small loan made a big difference*. Kids Can Press.

TGC. (2010, April 4). *Pennies a day* [Video]. YouTube. https://www.youtube.com/watch?v=veaVikY3u98

Whitlock, A. M. (2015). Economics through inquiry: Creating social businesses in fifth grade. *The Social Studies, 106*(3), 117–125.

Whitlock, A. M. (2017). Teaching about social business: The intersection of economics instruction and civic engagement. *Journal of Social Studies Research, 41(3)*, 235–242.

Whitlock, A. M. (2019). Elementary school entrepreneurs. *Interdisciplinary Journal of Project-Based Learning, 13*(1). https://doi.org/10.7771/1541-5015.1780

Whitlock, A. M., & Fox, K. (2014). One Hen: Using children's literature in project-based learning. *Social Studies and the Young Learner, 26*(4), 26–29.

178 HOLLYWOOD OR HISTORY?

APPENDIX A

Microfinance Vocabulary Handout

Complete the 2nd column in the chart with what you THINK each one of these words means. Fill in the 3rd column throughout the lesson once you have found the actual meaning.

Vocabulary Word	What I Think It Means	What It Means
Borrow		
Lend		
Loan		

Chapter 7: Production, Distribution, and Consumption   179

Interest		
Microfinance		
Entrepreneur		

180 HOLLYWOOD OR HISTORY?

APPENDIX B

Microfinance Profiles

Vivian Adama
Accra, Ghana

In 1990, Vivian Adama's husband died, leaving her alone with a little baby. She needed to work to take care of her baby but could not find a daycare facility that would take care of her child while she worked. Then she had a brilliant idea! Why not take care of her own child, and provide the same service for her neighbors?

Vivian started a daycare for babies out of her home. As it grew, she added toddlers and then moved out of her house into a new building as she saved up money. Over the years, she has turned her daycare into a full school. She started a primary and junior secondary school, adding grades as she was able to save the money for classrooms and teachers.

In 2001, Vivian received a microfinance loan from Opportunity International. She used her loan to buy a freezer and food to provide meals for her students.

Today she has 360 students, 19 permanent teachers and five visiting teachers. With her current loan, she is building a second floor to one of the buildings so that she can grow the school to serve 560 students.

The school makes enough profit to operate from school fees and by selling food. Vivian's school fees are lower than others so that even poor children can attend. She says that her neighborhood is poor, which is why other schools would not come there. Because her school is the only good one in that neighborhood, she gets a lot of students. Her plan, after she finishes building her school, is to also own a farm.

Alba Cerrato
Honduras

Alba Cerrato makes shoes in her home country of Honduras with the help of her husband, Raul. Since she got her first loan of $92 from Opportunity International, Alba has repaid her loan, tripled her sales, and received more loans to continue growing her business. She used her loans to buy three sewing machines and a polishing machine. With these, she can make

Chapter 7: Production, Distribution, and Consumption   181

more shoes. She now makes 24 pairs of shoes per week. Before she got her first loan, she made only eight pair of shoes. Raul helps by selling the shoes in the surrounding villages or in Nicaragua, a nearby country.

Alba has become a leader in her trust group and in her community. Many members of her trust group come to her for advice. She also helps her neighbors by teaching them how to start a business and showing them where they can buy materials at a lower cost. Her family and neighbors respect her because she works to bring hope to her community.

Alba's business has completely changed the lives of her children. Her son finished high school and is now in college, while her daughter is in fifth grade. The family is healthier because they can now pay to see a doctor when they are sick and have enough money to buy medicine. They have also bought land and are building a home. Alba describes her transformation by saying, "We have everything because of God. We have been given the opportunity."

Thiembe Radebe
Durban, South Africa

Thiembe Radebe owns two businesses in Claremont Township, just outside Durban, South Africa. His first business is welding and construction. His second is a small supply shop run by his two sons, who sell bread, chicken feed and other groceries.

He almost lost his business because he did not have enough money to buy the supplies he needed for his business. One day as he passed Opportunity South Africa's Pinetown branch, and saw the sign that said Opportunity, he felt hope in his heart, and he went inside to apply for a small loan. With cash in hand, Mr. Radebe bought materials so he could complete the job he was working on. He now has the money to do larger jobs and has increased the variety of items that he sells in his supply store, which is already bringing in more customers.

Hollywood or History?

Summarize the entrepreneur your group read about and put important ideas in the first column. Then write down how Nelson benefits from a microfinance loan in "Loan-a Lisa." In the middle, write what they have in common. At the end, write your opinion on whether you think Nelson is like the microfinance entrepreneur your group read about. Use as many vocabulary words as you can in your paragraph.

Microfinance Entrepreneur	Both	Nelson Muntz

What Do You Think? Hollywood or History?

Chapter 7: Production, Distribution, and Consumption   183

For Further Viewing

With over 700 episodes to choose from, there are more episodes of *The Simpsons* that could be used to teach the theme of Production, Distribution, and Consumption.

Entrepreneurship

There are many other times when the Simpson family invests in small businesses. "Loan-a Lisa" isn't the only episode that features microlending either! Here are some examples:

Oh Brother, Where Art Thou? (1991, Season 2, Episode 15)
Homer discovers he has a half-brother Herb who is an auto executive in Detroit. Herb invests in Homer's idea for a car design, and it fails miserably. (Written by Jeff Martin, Directed by W. M. "Bud" Archer)

Brother Can You Spare Two Dimes? (1992, Season 3, Episode 24)
After ruining his half-brother Herb's career with his failed car design in Season 2 (see above), Homer repays him by investing in Herb's idea for a baby translator, which gives Homer a return on his investment and restores Herb's career. (Written by John Swartzwelder, Directed by Rich Moore)

The Twisted World of Marge Simpson (1997, Season 8, Episode 11)
Marge joins an investment group where women of Springfield pool their money together to finance a small business. After the group dismisses her for being too cautious with her investments, Marge opens up her own pretzel franchise. (Written by Jennifer Crittenden, Directed by Chuck Sheetz)

Mr. Burns

Mr. Burns has been the center of several shady business practices in Springfield as a result of his relentless pursuit of profits. These episodes are the best of Mr. Burns being an evil capitalist.

Trouble with Trillions (1998, Season 9, Episode 20)
Mr. Burns stole a trillion-dollar bill from the U. S. government and Homer is recruited to get it back as retribution for his own tax fraud. (Written by Ian Maxtone-Graham, Directed by Swinton O. Scott III)

184 HOLLYWOOD OR HISTORY?

Who Shot Mr. Burns? Part One (1995, Season 6, Episode 25)
Who Shot Mr. Burns? Part Two (1995, Season 7, Episode 1)
When oil is found underneath Springfield Elementary, Mr. Burns taps the oil well first, taking the money for himself. He then blacks out the sun so that Springfield has no choice but to receive power from his nuclear plant. He even steals candy from a baby—and that's all in one episode! When Mr. Burns is shot at the end of Part One, the entire town is a suspect. In the summer of 1995, the country was obsessed with determining who shot Mr. Burns as *The Simpsons* ran a tie-in contest over the Internet, the first of its kind. (Writte by Bill Oakley and Josh Weinstein, Part One directed by Jeffrey Lynch, Part Two directed by Wes Archer)

Old Man and the Lisa (1997, Season 8, Episode 21)
Mr. Burns goes bankrupt and enlists Lisa to help him regain his fortune by opening a recycling plant. He makes his fortune back, only to turn on his promise to do well by the environment by catching fish to turn into slurry. (Written by John Swartzwelder, Directed by Mark Kirkland)

CHAPTER 8

SCIENCE, TECHNOLOGY, AND SOCIETY

*T*he *Simpsons* spans many decades and generations. Everyone from Gen X to Gen Z had the show as part of their television viewing choice during formative parts of their lives. These same generations have also seen a rapid boom in scientific advancement and technologies as well, and *The Simpsons* have grown along with them. From being one of the first shows to tie in Internet content and TV with the "Who Shot Mr. Burns?" contest (Cuprisin, 1995) to experimenting with different animation styles like Homer becoming 3-D (Cohen et al., 1995) and Katy Perry guest starring as her non-animated self (Castelleneta et al., 2010).

However, studying science and technology in the subject of social studies involves critically examining technology's progress. Certainly, advances in science have led to medical advancements that save lives and smartphones have made everything convenient—but at what cost to our mental health, our relationships, and our privacy? The COVID-19 pandemic is a great current example. The vaccine saved lives, but the increase in virtual personal interactions has taken a toll on our work—and not necessarily for the better. Of course, *The Simpsons* predicted everything from vaccine hesitancy to virtual schooling, and there are several episodes that cause us to examine the benefits and drawbacks to technological progress.

Erin C. Adams's lesson on technoskepticism in STEM education gives students practice in evaluating who is being "duped" by technology in the episode "The Miseducation of Lisa Simpson" from 2020 (Burns & Nastuk, 2020). By this time, K–12 students have consistently heard about getting jobs in "STEM fields," such as technology jobs or engineering for their high pay and evolving fields—this episode subverts what counts as a STEM

Hollywood or History?: An Inquiry-Based Strategy for Using The Simpsons to Teach Social Studies, pp. 185–230
Copyright © 2024 by Information Age Publishing
www.infoagepub.com
All rights of reproduction in any form reserved.

185

education. For example, as Adams poses in this lesson, are social media influencers considered working in a STEM field?

We may think of scientific and technological advancements as "new," but an examination of any other social studies discipline shows how science and technology have been defining society since the beginning of time (there is a reason why we say "don't reinvent the wheel"). The process of examining technology doesn't have to be done in a current events class. Chapter author Daniel G. Krutka is a founder of the Civics of Technology project—curriculum and professional development that "aims to empower students and educators to critically inquire into the effects of technologies on their individual and collective lives" (https://www.civicsoftechnology. org). He wrote two lessons for this chapter. In the first, Krutka uses the "Treehouse of Horror XII" episode segment "House of Whacks" (Frink et al., 2001) to help students critique the ubiquitous use of home technologies like Alexa or Google Nest. *The Simpsons* was satirizing these technologies in 2001 before they became a staple in homes for real.

Another component to science and technology is media literacy. Media literacy is the ability to discern information one sees online, be able to make informed decisions about what is accurate and helpful, and to create media in a responsible way (medialiteracynow.org, n.d.). Technology has advanced in such a way that any information can be accessed and spread at rapid rates, including falsehoods that can be potentially dangerous to democracy if taken at face value. Although media literacy is important to have when studying any subject, it has a natural fit in social studies, a subject that teaches critical thinking and questioning explicitly. Krutka uses a classic episode "The Computer Wore Menace Shoes" (Swartzwelder & Kirkland, 2000) to show how misinformation is easily spread when Homer creates a website and makes up content to share.

In the "For Further Viewing" section, there are other episodes that can be used to teach historical and contemporary examples of scientific advancement in order to give students practice in their critique of progress—or see how well *The Simpsons* already did it!

REFERENCES

Burns, J. S. (Writer), & Nastuk, M. (Director). (2020, February 16). The miseducation of Lisa Simpson (Season 31, Episode 12) [TV series episode]. In A. Jean, M. Scully, J. L. Brooks, M. Groening, & S. Simon (Executive Producers), *The Simpsons*. Gracie Films; Twentieth Century Fox Film Corporation.

Castelleneta, D. (Writer), Locusta, D. (Writer), Anderson, B. (Director), & Schofield, M. (Director). (2010, December 5). The fight before Christmas (Season 22, Episode 8) [TV series episode]. In A. Jean, M. Scully, J. L. Brooks, M.

Chapter 8: Science, Technology, and Society   187

Groening, & S. Simon (Executive Producers), *The Simpsons*. Gracie Films; Twentieth Century Fox Film Corporation.

Civics of Technology Project. (n.d.). *About us*. https://www.civicsoftechnology.org/aboutus

Cohen, D. X. (Writer), Anderson, B., & Mirkin, D. (Directors). (1995, October 29). Treehouse of horror VI: Homer[3] (Season 7, Episode 6) [TV series episode]. In B. Oakley, J. Weinstein, M. Scully, J. L. Brooks, M. Groening, & S. Simon (Executive Producers), *The Simpsons*. Gracie Films; Twentieth Century Fox Film Corporation.

Cuprisin, T. (1995, August 10). Broadcast bucks, events get bigger—Networks step up battle with cable to get viewers to tune in. *Milwaukee Journal Sentinel*, 3.

Frink, J. (Writer), Payne, D. (Writer), & Reardon, J. (Director). (2001, November 6). Treehouse of horror XII: House of whacks (Season 13, Episode 1) [TV series episode]. In A. Jean, M. Scully, J. L. Brooks, M. Groening, & S. Simon (Executive Producers), *The Simpsons*. Gracie Films; Twentieth Century Fox Film Corporation.

Media Literacy Now. (n.d.). *What is media literacy?* https://medialiteracynow.org/what-is-media-literacy/

Swartzwelder, J. (Writer), & Kirkland, M. (Director). (2000, December 3). The computer wore menace shoes (Season 12, Episode 6) [TV series episode]. In M. Scully, J. L. Brooks, M. Groening, & S. Simon (Executive Producers), *The Simpsons*. Gracie Films; Twentieth Century Fox Film Corporation.

STEM, Human Capital, and the Future of Work

Erin C. Adams

EPISODE(S):
"The Miseducation of Lisa Simpson" (2020, Season 31, Episode 12)

Grade	Subject	Topic
6–12	Social Studies and Science	Economics, Science, and Technology

Estimated Time Needed for Lesson
55 minutes

State Standards

State	Standards and Descriptions
Georgia	SSEF6. Explain how productivity, economic growth, and future standards of living are influenced by investment in factories, machinery, new technology, and health, education, and training of people.
	SSUSH23. Assess the political, economic, and technological changes during the Reagan, George H.W. Bush, Clinton, George W. Bush and Obama administrations.
	IT-FAI-3. Identify and describe the most current applications of artificial intelligence.
	IT-FAI-7. Describe and research the social and ethical impacts of artificial intelligence.
	IT-IDT-10. Describe, analyze, develop, and follow policies for managing ethical and legal issues in the business world and in a technology-based society.
Kansas	Computer Science- L1.IC.C.01. Evaluate the ways computing impacts personal, ethical, social, economic, and cultural practices.
New Hampshire	SS:HI:12:4.3: Explain how the development of technology has both simplified and complicated work.

Next Generation Science Standards

Standard	Description
HS-ETS1-3	Evaluate a solution to a real-world problem on prioritized criteria and tradeoffs that account for a range of constraints, including cost, safety, reliability, and aesthetics as well as possible social, cultural, and environmental impacts.

NCSS C3 Framework

Dimension	Description
Applying Disciplinary Concepts and Tools (Civics)	D2.Civ.13.9-12. Evaluate public policies in terms of intended and unintended outcomes, and related consequences. D2.Civ.14.9-12. Analyze historical, contemporary, and emerging means of changing societies. Promoting the common good and protecting rights.
Applying Disciplinary Concepts and Tools (Economics)	D2.Eco.1.9-12. Analyze how incentives influence choices that may result in policies with a range of costs and benefits for different groups. D2.Eco.13.9-12. Explain why advancements in technology and investments in capital good and human capital increase economic growth and standards of living.

NCSS Core Themes and Description

Theme	Description
VIII. Science, Technology, and Society	By exploring the relationships among science, technology, and society, students develop an understanding of past and present advances in science and technology and their impact.

Handouts/Materials/Web Links

Handout/Materials:

- Hollywood or History? Graphic Organizer

190 HOLLYWOOD OR HISTORY?

Episode Clips and Video Content:
- "The Miseducation of Lisa Simpson," Season 31, Episode 12
  - o **Clip 1:** 3:46–6:39
  - o **Clip 2:** 7:13–9:59
  - o **Clip 3:** 9:59–12:18'
  - o **Clip 4:** 12:19–13:10
  - o **Clip 5:** 15:37–17:35
  - o **Clip 6:** 13:15–15:36
  - o **Clip 7:** 13:35–19:15
- Shipt. (2021, November 9). *Kristen Bell's a fan* [Video]. YouTube. https://www.youtube.com/watch?v=75J1XuKmf_4
- Three Minute Theory. (2020, May 3). Three minute theory: What is immaterial labor? [Video]. YouTube. https://www.youtube.com/watch?v=LLo_9WkpS9g&t=33s

Secondary Sources:
- Adamson, J. (n.d.). *Oh, the humanities! Why STEM shouldn't take precedence over the arts.* Arizona State University Project Humanities. https://projecthumanities.asu.edu/content/oh-humanities-why-stem-shouldnt-take-precedence-over-arts
- Bharadwaj, A., & Dvorkin, M. A. (2019, July 10). The rise of automation: How robots may impact the U.S. labor market. *Regional Economist.* https://www.stlouisfed.org/publications/regional-economist/second-quarter-2019/rise-automation-robots
- Cox-Smith, S. (2017, June 13). Why we shouldn't teach girls to code. *LinkedIn.* https://www.linkedin.com/pulse/why-we-shouldnt-teach-girls-code-susan-cox-smith/?trk=public_profile_article_view
- Davidson, A. (Host). (2015, May 3). The machine comes to town (Episode 623) [Audio podcast episode]. In *Planet Money.* NPR. https://www.npr.org/sections/money/2015/05/13/406461675/episode-623-the-machine-comes-to-town
- Ferlazzo, L. (2012, February 26). *The dangers of "gamification" in education.* Larry Ferlazzo's Websites of the Day. https://larryferlazzo.edublogs.org/2012/02/26/the-dangers-of-gamification-in-education/
- Frazer, J. (2019, February 15). How the gig economy is reshaping careers for the next generation. *Forbes.* https://www.forbes.com/sites/johnfrazer1/2019/02/15/how-the-gig-economy-is-reshaping-careers-for-the-next-generation/?sh=49340a0449ad

Chapter 8: Science, Technology, and Society   191

- Funk, C., & Parker, K. (2018). *Most Americans evaluate STEM education as middling compared with other developed nations.* Pew Research Center https://www.pewresearch.org/social-trends/2018/01/09/5-most-americans-evaluate-stem-education-as-middling-compared-with-other-developed-nations/
- Kim, M. (2017, March 23). Let robots handle your emotional burnout at work. *NEXT.* https://www.howwegettonext.com/let-robots-handle-your-emotional-burnout-at-work/
- Merrilees, K. (2020, April 12). *The great ratings war of 2020.* Medium.com. https://medium.com/swlh/the-great-ratings-war-of-2020-e47392d9e169
- Parkin, S. (2016, November 18). Was gamification a terrible lie? *NEXT.* https://www.howwegettonext.com/was-gamification-a-terrible-lie/
- Perkins, D. (2020, February 16). A bewilderingly atonal *Simpsons* ditches the deep for the STEM. *AV Club.* https://www.avclub.com/a-bewilderingly-atonal-simpsons-ditches-the-deep-for-th-1841735235
- Rampell, C. (2013, November 15). Women gain in some STEM fields, but not computer science. *The New York Times.* https://archive.nytimes.com/economix.blogs.nytimes.com/2013/11/15/women-gain-in-some-stem-fields-but-not-computer-science/
- Scharpf, E. (2017, June 14). Why teaching girls to code is not the (only) answer. *Pacific Standard.* https://psmag.com/education/why-teaching-girls-to-code-is-not-the-only-answer

Guiding Questions

Primary Questions:
- What is the purpose of school? What does it mean to be educated? Miseducated?
- How much investment should schools make in STEM? What are the pros and cons of such investments? Who do you think benefits the most? (e.g., communities, corporations, students, schools, society).
- Why did the townspeople find Marge and John Legend's arguments for STEM convincing? Why is STEM so popular and why do people support it?

192   HOLLYWOOD OR HISTORY?

- How realistic is the episode, specifically the treatment of Lisa and Bart? Do you see similar tactics employed in your school (e.g., tracking, algorithms, personalized learning)?
- How did the episode preview or predict the Kristen Bell Shipt commercial? Consider Bell's "compliments" and commentary as well as the use of celebrity spokespersons like Bell, Legend, and Teigen.

Secondary Questions:
- What is the role of gender and economic privilege in STEM? Is it the great equalizer or divider?
- Why do some warn that coding and other STEM pursuits are not necessarily a good deal for girls?
- How does the episode use Lisa and Bart and John and Chrissy to subvert gender stereotypes?
- It has been argued that women are responsible for much of the cultural content (and therefore value) of the Internet and yet their contributions aren't seen as serious STEM work (see Terranova, 2000). As an Instagrammer, does Teigen work in STEM?
- Why was Lisa's resistance to automation and technology more effective than Homer's?
- How do algorithms and nudging complicate the notion of free will? How much free will or free choice did the characters have? Was anyone being manipulated?

Important Vocabulary

Algorithm: A computer-implementable sequence or set of instructions.
App(lication): Software that runs on a mobile device.
Automation: The operation of a device or completion of a task that replaces or does not use human labor.
Gamification: Using game-like techniques (e.g., competition, earning rewards) in non-game settings. See Ferlazzo (2012).
Gig Economy: Work that is (allegedly) mostly flexible, independent, temporary, or part-time, and often contracted using apps that interface between customers and workers. Examples include driving for Uber and shopping for Instacart. Also known as the sharing economy or 1099 economy.
Human Capital: The skills, education, and know-how people possess and that increases the value of a person's labor and that adds value

to those buying it (examples include school, a college education, training a company provides for their employees).

Immaterial Labor: Work that uses tacit knowledge to create value but that is often unseen or unrecognized. Emotional labor and customer service are examples. This is often work that is uniquely human and difficult to outsource to machines. Immaterial laborers use intellect, assume risk, and make decisions. Bart's classmates performed immaterial labor by squeezing fruit to determine ripeness. Even though immaterial labor is not unskilled labor, it might be viewed (and compensated) that way.

LaPerruque: "The wig" in French. The subversion of a system from the inside. It refers to a resistance strategy wherein the worker operates from the inside out, within the bounds of employment or the system, thus disguising resistance and even making it look like compliance (possibly in an exaggerated form). Resource reallocation or diversion is one example. Using a system's algorithms against it is another (see also Adams et al., 2021).

Nudge/Nudging: Creating conditions that cause people to unconsciously choose a desired outcome or choice.

Platform Economies: Multisided digital frameworks that "shape the terms on which participants interact with one another." A platform economy is the (re)organization of the economy, labor and work around platforms rather than other entities such as the factory. In this system platform owners organize and solicit labor.

Satire: Uses exaggeration and humor to critique foolish or nonsensical behavior or systems.

STEM: Refers to coursework and careers focused on science, technology, engineering and math. Sometimes art is included as STEAM.

Technoskepticism: The direction of attention to the downsides, constraints, or cultural characteristics that technologies extend, amplify, or create. See (Krutka et al., 2020) and https://thetechnoskeptic.com/

Assessment Strategies

Formative Assessments:
- Gallery walk
- Hollywood or History? Graphic Organizer

Summative Assessments:
- Hollywood or History Graphic Organizer (What do you think? section)
- Essays and recommendations/PSA

194 HOLLYWOOD OR HISTORY?

Sparking Strategy/Warm-Up

Lesson Introduction

Begin with a gallery walk. Students will respond to a question, quote or graph related to STEM and schooling. Each question or prompt should be written on a large piece of paper or sticky pad paper. Students walk around the room responding to each one in any order they like. Then, students should take a second trip around the room. This time they should engage with their classmates' responses by posing questions, asking for clarification (e.g., "do you mean ___," offering counter arguments, and offering answers). These questions and prompts will be revisited at the end of the lesson. (10 min)

- *What is the purpose of school?*
- *Should schools prepare students for work? If so, what kind?*
- Former Florida Governor Rick Scott stated in an interview "I want to spend our money getting people science, technology, engineering and math degrees…. That's what our kids need to focus all of their time and attention on: those type of degrees that when they get out of school, they can get a job." *What do you think about Scott's idea? Do you agree or disagree? Why?*
- Display the following graphs from the Rampell (2013) article (see above for link): "Percent of B.A.s in a field received by women" and "Median earnings by discipline." Ask: *What do you notice? What is the relationship between salary and degree choice and why is that significant for women?*
- The next two prompts use graphs from the Pew Research Center study (see above for link). Display "Americans see range of problems in K–12 STEM education." Ask: *How is your experience similar or different than what the data shows? Do you think STEM education should be improved? If so, how? What other factors hinder STEM besides what is listed?* Display "Most Americans give average or lower marks to K–12 education generally, STEM education specifically." Ask: *What do you think? Do you agree with the respondents?*

Lesson Procedures

1. Debrief the gallery walk. Give each group of students one of the prompts. Each group should summarize the responses for the class and try to draw conclusions, if possible (e.g., most students agreed that __ but a few said ___). (10 min)

2. Introduce the Hollywood or History? graphic organizer handout and work with students to detail how they can use the outline to record information during the film clip and document analyses. Break the students into groups. Explain that each group will view a clip from "The Miseducation of Lisa Simpson." As they watch, they should determine whether the scenes are History, Hollywood, or both by drafting a short statement/paragraph citing evidence from each source (scene). Space is included on the graphic organizer handout. In this case, think of history as real and Hollywood as fiction. How close is the clip to depicting what could really happen or what is currently happening? Hollywood means the content was invented for television and is very loosely, or not at all, based in reality. Allow time for students to discuss their findings as a group. (15 min)

3. Students extend their understanding by examining new information related to issues in STEM and STEM education (see Secondary Sources above). Start by showing the Kristen Bell Shipt commercial. Ask students how the commercial connected, extended or challenged their views on the episode and how the episode extended their thinking about companies like Shipt or Instacart. Provide students with additional resources and readings or let them choose from among the list provided. Students should again review their Hollywood or History? organizers to determine how much the new information connects, extends or challenges their initial viewpoints. For more on this strategy see Project Zero: https://pz.harvard.edu/resources/connect-extend-challenge

4. Social studies teachers might collaborate with ELA or media teachers for this portion of the lesson. Provide students with the definition of satire. Explain that many consider *The Simpsons* the epitome of satire (Henry, 2012; Methven, 2014). Ask students to review their Hollywood or History? analyses and use their vocabulary words (e.g., gig economy) to identify examples of satire in the episode. Students should support their claims with evidence drawn from the gallery walk and from their own experience and research. Crucially, teachers need to challenge students to ask *Who is being satirized here?* In satire, people's vices or perceived lack of intelligence is ridiculed for the purpose of social commentary and to raise questions about particular issues or phenomena. However, this time gifted individuals like Legend and Lisa and the teachers are the ones being duped and those often seen as vapid, self-absorbed (e.g., social media celebrities like Teigen) or stupid (e.g., Bart) pragmatically use STEM even

196 HOLLYWOOD OR HISTORY?

while they understand that it uses them right back. The following lesson and handout from *Read, Write, Think* "Satirizing the Simpsons" can be used as guide: https://www.readwritethink.org/classroom-resources/lesson-plans/exploring-satire-simpsons (10 min)

5. To conclude the lesson, students should choose one or two of the primary questions to answer. Then, students can work together to create a public service announcement, brochure or school improvement plan describing the pros and cons of STEM education. For both assignments, students should use the lesson's vocabulary words (e.g., gig economy) and support their claims with evidence from the sources and anecdotes from real life.
(10 min and/or assigned for homework)

Differentiation

Scaffolds: The majority of this lesson should be taught in small groups. It may be helpful to have students of varying ability levels work together. The text in the secondary source articles may be too technical for some students. The teacher may consider shortening the article or only using excerpts for students who may struggle with comprehension of the whole text as well as showing the images to the entire class.

ESL Interventions: In addition to the possible suggested scaffolds, teachers may wish to provide students with simplified definitions of vocabulary and key terms. As opposed to the assigned articles, the teacher may assign less technical and shorter articles to use. Some articles and documentaries may provide translations or subtitles, but teachers should check for their accuracy.

Extensions:
- The lesson can be extended by exploring the secondary questions and creating their own STEM satire. For example, they might create a video satirizing Bell's Shipt commercial or write or storyboard an additional episode scene depicting an issue in one of the supplemental texts (e.g. a commercial about teaching girls to code).

REFERENCES

Adams, E. C., Wurzburg, E., & Kerr, S. L. (2021). The tip of the iceberg: Immaterial labor, technoskepticism and the teaching profession. *Contemporary Issues in Technology and Teacher Education, 21*(1), 126–154.

Chapter 8: Science, Technology, and Society 197

Adamson, J. (n.d.). *Oh, the humanities! Why STEM shouldn't take precedence over the arts.* Arizona State University Project Humanities. https://projecthumanities.asu. edu/content/oh-humanities-why-stem-shouldnt-take-precedence-over-arts

Bharadwaj, A., & Dvorkin, M. A. (2019, July 10). The rise of automation: How robots may impact the U.S. labor market. *Regional Economist.* https://www. stlouisfed.org/publications/regional-economist/second-quarter-2019/rise-automation-robots

Burns, J. S. (Writer), & Nastuk, M. (Director). (2020, February 16). The miseducation of Lisa Simpson (Season 31, Episode 12) [TV series episode]. In A. Jean, M. Scully, J. L. Brooks, M. Groening, & S. Simon (Executive Producers), *The Simpsons.* Gracie Films; Twentieth Century Fox Film Corporation.

Cox-Smith, S. (2017, June 13). Why we shouldn't teach girls to code. *LinkedIn.* https://www.linkedin.com/pulse/why-we-shouldnt-teach-girls-code-susan-cox-smith/?trk=public_profile_article_view

Davidson, A. (Host). (2015, May 3). The machine comes to town (Episode 623) [Audio podcast episode]. In *Planet Money.* NPR. https://www.npr.org/sections/money/2015/05/13/406461675/episode-623-the-machine-comes-to-town

Ferlazzo, L. (2012, February 26). *The dangers of "gamification" in education.* Larry Ferlazzo's Websites of the Day. https://larryferlazzo.edublogs.org/2012/02/26/the-dangers-of-gamification-in-education/

Frazer, J. (2019, February 15). How the gig economy is reshaping careers for the next generation. *Forbes.* https://www.forbes.com/sites/johnfrazer1/2019/02/15/how-the-gig-economy-is-reshaping-careers-for-the-next-generation/?sh=49340a0449ad

Funk, C., & Parker, K. (2018). *Most Americans evaluate STEM education as middling compared with other developed nations.* Pew Research Center. https://www.pewresearch.org/social-trends/2018/01/09/5-most-americans-evaluate-stem-education-as-middling-compared-with-other-developed-nations/

Henry, M. A. (2012). The Simpsons, satire, and American culture. In M. A. Henry (Ed.), *The Simpsons, satire, and American culture.* Palgrave Macmillan.

Kim, M. (2017, March 23). Let robots handle your emotional burnout at work. *NEXT.* https://www.howwegettonext.com/let-robots-handle-your-emotional-burnout-at-work/

Krutka, D. G., Heath, M. K., & Mason, L. E. (2020). Technology won't save us – A call for technoskepticism in social studies [Editorial]. *Contemporary Issues in Technology and Teacher Education, 20*(1), 108–120.

Merrilees, K. (2020, April 12). *The great ratings war of 2020.* Medium.com. https://medium.com/swlh/the-great-ratings-war-of-2020-e47392d9e169

Methven, J. (2014, May 4). The Simpsons at 25: Satire in serious times. *Al Jazeera America.* http://america.aljazeera.com/articles/2014/5/4/the-simpsons-at-25satireinserioustimes.html

Parkin, S. (2016, November 18). Was gamification a terrible lie? *NEXT.* https://www.howwegettonext.com/was-gamification-a-terrible-lie/

Perkin, D. (2020, February 16). A bewilderingly atonal *Simpsons* dithes the deep for the STEM. *AV Club.* https://www.avclub.com/a-bewilderingly-atonal-simpsons-ditches-the-deep-for-th-1841735235

198 HOLLYWOOD OR HISTORY?

Rampell, C. (2013, November 15). Women gain in some STEM fields, but not computer science. *The New York Times.* https://archive.nytimes.com/economix.blogs.nytimes.com/2013/11/15/women-gain-in-some-stem-fields-but-not-computer-science/

Scharpf, E. (2017, June 14). Why teaching girls to code is not the (only) answer. *Pacific Standard.* https://psmag.com/education/why-teaching-girls-to-code-is-not-the-only-answer

Shipt. (2021, November 9). *Kristen Bell's a fan* [Video]. YouTube. https://www.youtube.com/watch?v=75J1XuKmf_4

Terranova, T. (2000). Free Labor: Producing Culture for the Digital Economy. *Social Text, 18*(2), 33-58. https://web.mit.edu/schock/www/docs/18.2terranova.pdf

The Technoskeptic. (n.d.). *About.* https://thetechnoskeptic.com/about/

Three Minute Theory. (2020, May 3). Three minute theory: What is immaterial labor? [Video]. YouTube. https://www.youtube.com/watch?v=LLo_9WkpS9g&t=33s

Wright, J. (n.d.). Exploring satire with The Simpsons. *Read, Write, Think.* https://www.readwritethink.org/classroom-resources/lesson-plans/exploring-satire-simpsons

Chapter 8: Science, Technology, and Society   199

Hollywood or History?

Compare what you learned from the sources about STEM education from the gallery walk and the clip from "The Miseducation of Lisa Simpson" that your group was given. In the section located at the bottom of the page, explain whether you think the clip is an accurate account of what is happening ("history"), pure Hollywood creation, or a mixture of both. Use examples from your sources/documents to explain your answer.

Sources	"The Miseducation of Lisa Simpson"

200 HOLLYWOOD OR HISTORY?

What Do You Think? Hollywood or History?

Chapter 8: Science, Technology, and Society   201

"Trusting Every Aspect of Our Lives to a Giant Computer was the Smartest Thing We Ever Did:" Are Smart Technologies Worth the Cost?

Daniel G. Krutka

EPISODE(S):
"Treehouse of Horror XII: House of Whacks" (2001, Season 13, Episode 1)

Grade	Subject	Topic
9–12	Social Studies	Technology

Era Under Study	Estimated Time Needed for Lesson
Present and Future Age of Artificial Intelligence	120 minutes (2 60-minute class periods)

State Standards

State	Standards and Descriptions
Indiana	Geography and History of the World-6.4. Analyze how transportation and communication changes have led to both cultural convergence and divergence in the world. Examples: railroads; automobiles and airplanes; computer technology; television; cell phones; satellite communications; virtual reality; artificial intelligence
Mississippi	Sociology-5. Describe the impact of modern technology on cultures throughout the world.
New Jersey	U.S. History-6.1.12.EconNE.16.b: Evaluate the economic, political, and social impact of new and emerging technologies on individuals and nations.

Common Core Standards

Standard	Description
CCSS.ELA-LITERACY. RH.9-10.9	Compare and contrast treatments of the same topic in several primary and secondary sources.

202 HOLLYWOOD OR HISTORY?

CCSS.ELA-LITERACY. RH.11-12.2	Determine the central ideas or information of a primary or secondary source; provide an accurate summary that makes clear the relationships among the key details and ideas.
CCSS.ELA-LITERACY. RH.11-12.7	Integrate and evaluate multiple sources of information presented in diverse formats and media (e.g., visually, quantitatively, as well as in words) in order to address a question or solve a problem.

NCSS C3 Framework

Dimension	Description
Developing Questions and Planning Inquiries	D1.2.9-12. Explain points of agreement and disagreement experts have about interpretations and applications of disciplinary concepts and ideas associated with a compelling question.
Applying Disciplinary Concepts and Tools (Civics)	D2.Civ.14.9-12. Analyze historical, contemporary, and emerging means of changing societies, promoting the common good, and protecting rights.
Evaluating Sources and Using Evidence	D3.4.9-12. Refine claims and counterclaims attending to precision, significance, and knowledge conveyed through the claim while pointing out the strengths and limitations of both.
Communicating Conclusions and Taking Informed Action	D4.7.9-12. Assess options for individual and collective action to address local, regional, and global problems by engaging in self-reflection, strategy identification, and complex causal reasoning.

NCSS Core Themes and Description

Theme	Description
VIII. Science, Technology, and Society	By exploring the relationships among science, technology, and society, students develop an understanding of past and present advances in science and technology and their impact.

Handouts/Materials/Web Links

Handout/Materials:

- Supporting Question 3 Performance Task Handout

Chapter 8: Science, Technology, and Society   203

- Summative Extension Activity Handout
- Taking Informed Action Handout
- Hollywood or History? Graphic Organizer

Episode Clips and Video Content:
- "Treehouse of Horror XII," Season 13, Episode 1
  - o **House of Whacks Clip:** 7:50–15:27

Primary Sources:
- SmartHome. (2016, August 5). Introducing Amazon Echo [Video]. *YouTube.* https://www.youtube.com/watch?v=CYtb8RRj5r4
- Primary sources are included within "Episode 382: The ELIZA effect" found below

Secondary Sources:
- BBC News (2021, December 28). Alexa tells 10-year-old girl to touch live plug with penny. *BBC News.* https://www.bbc.com/news/technology-59810383
- Hall, D. (2019, December 10). The ELIZA effect (Episode 382) [Audio podcast episode]. In *99% Invisible.* https://99percentinvisible.org/episode/the-eliza-effect/
- Lynskey, D. (2019, October 9). *'Alexa, are you invading my privacy?'—the dark side of our voice assistants.* The Guardian.
- *Wikipedia.* (2021, December 26). *Internet of things.* https://en.wikipedia.org/wiki/Internet_of_things

Guiding Questions

Primary Question:
- Are "smart" technologies worth the cost?

Secondary Questions:
- What are "smart" technologies?
- What harms and benefits of the Ultrahouse 3000 could happen?
- What are the harms and benefits of "smart" technologies?
- What is a primary/secondary source?
- What type of source is *The Simpsons?*

Important Vocabulary

Artificial Intelligence (AI): Displayed by machines which use experience and new data to improve their ability to complete tasks.

Internet of Things (IoT): Technologies which share data about their use via a connection to the Internet.

Machine Learning: A form of artificial intelligence (AI) in which computer algorithms use data and experience complete tasks without direct instructions to do so.

Smart Technologies: A type of Internet of Technology (IoT) technology most often associated with home appliances or other products that share data through their connection to the Internet.

Surveillance Technologies: A range of devices that collect image, location, communication, and other data, which increasingly include Internet of Things technologies.

Assessment Strategies

Formative Assessments:
- Hollywood or History? Graphic Organizer
- Supporting Question 3 Performance Task Handout

Summative Assessments:
- Students will conclude by using evidence to answer the primary/compelling question in a whole class discussion.

Sparking Strategy/Warm-Up

Lesson Introduction

The teacher can open by asking students to view three devices and answer: *What do these devices have in common? What are the costs of each device?*
- Virtual Assistant Technology: https://pixabay.com/photos/alexa-echo-smart-home-box-jukebox-4758340/
- Surveillance Doorbell: https://images-na.ssl-images-amazon.com/images/G/01/vince/boost/detailpages/eradoorbell4a.jpg
- Smartphone: https://pixabay.com/photos/samsung-smartphone-hand-holding-1283938/

Chapter 8: Science, Technology, and Society   205

If students focus solely on price, then the teacher might say: The costs of a product can include more than just money. *What other "costs" besides price come with these products? How else do we "pay" for them in our lives?*

The teacher can then clarify that this inquiry focuses on "smart" technologies, which are also called Internet of Things (IoT). Those who are more pessimistic about their purposes and effects may call them surveillance technologies.

- *Can anyone define or provide examples of these types of technologies?*
- *Do you own or use these types of technologies?*
- *Do you feel like these technologies benefit or harm your life? Do they benefit or harm society?*

The teacher will explain that the primary or compelling question for this lesson is: *Are "smart" technologies worth the cost?* (30 min)

Lesson Procedures

Day 1

1. Students will answer Supporting/Secondary Question 1: *What are "smart" technologies?* Individually or in small groups, students should review the Wikipedia page for "Internet of Things" and answer the following questions: *What are Internet of Things technologies? What are examples of Internet of Things technologies? To what degree do you find the IoT Wikipedia entry credible?* Students should be prepared to discuss these answers in a whole class discussion. (20–30 min)

Day 2

1. Students will answer Supporting/Secondary Question 2: *What harms and benefits of the Ultrahouse 3000 could happen?* Students will watch the "House of Whacks" segment from the "Treehouse of Horror XII" episode of *The Simpsons*. After watching the segment of *The Simpsons*, answer the following questions on their Hollywood or History? Graphic Organizer: *In what ways is the Ultrahouse 3000 a "smart" technology? What are the harms and benefits of the Ultrahouse 3000? Is this Ultrahouse 3000 episode real, true to life, or is it fictional? How accurate is Ultrahouse 3000 to "smart" technologies today? What lessons can we learn today from this 2001 dystopian segment?* (20 min)

206   HOLLYWOOD OR HISTORY?

2. If time, have students share these answers in a whole class discussion. (5 min)
3. Students will answer Supporting/Secondary Question 3: *What are the harms and benefits of "smart" technologies?* Students can review sources including the article and podcast on "The ELIZA effect" from the *99% Invisible* podcast; the primary source commercial, "Introducing Amazon Echo," Amazon, 2014; the article, "'Alexa, are you invading my privacy?'—the dark side of our voice assistants" from *The Guardian*; a tweet from McKinsey & Company, and the short "Alexa tells 10-year-old girl to touch live plug with penny" from the BBC News. The first two sources are long and the teacher could choose to just use one. The final source provides a short, more recent example of a problem with the voice assistant Alexa that students might find comparable to the Ultrahouse 3000. After reviewing the sources, complete the other half of the Hollywood or History Graphic Organizer comparing these smart technologies to the Ultrahouse 3000 from "House of Whacks." (30 min)
4. Students draw on evidence from sources to participate in a whole class discussion around the bottom part of the Hollywood or History Graphic Organizer that answers the primary question: *Are "smart" technologies worth the cost?* (30 min)

Differentiation

Scaffolds: The majority of this lesson should be taught in small groups. It may be helpful to have students of varying ability levels work together. The text in the primary and secondary source articles may be too technical for some students. The teacher may consider shortening the article or only using excerpts for students who may struggle with comprehension of the whole text as well as showing the images to the entire class.

ESL Interventions: In addition to the possible suggested scaffolds, teachers may wish to provide students with simplified definitions of vocabulary and key terms. As opposed to the assigned articles, the teacher may assign less technical and shorter articles to use for the comparison activity.

Extensions:

- In small groups, students should identify a "smart" technology that is important to them and society and ask the following critical questions about technology:
    - o *What does society give up for the benefits of the technology?*

Chapter 8: Science, Technology, and Society   207

- o *Who is harmed and who benefits from the technology?*
- o *What does the technology need?*
- o *What are the unintended or unexpected changes caused by the technology?*
- o *Why is it difficult to imagine our world without the technology?*

After discussing and researching these questions on the Five Critical Questions Handout, students should share with the whole class.

- Students can take informed action as individuals and citizens by answering the following questions:
  - o *What is one "smart" technology with which you would like to change your relationship to more align with your values? How can you better align your values with your use (or non-use) of the technology?*
  - o *What is one "smart" technology in which our society needs to place limits or even ban? Which groups or people are already working toward more just relationships with technology? What action will you take to support the efforts of that group?*
    - § Students can start by reviewing the work of groups like the Electronic Frontier Foundation, Algorithmic Justice League, Data 4 Black Lives, or other people, groups, or organizations working for more just relationships with technology.

REFERENCES

BBC News (2021, December 28). Alexa tells 10-year-old girl to touch live plug with penny. *BBC News*. https://www.bbc.com/news/technology-59810383

Frink, J. (Writer), Payne, D. (Writer), & Reardon, J. (Director). (2001, November 6). Treehouse of horror XII: House of whacks (Season 13, Episode 1) [TV series episode]. In A. Jean, M. Scully, J. L. Brooks, M. Groening, & S. Simon (Executive Producers), *The Simpsons*. Gracie Films; Twentieth Century Fox Film Corporation.

Hall, D. (2019, December 10). The ELIZA effect (Episode 382) [Audio podcast episode]. In *99% Invisible*. https://99percentinvisible.org/episode/the-eliza-effect/

Lynskey, D. (2019, October 9). *'Alexa, are you invading my privacy?'—the dark side of our voice assistants*. The Guardian. https://www.theguardian.com/technology/2019/oct/09/alexa-are-you-invading-my-privacy-the-dark-side-of-our-voice-assistants

208   HOLLYWOOD OR HISTORY?

McKinsey & Company [@McKinsey]. (2022, January 5). *Up to 45 percent of the world's population doesn't get enough #sleep. Can the burgeoning #sleeptech industry provide solutions?* Twitter. https://twitter.com/mckinsey/status/1478924285683109889?s=21

SmartHome. (2016, August 5). Introducing Amazon Echo [Video]. *YouTube.* https://www.youtube.com/watch?v=CYtb8RRj5r4

Wikipedia. (2021, December 26). *Internet of things.* https://en.wikipedia.org/wiki/Internet_of_things

APPENDIX A

Supporting Question 3 Performance Task Handout

Name: _____   **Date**: _____

Directions: After reviewing the sources, complete the T-chart below to identify harms and benefits of smart technologies.

Benefits	Harms

Chapter 8: Science, Technology, and Society   209

Then answer the compelling question: Are "smart" technologies worth the cost?

APPENDIX B

Extension Activity Handout

Directions: In small groups, identify an Internet of Things (IoT) technology that is important to your group and society which you want to examine.

Group Members: _____

Technology: _____

Use this handout (tinyurl.com/FiveCriticalTechnologyQs) to consider critical questions citizens can ask about technologies. Then answer the following questions for the technology your group chose.

Critical Questions about Technology	Answers for Your Technology
1. What does society give up for the benefits of the technology?	

210   HOLLYWOOD OR HISTORY?

2. Who is harmed and who benefits from the technology?	
3. What does the technology need?	
4. What are the unintended or unexpected changes caused by the technology?	
5. Why is it difficult to imagine our world without the technology?	

APPENDIX C

Taking Informed Action Handout

Directions: Students can take informed action as individuals and citizens. Answer the following questions to plan the action you will take.

Individual Action Questions: What is one "smart" technology with which you would like to change your relationship to more align with your values? How can you better align your values with your use (or non-use) of the technology?

Chapter 8: Science, Technology, and Society   211

Societal Action Question: What is one "smart" technology in which our society needs to place limits or even ban? Which groups or people are already working toward more just relationships with technology? How action will you take to support the efforts of that group?

Hollywood or History?

Are Smart Technologies Worth the Cost?

Hollywood has a long history of predicting the benefits and harms which technologies may cause us in the past, present, and future. In the optimistic cases, Hollywood envisions technology utopias. In the pessimistic portrayals, they offer us dystopian warnings to avoid. In this inquiry lesson, students will investigate what to make of how *The Simpsons* portrays "smart" technologies. Students will draw on primary and secondary source materials in their analysis.

Evaluate each source provided and summarize your observations and analysis in corresponding spaces provided. In the section located at the bottom of the page, explain whether you think the scenes from the 2001 "House of Whacks" segment from "Treehouse of Horror XII" (Season 13, Episode 1) *of The Simpsons* are to be evaluated as real, true to life, or fictional? Use examples from your sources/documents to explain your answer.

Primary Source	Clips from The Simpsons	Secondary Source
Source: "Introducing Amazon Echo," Amazon, 2014 Source: #sleeptech tweet, McKinsey & Company, 2021 Source: "Alexa tells 10-year-old girl to touch live plug with penny," BBC News, 2021.	Source: "House of Whacks" segment from "Treehouse of Horror XII (Season 13, Episode 1)" of *The Simpsons*, 2001.	Source: Internet of things Wikipedia entry: https://en.wikipedia.org/wiki/Internet_of_things Source: "Episode 382: The ELIZA effect," *99% Invisible* podcast, 2019. Source: "'Alexa, are you invading my privacy?'—the dark side of our voice assistants," *The Guardian*, 2019.

Chapter 8: Science, Technology, and Society 213

What Do You Think? Hollywood or History?

"Well, Kids, Aren't You Glad We Don't Believe in Inoculations?": Does New Media Provide More "Real News?"

Daniel G. Krutka

EPISODE(S):
"The Computer Wore Menace Shoes" (2000, Season 12, Episode 6)

Grade	Subject	Topic
9–12	Social Studies	Technology

Era Under Study	Estimated Time Needed for Lesson
New and Old Media (21st century)	150 minutes (2 60 minute lessons, and 30 min for the assessment)

State Standards

State	Standards and Descriptions
Indiana	USH.9.4 Reflect on the role of media and social media in the democratic process.
Mississippi	7C.2.1. Compare the positive and negative impacts of changing technologies on expanding the role of citizens throughout the world and the challenges posed by new media sources to obtaining reliable information upon which to make decisions.
	WH.12.5. Debate the impact of modern technology as a prompter of immediate reactions to government policies and discuss the influence of social media on various facets of society and culture.
	USG.6.8. Evaluate the role of journalism including internet vs. traditional media on the political process.
Ohio	8.21. Informed citizens understand how media and communication technology influence public opinion.

Common Core Standards

Standard	Description
CCSS.ELA-LITERACY.RH.9-10.3	Analyze in detail a series of events described in a text; determine whether earlier events caused later ones or simply preceded them.
CCSS.ELA-LITERACY.RH.11-12.2	Determine the central ideas or information of a primary or secondary source; provide an accurate summary that makes clear the relationships among the key details and ideas.
CCEE.ELA-LITERACY.RH.11-12.7	Integrate and evaluate multiple sources of information presented in diverse formats and media (e.g., visually, quantitatively, as well as in words) in order to address a question or solve a problem.

NCSS C3 Framework

Dimension	Description
Developing Questions and Planning Inquiries	D1.5.9-12. Determine the kinds of sources that will be helpful in answering compelling and supporting questions, taking into consideration multiple points of view represented in the sources, the types of sources available, and the potential uses of the sources.
Applying Disciplinary Concepts and Tools (Civics)	D2.Civ.1.6-8. Distinguish the powers and responsibilities of citizens, political parties, interest groups, and the media in a variety of governmental and nongovernmental contexts.
Evaluating Sources and Using Evidence	D3.4.9-12. Refine claims and counterclaims attending to precision, significance, and knowledge conveyed through the claim while pointing out the strengths and limitations of both.
Communicating Conclusions and Taking Informed Action	D4.7.9-12. Assess options for individual and collective action to address local, regional, and global problems by engaging in self-reflection, strategy identification, and complex causal reasoning.

NCSS Core Themes and Description

Theme	Description
VIII. Science, Technology, and Society	By exploring the relationships among science, technology, and society, students develop an understanding of past and present advances in science and technology and their impact.

216   HOLLYWOOD OR HISTORY?

Handouts/Materials/Web Links

Handout/Materials:
- Supporting Question 1 Performance Task Handout
- Supporting Question 2 Performance Task Handout
- Summative Extension Activity Handout
- Five Critical Questions about Technology Handout (tinyurl.com/FiveCriticalTechnologyQs)
- Taking Informed Action Handout
- Hollywood or History? Graphic Organizer

Episode Clips and Video Content:
- "The Computer Wore Menace Shoes," Season 12, Episode 6
- PBS Origins. (2019, August 7). *When did the news start?* [Video]. YouTube. https://www.youtube.com/watch?v=zUFV3T2XQw4
- TED-Ed. (2014, June 5). *How to choose your news—Damon Brown* [Video]. YouTube. https://www.youtube.com/watch?v=q-Y-z6HmRgI

Primary Sources:
- Buzzfeed. (n.d.). *Home.* https://www.buzzfeed.com
- The New York Times. (n.d.). *Home.* https://www.nytimes.com

Secondary Sources:
- Pew Research Center. (1999, March 30). *Section I: The core principles of journalism.* Pew Research Center. https://www.pewresearch.org/politics/1999/03/30/section-i-the-core-principles-of-journalism/
- Sherman, A. (2020, June 5). *Old and new media continue to be dogged by 'both sides' philosophy.* CNBC. https://www.cnbc.com/2020/06/05/old-and-new-media-continue-to-be-dogged-by-both-sides-philosophy.html

Guiding Questions

Primary Question:
- Does new media provide more "real news?"

Secondary Questions:
- How has news changed over time?

Chapter 8: Science, Technology, and Society   217

- How is Mr. X's "news" similar tp and different from media of the past and present?
- What is a primary and secondary source?
- What type of source is *The Simpsons*?

Important Vocabulary

New Media: Developing forms of media, usually electronic, regarded as being experimental.

Old Media: Media in existence before the arrival of the internet, such as newspapers, books, television, and cinema.

Social Media: Communication platforms that allow users to access networks of other accounts instantaneously.

Web 2.0: A term that was used, particularly just after the turn of the 21st century, to describe websites or blogs where people can produce content and interact with other users.

Assessment Strategies

Formative Assessments:
- Hollywood or History? Graphic Organizer
- Supporting Question 1 Performance Task (Venn Diagram)

Summative Assessments:
- Students will conclude by using evidence to answer the compelling question in a whole class discussion.

Sparking Strategy/Warm-Up

Lesson Introduction

The teacher can draw on students' prior experiences by asking, *Where do you get news?* The teacher can ask various clarification and follow up questions, such as, *What makes something news?*

Teachers can ask students to review *The New York Times* and *BuzzFeed* to decipher differences between old and new media primary sources. Teachers should be careful to explain that quality and focus can vary for old and new media, but to focus on differences that might be more common.

218 HOLLYWOOD OR HISTORY?

The teacher will explain that the compelling/primary question for this lesson is: *Does new media provide more "real news?"* (20 min)

Lesson Procedures

Day 1

1. Students will answer Supporting/Secondary Question 1: *How has news changed over time?* Individually or in small groups, students should define "old" and "new" media using the Dictionary.com definitions. Have the students enter the basic definitions into the Venn Diagram on the Supporting Question 1 Handout. (20 min)
2. In small groups, have the students view the "When did the news start?" video, and read the CNBC article. Using these sources, students should then add to their Venn diagram. Afterward, engage the whole class in a discussion of the question: *How has news changed over time?* (20 min)

Day 2

1. Begin Day 2 by having students read the "Core Principles of Journalism" article. Teachers could choose to have the class jigsaw the article, where small groups each take one principle to become an expert on, then teach it to a separate group. Or students could read the article in its entirety. (20 min)
2. Students will answer Supporting/Secondary Question 2: *How is Mr. X's "news" similar and different from media of the past and present?* "The Computer Wore Menace Shoes" episode of *The Simpsons* was released in 2000 at a time when web publishing tools made it easier for people without programming knowledge to create personal websites and blogs. Students will watch the episode and should answer the following questions on their Supporting Question 2 Handout:

   - *What characteristics of old and new media does Mr. X represent?*
   - *Which principles of journalism, if any, does Mr. X exhibit?*
   - *Would the three online evaluation strategies from the Civic Online Reasoning site help citizens of Springfield evaluate Mr. X's claims?*

Chapter 8: Science, Technology, and Society   219

3. Students should be prepared to discuss these answers in a whole class discussion. (30 min for the episode, 10 minutes for discussion)

Day 3

1. For the final assessment, students should complete the Hollywood or History? Graphic organizer using the primary sources, secondary sources, and the *Simpsons* episode. Students draw on evidence from sources to participate in a whole class discussion that answers the compelling question: *Does new media provide more "real news?"* and the bottom of their Hollywood or History graphic organizer about whether *The Simpsons'* portrayal of new media is Hollywood, history, or both. (30 min or could be assigned for homework)

Differentiation

Scaffolds: The majority of this lesson should be taught in small groups. It may be helpful to have students of varying ability levels work together. The text in the secondary source articles or videos may be too technical for some students. The teacher may consider shortening the article or only using excerpts for students who may struggle with comprehension of the whole text as well as showing the images to the entire class.

ESL Interventions: In addition to the possible suggested scaffolds, teachers may wish to provide students with simplified definitions of vocabulary and key terms. As opposed to the assigned articles or videos, the teacher may assign a less technical and shorter articles to use for the comparison activity.

Extensions:
- Have students identify a media technology that is important to them (individually or in small groups) and to society. Have them answer the Five Critical Questions about technology using the Summative Extension Activity Handout.
- Students can take informed action as individuals and citizens by answering the following questions in the Taking Informed Action Handout:
    - o   *What is one way you can be a more responsible consumer and producer of news on- and offline?*

220   HOLLYWOOD OR HISTORY?

o   *What is one way you can advocate for a more responsible media environment?*

§ Students start by reviewing the work of groups like the Stanford History Project's Civic Online Reasoning, Michael Caulfield's SIFT method, or the News Literacy Project working for better online environments.

REFERENCES

Buzzfeed. (n.d.). *Home*. https://www.buzzfeed.com

Civic Online Reasoning. (n.d.). *Curriculum*. https://cor.stanford.edu/curriculum/

News Literacy Project. (n.d.). *About*. https://newslit.org/about/

New York Times. (n.d.). *Home*. https://www.nytimes.com

PBS Origins. (2019, August 7). *When did the news start?* [Video]. YouTube. https://www.youtube.com/watch?v=zUFV3T2XQw4

Pew Research Center. (1999, March 30). *Section I: The core principles of journalism*. Pew Research Center. https://www.pewresearch.org/politics/1999/03/30/section-i-the-core-principles-of-journalism/

Sherman, A. (2020, June 5). *Old and new media continue to be dogged by 'both sides' philosophy*. CNBC. https://www.cnbc.com/2020/06/05/old-and-new-media-continue-to-be-dogged-by-both-sides-philosophy.html

Swartzwelder, J. (Writer), & Kirkland, M. (Director). (2000, December 3). The computer wore menace shoes (Season 12, Episode 6) [TV series episode]. In M. Scully, J. L. Brooks, M. Groening, & S. Simon (Executive Producers), *The Simpsons*. Gracie Films; Twentieth Century Fox Film Corporation.

TED-Ed. (2014, June 5). *How to choose your news—Damon Brown* [Video]. YouTube. https://www.youtube.com/watch?v=q-Y-z6HmRgI

University Libraries. (n.d.). *SIFT: Source analysis*. University of Oklahoma. https://guides.ou.edu/sift

APPENDIX D

Supporting Question 1 Performance Task Handout

Name(s): _____ **Date**: _____

Directions: After reviewing the sources, define "old" and "new" media and then identify similarities and differences between each.

Chapter 8: Science, Technology, and Society   221

Definitions	
Old Media	
New Media	

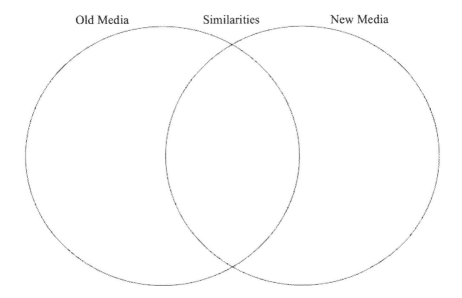

How has the news changed over time?

222   HOLLYWOOD OR HISTORY?

APPENDIX E

Supporting Question 2 Performance Task Handout

Name(s): _____**Date**: _____

Directions: "The Computer Wore Menace Shoes" episode of *The Simpsons* was released in 2000 at a time when web publishing tools made it easier for people without programming knowledge to create personal websites and blogs. Students should answer the following questions:

1. What characteristics of old and new media does Mr. X represent?

2. Which principles of journalism, if any, does Mr. X exhibit?

3. Would the three online evaluation strategies from the Civic Online Reasoning site help citizens of Springfield evaluate Mr. X's claims?

1. Who's behind the information?

2. What's the evidence?

3. What do other sources say?

Chapter 8: Science, Technology, and Society   223

APPENDIX F

Summative Extension Activity Handout

Directions: In small groups, identify a media technology that is important to your group and society which you want to examine.

Group Members: _____

Technology: _____

Use this handout (tinyurl.com/FiveCriticalTechnologyQs) to consider critical questions citizens can ask about technologies. Then answer the following questions for the technology your group chose.

Critical Questions about Technology	Answers for Your Technology
1. What does society give up for the benefits of the technology?	
2. Who is harmed and who benefits from the technology?	
3. What does the technology need?	

224 HOLLYWOOD OR HISTORY?

4. What are the unintended or unexpected changes caused by the technology?	
5. Why is it difficult to imagine our world without the technology?	

APPENDIX G

Taking Informed Action Handout

Directions: Students can take informed action as individuals and citizens. Answer the following questions to plan the action you will take.

Individual Action Questions: What is one way you can be a more responsible consumer and producer of news on- and offline?

Chapter 8: Science, Technology, and Society   225

Societal Action Question: What is one way you can advocate for a more responsible media environment?

[Note: Students start by reviewing the work of groups like the Stanford History Project's Civic Online Reasoning, Michael Caulfield's SIFT method, or the News Literacy Project working for better online environments.]

Hollywood or History?

Does New Media Provide More "Real News?

Hollywood has a long history of predicting the benefits and harms which media technology may cause us in the past, present, and future. In the optimistic cases, Hollywood shows newspaper journalists exposing corruption or evil. In the pessimistic portrayals, the media is part of the problem—covering up corruption or evil. In this inquiry lesson, students will investigate what to make of how *The Simpsons* portrays new media such as blogs. Students will draw on primary and secondary source materials in their analysis.

Evaluate each source provided and summarize your observations and analysis in corresponding spaces provided. In the section located at the bottom of the page, explain whether you think the scenes from the 2000 "The Computer Wore Menace Shoes" episode (Season 12, Episode 6) of *The Simpsons* are be evaluated as real, true to life, or fictional? Use examples from your sources/documents to explain your answer.

Primary Source	Clips from The Simpsons	Secondary Source
Source 1 (old media): The New York Times Source 2 (new media): BuzzFeed	Source: The Computer Wore Menace Shoes (Season 12, Episode 6), of The Simpsons, 2000	Source 1: "When did the News Start?," Origins of Everything, 2019 Source 2: "The Core Principles of Journalism," PEW Research Center, 1999 Source 3: Old Media and New Media, Dictionary.com, n.d. Source 4: "Old and new media continue to be dogged by 'both sides' philosophy," CNBC, 2020 Source 5: "How to choose your news," TED-Ed, 2014

Chapter 8: Science, Technology, and Society   227

What Do You Think? Hollywood or History?

228 HOLLYWOOD OR HISTORY?

For Further Viewing

With over 700 episodes to choose from, there are more episodes of *The Simpsons* that could be used to teach the theme of Science, Technology, and Society.

Satirizing Technology

The Simpsons has made fun of different technological innovations over the years. Sometimes it's a small throwaway joke; other times they devote a whole episode to satirizing technology. Often, their satire has become real concerns as technology evolves, just like the home tech in "House of Whacks." Here are several episodes that, at minimum, have a passing reference to technology satire.

Lisa on Ice (1994, Season 6, Episode 8)
As you can see in the episodes listed in this section, *The Simpsons* can't resist an opportunity to make fun of Apple. Although this episode has nothing to do with technology, there is a passing joke about the poor handwriting recognition of the Apple Newton, showing that the show was always ready to satirize the latest technology, even in the early 90s. (Written by Mike Scully, Directed by Bob Anderson)

Lisa's Date with Density (1996, Season 8, Episode 7)
Homer finds an auto dialer machine and uses the technology to scam people into sending him money, a comment on how technology is so convenient, it can be used to easily aid criminal behavior. (Written by Mike Scully, Directed by Susie Deitter)

Make Room for Lisa (1999, Season 10, Episode 16)
Although this episode is mainly about Homer and Lisa's relationship, there are a few references to the dangers of technology. Homer has a cell phone tower installed in Lisa's room to pay his debts, and Marge eavesdrops on her neighbors via a baby monitor. (Written by Brian Scully, Directed by Matthew Nastuk)

Thirty Minutes Over Tokyo (1999, Season 10, Episode 23)
The family loses all of their money when they go to a cybercafé to use the public Internet and jailbird Snake uses technology to drain their bank account with an illegal download. (Written by Donick Cary and Dan Greaney, Directed by Jim Reardon)

Chapter 8: Science, Technology, and Society   229

MyPods & Boomsticks (2008, Season 20, Episode 7)
In the B-story of this episode, Lisa becomes addicted to her "MyPod" and is forced to work off her debt to "Steve Mobbs" by advertising for the device. Clearly, this entire subplot is a satire of society's addiction to Apple products. (Written by Marc Wilmore, Directed by Steven Dean Moore).

Four Regrettings and a Funeral (2013, Season 25, Episode 3)
This episode is about things Springfieldians regret—Homer's regret is selling his Apple stock due to his inability to foresee the tech company's growth. There is also a Siri joke in this episode about how poor the voice recognition is. (Written by Marc Wilmore, Directed by Mark Kirkland)

Specs and the City (2014, Season 25, Episode 11)
Mr. Burns gives his nuclear plant employees "Oogle Goggles" (a play on Google Glass) to spy on them. Of course, Homer becomes addicted to the virtual reality glasses. (Written by Brian Kelley, Directed by Lance Kramer)

Science Education

In addition to the many episodes about public education in Springfield (see Chapter 11 in this book), there are two episodes about science and technology education specifically:

The Monkey Suit (2006, Season 17, Episode 21)
Ned Flanders and Reverend Lovejoy successfully get the teaching of evolution in school to be made illegal. Lisa teaches evolution in secret, which gets her arrested. The rest of the episode is a parody of the Scopes Monkey Trial and the creationism vs. evolution debate. (Written by J. Stewart Burns, Directed by Raymond S. Persi)

The Girl Code (2016, Season 27, Episode 10)
Lisa joins a coding class and becomes the protégé of a fellow female coder due to lack of gender diversity in the field. Lisa gets so good at coding that she ends up creating an app that comes to life with human intelligence and feelings. (Written by Rob LaZebnik, Directed by Chris Clements)

Predicting Tech

In the "For Further Viewing" section in Chapter 2, I listed two episodes that call forward into the near and distant future to imagine what life must be like. Of course, technology is a big part of dreaming about the future,

230   HOLLYWOOD OR HISTORY?

and *The Simpsons* has predicted technological advancements many times. Here are examples:

Lisa's Wedding (1995, Season 6, Episode 19)
This episode looks into the future of 2010 (which of course is now the past). In 1995, the show predicted the future technology of FaceTime, vending machines that take credit cards, holograms, automated jobs, virtual reality, Apple Watches, and virtual schooling. (Written by Greg Daniels, Directed by Jim Reardon)

Bart to the Future (2000, Season 11, Episode 17)
This episode takes place in 2030 where Lisa is President of the United States and Bart is her deadbeat brother looking for a job in her administration. This episode predicted a future of hologram telegrams, hover buses, and "virtual fudge." How much of this will come true? (Written by Dan Greaney, Directed by Michael Mercantel)

CHAPTER 9

GLOBAL CONNECTIONS

Social studies is made up of many interconnecting disciplines that all compliment each other. When engaging in any inquiry, students may be applying skills from many disciplines. This chapter focuses on those connections among disciplines through a global context. In this theme, students learn about how global issues such as poverty, human rights, environmental issues, and conflict can be examined from different social studies lenses (NCSS, n.d.). The theme also highlights for students the ways we all are globally connected. Studying issues like the COVID-19 pandemic or climate change can show students how what happens globally also has an impact locally.

The Simpsons has featured many different countries in episodes over the years, and not always in the best light (see Chapter 1 for more on stereotypical representations of cultures on the show). There have been times when episodes show the impact of individual actions, such as when Bart releases toads in Australia that destroy the ecosystem there (Oakley et al., 1995) or when Homer destroys ancient ruins in Italy (Frink & Kirkland, 2005). There are also examples of when *The Simpsons* address how global issues impact them locally–*The Simpsons Movie* from 2007 (Silverman, 2007) is about the Environmental Protection Agency stepping in to stop the extensive pollution in Springfield. Of course, the show itself is a global connection. It airs all over the world and is broadcast and dubbed in over 25 languages (Logan, 2015). It appears that themes from the episodes–family, work life, and small communities—are understood globally.

This chapter focuses on two episodes that show the characters engaging in more global systems. In "Kiss Kiss, Bang Bangalore" (Castellaneta et al., 2006), Mr. Burns outsources the work of the Springfield Nuclear Power Plant to India and Homer goes to India to manage the new plant

---

Hollywood or History?: An Inquiry-Based Strategy for Using The Simpsons to Teach Social Studies, pp. 231–253
Copyright © 2024 by Information Age Publishing
www.infoagepub.com
All rights of reproduction in any form reserved.

232 HOLLYWOOD OR HISTORY?

there. This lesson looks at global connections through an economics lens, as students explore the benefits and costs of outsourcing jobs to India—more specifically, *who* benefits from outsourcing and who does not. In the episode, Homer actually gives his Indian workers fair wages, benefits, vacation time, and severance, which allows students to consider taking action against companies that perhaps do not have fair labor practices in other countries.

The second lesson in this chapter asks students to examine the creation of the United Nations—the ultimate example of global cooperation. The lesson features "Simpson Tide" (Ventimilia & Sternin, 1998), an episode where Homer joins the navy and is accidentally part of a global conflict during a training exercise. The United Nations must intervene as Homer's blunder triggers a renewal of the communist Soviet Union. For other ways the family has connected with the world beyond Springfield, including other ways to use episodes already featured in previous chapters, see the "For Further Viewing" section.

REFERENCES

Castellaneta, D. (Writer), Lacusta, D., & Kirkland, M. (Director). (2006, April 9). Kiss, kiss, bang, Bangalore (Season 17, Episode 17) [TV series episode]. In A. Jean, J. L. Brooks, M. Groening, & S. Simon (Executive Producers), *The Simpsons*. Gracie Films; Twentieth Century Fox Film Corporation.

Frink, J. (Writer), & Kirkland, M. (Director). (2005, December). The Italian bob (Season 17, Episode 8) [TV series episode]. In A. Jean, J. L. Brooks, M. Groening, & S. Simon (Executive Producers), *The Simpsons*. Gracie Films; Twentieth Century Fox Film Corporation.

Logan, M. (2015, November 16). *Why 'The Simpsons' is the most powerful TV show of all time*. TV Insider. https://www.tvinsider.com/53856/why-the-simpsons-is-the-most-powerful-tv-show-of-all-time/

Oakley, B. (Writer), Weinstein, J. (Writer), & Archer, W. (Director). (1995, February 19). Bart vs. Australia (Season 6, Episode 16) [TV series episode]. In D. Mirkin, J. L. Brooks, M. Groening, & S. Simon (Executive Producers), *The Simpsons*. Gracie Films; Twentieth Century Fox Film Corporation.

Silverman, D. (Director). (2007). *The Simpsons movie* [Film]. Gracie Films & 20th Century Fox Animation.

Ventimilia, J. (Writer), & Sternin, J (Director). (1998, March 29). Simpson tide (Season 9, Episode 18) [TV series episode]. In M. Scully, J. L. Brooks, M. Groening, & S. Simon (Executive Producers), *The Simpsons*. Gracie Films; Twentieth Century Fox Film Corporation.

Chapter 9: Global Connections 233

"Is Anything in This Bar Made in America?"

Annie McMahon Whitlock

EPISODE(S):
"Kiss Kiss, Bang Bangalore" (2006, Season 17, Episode 17)

Grade	Subject	Topic
11–12	Economics	Outsourcing, responsible labor practices

Estimated Time Needed for Lesson
150 minutes (three 50-minute class periods)

State Standards

State	Standards and Descriptions
Arizona	HS.E5.2. Explain how interdependence impacts individuals, institutions, and societies.
Michigan	E3.1.4. Impact of Transitional Economies—analyze the impact of transitional economies, such as in China and India, on the global economy in general and the American economy in particular.
North Carolina	EPF.E.4. Understand factors of economic interdependence and their impact on nations.

Common Core Standards

Standard	Description
CCSS.ELA-LITERACY. W.11-12.1.B	Develop claim(s) and counterclaims fairly and thoroughly, supplying the most relevant evidence for each while pointing out the strengths and limitations of both in a manner that anticipates the audience's knowledge level, concerns, values, and possible biases.

234 HOLLYWOOD OR HISTORY?

| CCSS.ELA-LITERACY. SL.11-12.5 | Present information, findings, and supporting evidence, conveying a clear and distinct perspective, such that listeners can follow the line of reasoning, alternative or opposing perspectives are addressed, and the organization, development, substance, and style are appropriate to purpose, audience, and a range of formal and informal tasks. |

NCSS C3 Framework

Dimension	Description
Developing Questions and Planning Inquiries	D1.3.9-12. Explain points of agreement and disagreement experts have about interpretations and applications of disciplinary concepts and ideas associated with a supporting question.
Applying Disciplinary Concepts and Tools (Economics)	D2.Eco.15.9-12. Explain how current globalization trends and policies affect economic growth, labor markets, rights of citizens, the environment, and resource and income distribution in different nations.
Communicating Conclusions and Taking Informed Action	D4.1.9-12. Construct arguments using precise and knowledgeable claims, with evidence from multiple sources, while acknowledging counterclaims and evidentiary weaknesses.

NCSS Core Themes and Description

Theme	Description
VII. Production, Distribution, and Consumption	This theme provides for the study of how people organize for the production, distribution, and consumption of goods and services, and prepares students for the study of domestic and global economic issues.
IX. Global Connections	The realities of global interdependence require an understanding of the increasingly important and diverse global connections among world societies. The theme prepares students to study issues arising from globalization.

Chapter 9: Global Connections   235

Handouts/Materials/Web Links

Handout/Materials:
- Hollywood or History? Graphic Organizer

Episode Clips and Video Content:
- "Kiss Kiss, Bang Bangalore," Season 17, Episode 17
    - o **Clip 1:** 0:00–2:33
    - o **Clip 2:** 9:08–11:13
    - o **Clip 3:** 11:30–12:18
    - o **Clip 4:** 17:29–20:05
- Daraddicted. (2014, March 19). *Outsourcing: Is it good or bad?* [Video]. YouTube. https://www.youtube.com/watch?v=7qeehDLYa8g

Secondary Sources:
- Pahwa, A. (2022, June 10). *Outsourcing: Definition, types, pros, cons, & examples.* Feedough. https://www.feedough.com/outsourcing-definition-types-pros-cons-examples/

Guiding Questions

Primary Question:
- Is outsourcing good or bad?

Secondary Questions:
- What is outsourcing?
- What are the costs of outsourcing?

Important Vocabulary

Outsourcing: A business practice where a company hires a third-party to perform its tasks, operations, jobs, or processes, rather than doing the work in-house.

Assessment Strategies

Formative Assessments:
- Hollywood or History? Graphic Organizer

236   HOLLYWOOD OR HISTORY?

Summative Assessments:

- Students will answer this question in a short essay: *Is outsourcing good or bad?* They should include examples from the secondary sources and *The Simpsons* to back up their claims. They should also include specifics about who benefits and does not benefit from outsourcing.

Sparking Strategy/Warm-Up

Lesson Introduction

Read the definition of "outsourcing" to students and ask them to think of examples of outsourcing that they might know and whether these examples are positive or negative. (5 min)

Lesson Procedures

Day 1

1. Divide the students into three groups. Each group will take a section of the article from Feedough that goes over the types of outsourcing and the reasons why companies outsource. Each group will need to create a graphic that explains their section to their classmates. They can use digital tools to make an info-graphic, or a simple "mind-map" on paper and pencil can work too. (20 min+)
   Group 1: "Based on the Type of Activity"
   Group 2: "Based on Location"
   Group 3: "Reasons for Outsourcing"

2. Each group should present their work to their classmates. This can be done through a digital gallery walk or through formal presentations where students can explain their graphic to practice speaking and listening skills. (20 min+)
3. For an exit ticket, the class should answer the following questions in a short paragraph: *What is one thing new you learned from the presentations? What is one question you still have?* (10 min)

Day 2

1. Start this lesson by reviewing key concepts from the presentations that students may still have questions about. This information

Chapter 9: Global Connections   237

should come from the previous lesson's exit ticket. If need be, display the group's graphics again or have them easily accessible. (5 min)

2. Explain that you will be showing clips from the "Kiss Kiss, Bang Bangalore" episode of *The Simpsons* to show an example of outsourcing. Explain that the Springfield Nuclear Power Plant is outsourcing its operations to India and Homer Simpson must manage the workers overseas.

> **Clip 1:** 0:00–2:33
>
> After playing the clip, ask: *What was Mr. Burns's reason for outsourcing?* Have students write the reason on the far left side of their Hollywood or History? Graphic Organizer and the specific example from the episode that meets this definition.
>
> **Clip 2:** 9:08–11:13
> **Clip 3:** 11:30–12:18
>
> After playing these two clips, ask: *What types of outsourcing are shown?* Have the students write the types of outsourcing on the far left side of their Hollywood or History? Graphic Organizer and the specific example from the episode that answers this question. (20 min)

3. Put students in small groups. Based on what they know so far about outsourcing and what they have seen in the episode, they should discuss the question: *Is outsourcing good or bad? Why?* (5 min)

4. The small groups should watch the video "Outsourcing: Is it good or bad?" to get another opinion on the pros and cons of outsourcing. The rest of the Feedough article called "Outsourcing Pros and Cons" also has examples. Students should take notes in the bottom section of their Hollywood or History? Graphic Organizer. As they work, the students should share their opinions based on the evidence so far and start to formulate an evidence-based argument. (20 min)

Day 3

1. Explain that the students will be making their final claim in their argument on outsourcing in a summative assessment. Have them go back through their notes from the previous lesson to add a

238 HOLLYWOOD OR HISTORY?

little more detail around the question *Is outsourcing good or bad?* In a whole group discussion, ask the class: *Who benefits from outsourcing and who does not?* (10 min)

2. Play Clip 4 from the episode, then ask the whole class: *Ultimately, why does Mr. Burns move operations back to Springfield? Was Homer a good manager? Who benefited from outsourcing in this episode and who did not? Why?* (10 min)

> **Clip 4:** 17:29–20:05
>
> The students should note that when Homer treated the workers in India fairly (with good wages and paid vacation), it was no longer profitable for Mr. Burns to outsource. In this case, the Indian workers benefited from responsible outsourcing.

3. Students should complete the summative assessment essay: *Is outsourcing good or bad?* They should include examples from the secondary sources and *The Simpsons* to back up their claims. They should also include more specifics about who benefits and does not benefit from outsourcing. They could complete this in class or for homework. (30 min)

Differentiation

Scaffolds: Day 1 of this lesson could take several days if the pace needs to be slowed down for students to comprehend the definitions and display the definitions visually.

ESL Interventions: Captions on the YouTube video should be on, with opportunities for students to watch it in sections. *The Simpsons* can be watched in many languages.

Extensions:

- Students could research the "fast fashion" industry and how companies have outsourced labor to make clothing quickly. One example is the movement to boycott H&M clothing after it was discovered in 2018 that the conditions for its outsourced workers were terrible. https://turnaroundhm.org/wage-research-september-2018/

- Have students research a popular company that makes a product they're interested in. Research this company's outsourcing practices. *What type of outsourcing do they do (if any)? Do they have fair labor practices? Who benefits from outsourcing?*

REFERENCES

Castellaneta, D. (Writer), Lacusta, D., & Kirkland, M. (Director). (2006, April 9). Kiss kiss, bang Bangalore (Season 17, Episode 17) [TV series episode]. In A. Jean, J. L. Brooks, M. Groening, & S. Simon (Executive Producers), *The Simpsons*. Gracie Films; Twentieth Century Fox Film Corporation.

Daraddicted. (2014, March 19). *Outsourcing: Is it good or bad?* [Video]. YouTube. https://www.youtube.com/watch?v=7qeehDLYa8g

Pahwa, A. (2022, June 10). *Outsourcing: Definition, types, pros, cons, & examples.* Feedough. https://www.feedough.com/outsourcing-definition-types-pros-cons-examples/

Turnaround H&M. (n.d.). *Home.* https://turnaroundhm.org/

Hollywood or History?

Outsourcing in *The Simpsons*

As you read about outsourcing, take notes on the definitions and types of outsourcing you read about, as well as the specific examples you see in the "Kiss Kiss, Bang Bangalore" episode. Then, write your evidence about whether or not you believe outsourcing is good or bad and why.

Outsourcing Definitions	The Simpsons

Chapter 9: Global Connections   241

Is outsourcing good or bad?

Evidence that outsourcing is **good**	Evidence that outsourcing is **bad**
Who benefits from outsourcing?	Who does not benefit from outsourcing?

"It's My First Day!" The Creation of the United Nations

Annie McMahon Whitlock

EPISODE(S):
"Simpson Tide" (1998, Season 9, Episode 19)

Grade	Subject	Topic
9–12	U.S./ World History	Creation of the United Nations

Era Under Study	Estimated Time Needed for Lesson
Post-World War II United States 1945–1989	55 minutes + time for summative assessment if needed

State Standards

State	Standards and Descriptions
California	10.9.8. Students analyze the international developments in the post-World War II world. Discuss the establishment and work of the United Nations and the purposes and functions of the Warsaw Pact, SEATO, NATO, and the Organization of American States.
Massachusetts	USII.T3.5. Using primary sources such as news articles/ analyses, editorials, and radio/newsreel coverage, analyze one of the events that led to World War II, one of the major battles of the war and its consequences, or one of the conferences of Allied leaders following the war. USII.T3.6. Describe the Allied response to the persecution of the Jews by the Nazis before, during, and after the war.
Michigan	8.1.1. Origins and Beginnings of the Cold War— analyze the factors that contributed to the Cold War, including: diplomatic and political actions by both the United States and the U.S.S.R. in the last years of World War II and the years afterward.

Chapter 9: Global Connections   243

Common Core Standards

Standard	Description
CCSS.ELA-LITERACY. W.11-12.1.B	Develop claim(s) and counterclaims fairly and thoroughly, supplying the most relevant evidence for each while pointing out the strengths and limitations of both in a manner that anticipates the audience's knowledge level, concerns, values, and possible biases.

NCSS C3 Framework

Dimension	Description
Applying Disciplinary Concepts and Tools (History)	D2.His.1.9-12. Evaluate how historical events and developments were shaped by unique circumstances of time and place as well as broader historical contexts. D2.His.2.9-12. Analyze change and continuity in historical eras.
Communicating Conclusions and Taking Informed Action	D4.1.9-12. Construct arguments using precise and knowledgeable claims, with evidence from multiple sources, while acknowledging counterclaims and evidentiary weaknesses.

NCSS Core Themes and Description

Theme	Description
II. Time, Continuity, and Change	Through the study of the past and its legacy, learners examine the institutions, values, and beliefs of people in the past, acquire skills in historical inquiry and interpretation, and gain an understanding of how important historical events and developments have shaped the modern world.
IX. Global Connections	The realities of global interdependence require an understanding of the increasingly important and diverse global connections among world societies. This theme prepares students to study issues arising from globalization.

Handouts/Materials/Web Links

Handout/Materials:
- Hollywood or History? Graphic Organizer

Episode Clips and Video Content:
- "Simpson Tide," Season 9, Episode 19
  - o **Clip:** 17:36–20:55

Primary Sources:
- United Nations. (1945). *Charter of the United Nations*. General Records of the United States Government, National Archives. https://www.docsteach.org/documents/document/charter-united-nations
  - o Reading by Sir Lawrence Olivier: http://downloads.unmultimedia.org/radio/library/classics/ltd/mp3/unradioclassics-readingofthepreambletotheuncharter-olivier-copeland_2009_06_12t19_54_10_0021.mp3?s=4E791DEAF8715A84BCD98CB1B53F5D72&save

Secondary Sources:
- The Learning Network. (2011, October 24). October 24, 1945: United Nations is born. *New York Times*. https://archive.nytimes.com/learning.blogs.nytimes.com/2011/10/24/oct-24-1945-united-nations-is-born/
- United Nations. (n.d.). *Home*. www.un.org

Guiding Questions

Primary Question:
- What was the purpose behind the creation of the United Nations?

Secondary Questions:
- What does the United Nations do?

Important Vocabulary

Charter: A written grant by which a body such as a company, college, or city is founded and its rights and privileges defined.

United Nations: A global organization established after World War II in an attempt to maintain international peace and security, and to achieve cooperation among nations on economic, social, and humanitarian problems.

Assessment Strategies

Formative Assessments:
- Hollywood or History? Graphic Organizer

Summative Assessments:
- Students should complete the summative assessment at the bottom of the Hollywood or History? Graphic Organizer. Using evidence from the primary and secondary sources, students should answer the question: *Do you think the United Nations has been successful in its mission, as it was defined in the Preamble from 1945?*

Sparking Strategy/Warm-Up

Lesson Introduction

Start by playing the clip from "Simpson Tide." Explain that in this episode, Homer has joined the U. S. Navy, and during a training exercise, accidentally captains the submarine into Russian waters. After playing the clip, ask the students: *What do you know about what the United Nations does in real life?* (10 min)

Lesson Procedures

This lesson was adapted from a United Nations teaching resource called "The Birth of the UN" from this website: https://www.un.org/en/birth-un-background-information

1. Begin by explaining that the United Nations was created near the end of World War II. The Allied Powers believed that a global organization was needed to bring peace to the world and prevent future wars. In San Francisco in 1945, representatives from 50 countries met to develop the charter of the United Nations. This document, agreed upon by all attendees, was a guide to the mission and purpose of the group. (5 min)

246 HOLLYWOOD OR HISTORY?

2. Have students access the Preamble for the Charter for the United Nations. In partners or small groups, have students read the Preamble or listen to a reading by Sir Lawrence Olivier. After reading, have students answer the following questions in the "Primary Source" column of their Hollywood or History? Graphic Organizer. (15 min)

> *Who do you think is the audience of the text? How do you know?*
>
> *What is the purpose of the UN according to the preamble? Use your own words.*
>
> *The Charter opens with the words "WE THE PEOPLE OF THE UNITED NATIONS." What do the words "UNITED NATIONS" mean in this context?*

3. Have volunteers share their answers in the whole group. After that, hand out the short article from the *New York Times*. This is a secondary source that reports on the goals of the UN Charter from 1945. Have the students add any new information about what the purpose of the United Nations was in the "Secondary Sources" column from the Hollywood or History? Graphic Organizer. They should also add any information from the "Simpson Tide" clip. (10 min)
4. Finally, have students browse the United Nations website to get a sense of what the United Nations has accomplished and is still working on since 1945. The students should take notes in the "UN Since 1945" column of the Hollywood or History? Graphic Organizer. Students should share what they found with the whole group. (15 min)
5. For homework or with any leftover class time, the students should complete the summative assessment at the bottom of the Hollywood or History? Graphic Organizer. Using evidence from the primary and secondary sources, students should answer the question: *Do you think the United Nations has been successful in its mission, as it was defined in the Preamble from 1945?*

Differentiation

Scaffolds: If necessary, students can read selected excerpts from the *New York Times* article. Some students may need more structure and guidance on how to browse the United Nations website. Students could be paired with others to complete the website browsing activity.

Chapter 9: Global Connections   247

ESL Interventions: In addition to the scaffolds, ESL students can read the UN Charter Preamble AND listen to the reading at the same time.

Extensions:

- The United Nations has developed 17 Sustainable Development Goals to guide others in how to take care of the planet. Have students browse the website "The Lazy Person's Guide to Saving the World" and commit to doing one of the activities to help make a more sustainable environment. https://www.un.org/sustainabledevelopment/takeaction/

- The United States is the only United Nations member to not ratify the Convention on the Rights of the Child document. Read more about the CRC document from the UN website, as well as this article about why the United States has yet to ratify it. (https://atlascorps.org/the-united-states-has-not-ratified-the-un-convention-on-the-rights-of-the-child/#:~:text=Host%20Organization%20Spotlight-,The%20United%20States%20has%20not%20ratified%20the%20UN,the%20Rights%20of%20the%20Child&text=Huge%20number%20of%20States%20have,have%20not%20ratified%20the%20treaty.) If students feel compelled to, write to their U. S. Senators and ask them to bring the document to a vote.

REFERENCES

The Learning Network. (2011, October 24). October 24, 1945: United Nations is born. *New York Times.* https://archive.nytimes.com/learning.blogs.nytimes.com/2011/10/24/oct-24-1945-united-nations-is-born/

Minasyan, L. (2018, September 30). The United States has not ratified the UN Convention on the Rights of the Child. *AtlasCorps.* https://atlascorps.org/the-united-states-has-not-ratified-the-un-convention-on-the-rights-of-the-child/#:~:text=Host%20Organization%20Spotlight-,The%20United%20States%20has%20not%20ratified%20the%20UN,the%20Rights%20of%20the%20Child&text=Huge%20number%20of%20States%20have,have%20not%20ratified%20the%20treaty.

United Nations. (n.d.). The birth of the U.N.: Teaching guide and resources. *Teach the UN.* https://www.un.org/en/birth-un-background-information

United Nations. (n.d.). The lazy person's guide to saving the world. *Sustainable Development Goals.* https://www.un.org/sustainabledevelopment/takeaction/

United Nations. (n.d.). *Home.* www.un.org

United Nations. (1945). *Charter of the United Nations.* General Records of the United States Government, National Archives.

248 HOLLYWOOD OR HISTORY?

Ventimilia, J. (Writer), & Sternin, J (Director). (1998, March 29). Simpson tide (Season 9, Episode 18) [TV series episode]. In M. Scully, J. L. Brooks, M. Groening, & S. Simon (Executive Producers), *The Simpsons*. Gracie Films; Twentieth Century Fox Film Corporation.

Chapter 9: Global Connections   249

Hollywood or History?

The United Nations

Take notes in the columns on what you found from the primary and secondary sources on the founding of the United Nations in 1945, comparing them to what the United Nations has accomplished since 1945.

Primary Source—UN Charter from 1945	Secondary Sources—*NY Times, The Simpsons*	United Nations website
Who do you think is the audience of the text? How do you know?	*Who do you think is the audience of these text? How do you know?*	*What has the United Nations accomplished since its founding?*
What is the purpose of the UN according to the preamble? Use your own words.	*What is the purpose of the UN according to these sources? Use your own words.*	
The Charter opens with the words "WE THE PEOPLES OF THE UNITED NATIONS." What do the words "UNITED NATIONS" mean in this context?		

250 HOLLYWOOD OR HISTORY?

Do you think the United Nations has been successful in its mission, as it was defined in the Preamble from 1945?

Evidence that supports "Yes"	Evidence that supports "No"

Chapter 9: Global Connections   251

For Further Viewing

With over 700 episodes to choose from, there are more episodes of *The Simpsons* that could be used to teach the theme of Global Connections.

More About World War II

In the world of *The Simpsons*, Grandpa Abe Simpson is a veteran of World War II. For those looking for episodes to teach the World War II/Post-War era in general, these two episodes are great for a Hollywood or History? comparison:

Raging Abe Simpsons and His Grumbling Grandson in "The Curse of the Flying Hellfish" (1996, Season 7, Episode 22)
This episode flashes back to the end of the war when Grandpa's squadron, The Flying Hellfish, steal artwork from the Nazis (who stole them from people they murdered). Grandpa and Mr. Burns fight over who inherits the fortune, as they are the last surviving veterans. Use this to compare to real stories of missing art from the time period recovered by the Monuments Men. (Written by Johnathan Collier, Directed by Jeffrey Lynch)

Simpsons Christmas Stories (2005, Season 17, Episode 9)
Similar to the "Treehouse of Horror" episodes, this is a Christmas holiday-themed episode with three distinct story segments. In one, Grandpa recounts a story of getting shot down by Japanese planes with Mr. Burns during the war. Being that this is an unconventional Christmas episode, Santa Claus makes an appearance. (Written by Don Payne, Directed by Steven Dean Moore)

More About the United Nations

"Simpson Tide" is not the first time the United Nations makes an appearance on *The Simpsons*. Any clips from these episodes could also be used as secondary sources in the "It's My First Day!" lesson in this chapter.

Treehouse of Horror II (1991, Season 3 Episode 7)
In the first segment of this Halloween episode, the Simpsons travel to Marrakesh and buy a cursed monkey's paw that gives the family three wishes. The United Nations makes a brief appearance when Lisa wishes for world peace. ("The Monkey's Paw" written by Al Jean and Mike Reiss, Directed by Jim Reardon)

252 HOLLYWOOD OR HISTORY?

Das Bus (1998, Season 9, Episode 15)
This episode begins with the kids at Springfield Elementary in a Model U.N. club—before their bus crashes, stranding them on an island. A full lesson using this episode to teach about Power, Authority, and Governance is in Chapter 6. (Written by David X. Cohen, Directed by Pete Michels)

Global Impact

As mentioned in the opening of this chapter (as well as in Chapter 1), the Simpson family has traveled all over the world. At times, their impact on the places they visited have formed connections between Springfield and their vacation spots.

Bart vs. Australia (1995, Season 6, Episode 16)
When traveling to Australia, Bart brings a bullfrog into the country, which wreaks havoc on the ecosystem of the continent. At the end of the episode, a koala latches on to the family's escape plane, suggesting that the koala could have a similar effect on Springfield's ecosystem. For a full lesson on the cultural stereotypes in this lesson, see Chapter 1. (Written by Bill Oakley and Josh Weinstein, Directed by Wes Archer)

Thirty Minutes Over Tokyo (1999, Season 10, Episode 23)
The Simpsons travel to Japan on a discounted vacation and Homer and Bart are irresponsible tourists. Many Japanese people found this episode offensive to their culture. (Written by Donick Cary and Dan Greaney, Directed by Jim Reardon)

Simpson Safari (2001, Season 12, Episode 17)
The Simpsons travel to Africa and find that a primate researcher is using monkeys to mine for diamonds. (Written by John Swartzwelder, Directed by Mark Kirkland)

Goo Goo Gai Pan (2005, Season 16, Episode 12)
This episode shows the global connections of international adoption, as the family travels to China to help Selma adopt a baby, with Homer posing as her husband. (Written by Dana Gould, Directed by Lance Kramer)

Not An Episode, But ...

After years in development and after many requests from fans, *The Simpsons Movie* was released in 2007. In the movie Homer's poor environmental

Chapter 9: Global Connections   253

practices (dumping his pet pig's waste) has caused a global disaster. The only solution is for the Environmental Protection Agency to put the town of Springfield under a dome. Use this movie to look for examples of the United Nations' 17 Sustainable Development Goals.

REFERENCE

Silverman, D. (Director). (2007). *The Simpsons movie* [Film]. Gracie Films & 20th Century Fox Animation.

CHAPTER 10

CIVIC IDEALS AND PRACTICES

The 10th and final NCSS Social Studies theme presented in this book is "Civic Ideals and Practices." In other words—it is what we teach social studies for. In schools, students learn history, geography, civics, economics, and other social studies disciplines in order to be better citizens. This requires studying historical and contemporary issues of citizenship so that one can have "full participation" in society (NCSS, n.d.). Concepts of citizenship, democracy, community, and civic virtue are found in so many episodes of *The Simpsons*, that one could draw from any of the episodes already mentioned in this book to teach this theme. Mostly because these concepts are universal—how do people balance the needs of the individual and the needs of the group for the common good? How do we function in society with competing values? These are important questions for humans or cartoon humans.

The first lesson in this chapter is written by lifelong Simpsons fan, Anthony Salciccioli. He uses the episode "Much Apu About Nothing" (Cohen & Dietter, 1996) to show the conflicting value systems involved in the debate over welcoming immigrants to this country. In this episode, Apu becomes a naturalized U. S. citizen after facing potential deportation due to a xenophobic law in Springfield. It is fitting that we start this book with a lesson on Apu and how his representation as an Indian immigrant on the show has been a point of contention among South Asian Americans, and we end the book with Apu representing the struggle that many immigrants face over how much to adopt American culture while retaining their ethnic identities. Many times, this is in the face of extreme racism and xenophobia, as is demonstrated in this episode. Salciccioli's lesson asks students to look at the historical and contemporary connections to the issue of citizenship as it relates to immigration.

Hollywood or History?: An Inquiry-Based Strategy for Using The Simpsons to Teach Social Studies, pp. 255–280
Copyright © 2024 by Information Age Publishing
www.infoagepub.com
All rights of reproduction in any form reserved.

255

256 HOLLYWOOD OR HISTORY?

There are two parts to this NCSS theme—"Civic Ideals" and "Practices." It's not enough for students to learn about civic concepts, but they need experience practicing them. NCSS specifically states that this theme is also about "students learn[ing] by experience how to participate in community service and political activities and how to use democratic processes to influence public policy" (n.d.). The second lesson involves guiding students through a process of changing a public policy issue they disagree with using the "Team Homer" episode (Scully & Kirkland, 1996). In this lesson, 1st and 2nd grade students get two scaffolded examples of how two fictional schools—one being Springfield Elementary—addressed a school-wide issue. The rest of the lesson involves teachers guiding students to address a classroom or school problem of their own. This gives them the chance to truly practice civic ideals.

This chapter's "For Further Viewing" section has examples of how *The Simpsons* has demonstrated Civic Ideals and Practices, including more episodes about immigration and civic action. There are many more examples than what are featured here! Even small parts of episodes like the two minute clips from "Team Homer" can be used as examples of how students can live civic ideals (Scully & Kirkland, 1996).

REFERENCES

Cohen, D. S. (Writer), & Dietter, S. (Director). (1996, May 5). Much Apu about nothing (Season 7, Episode 23) [TV series episode]. In B. Oakley, J. Weinstein, M. Scully, J. L. Brooks, M. Groening, & S. Simon (Executive Producers), *The Simpsons*. Gracie Films; Twentieth Century Fox Film Corporation.

National Council for the Social Studies. (n.d.). *National curriculum standards for social studies: Chapter 2—the themes of social studies.* https://www.socialstudies.org/national-curriculum-standards-social-studies-chapter-2-themes-social-studies

Scully, M. (Writer), & Kirkland, M. (Director). (1996, January 7). Team Homer (Season 7, Episode 12) [TV series episode]. In B. Oakley, J. Weinstein, M. Scully, J. L. Brooks, M. Groening, & S. Simon (Executive Producers), *The Simpsons*. Gracie Films; Twentieth Century Fox Film Corporation.

Chapter 10: Civic Ideals and Practices   257

Springfield and the History of American Immigration

Anthony Salciccioli

EPISODE(S):
"Much Apu About Nothing" (1996, Season 7, Episode 23)

Grade	Subject	Topic
9–12	United States History	Immigration

Era Under Study	Estimated Time Needed for Lesson
The Development of an Industrial, Urban, and Global United States (1870–1930)	150 minutes (three 50–55-minute lessons)

State Standards

State	Standards and Descriptions
California	11.11 Students analyze the major social problems and domestic policy issues in contemporary American society. 1. Discuss the reasons for the nation's changing immigration policy, with emphasis on how the Immigration Act of 1965 and successor acts have transformed American society.
Michigan	6.1.1 Factors in the American Second Industrial Revolution —Analyze the factors that enabled the United States to become a major industrial power. 6.1.3 Urbanization—Explain the causes and consequences of urbanization, including: • the location and expansion of major urban centers and their • link to industry and trade • internal migration, including the Great Migration • the development of cities divided by race, ethnicity, and class the resulting tensions among and within groups • different perspectives about the immigrant experience

258 HOLLYWOOD OR HISTORY?

New York	Standard 1.3: Study about the major social, political, economic, cultural, and religious developments in New York State and United States history involves learning about the important roles and contributions of individuals and groups. Students: • compare and contrast the experiences of different ethnic, national, and religious groups, including Native American Indians, in the United States, explaining their contributions to American society and culture.

Common Core Standards

Standard	Description
CCSS.ELA-LITERACY. RH.6-8.1	Cite specific textual evidence to support analysis of primary and secondary sources.
CCSS.ELA-LITERACY. RH.9-10.2	Determine the central ideas or information of a primary or secondary source; provide an accurate summary of how key events or ideas developed the course of the text.
CCSS.ELA-LITERACY. RH.11-12.2	Determine the central ideas or information of a primary or secondary source; provide an accurate summary that makes clear the relationships among the key details and ideas.

NCSS C3 Framework

Dimension	Description
Applying Disciplinary Concepts and Tools (Civics)	D2.Civ.2.9-12. Analyze the role of citizens in the U. S. political system, with attention to various theories of democracy, changes in Americans' participation over time, and alternative models from other countries, past and present. D2.Civ.8.9-12. Evaluate social and political systems in different contexts, times, and places, that promote civic virtues and enact democratic principles.
Communicating Results and Taking Informed Action	D4.1.9-12. Construct arguments using precise and knowledgeable claims, with evidence from multiple sources, while acknowledging counterclaims and evidentiary weaknesses.

Chapter 10: Civic Ideals and Practices 259

NCSS Core Themes and Description

Theme	Description
I. Culture	Through the study of culture and cultural diversity, learners understand how human beings create, learn, share, and adapt to culture, and appreciate the role of culture in shaping their lives and society, as well the lives and societies of others.
II. Time, Continuity, and Change	Through the study of the past and its legacy, learners examine the institutions, values, and beliefs of people in the past, acquire skills in historical inquiry and interpretation, and gain an understanding of how important historical events and developments have shaped the modern world.
IV. Individual Development and Identity	Personal identity is shaped by family, peers, culture, and institutional influences. Through this theme, students examine the factors that influence an individual's personal identity, development, and actions.
V. Individuals, Groups, and Institutions	Institutions such as families and civic, educational, governmental, and religious organizations exert a major influence on people's lives. This theme allows students to understand how institutions are formed, maintained, and changed, and to examine their influence.
X. Civic Ideals and Practices	An understanding of civic ideals and practices is critical to full participation in society and is an essential component of education for citizenship. This theme enables students to learn about the rights and responsibilities of citizens of a democracy, and to appreciate the importance of active citizenship.

Handouts/Materials/Web Links

Handout/Materials:
- Upsides and Challenges Handout
- Hollywood or History? Graphic Organizer
- Immigration Data

Episode Clips and Video Content:
- "Much Apu About Nothing," Season 7, Episode 23
  - o Students will watch the entire episode, but educators will stop at the following points to engage in the different activities: **6:14, 9:20, 15:13, 19:45**

260 HOLLYWOOD OR HISTORY?

Primary Sources:

- Hallahan. (1921, May 7). An alien anti-dumping bill. *Providence Evening Bulletin*, 13. https://www.loc.gov/resource/cph.3a44285/
- Irish Central. (1910). *No Irish need apply.* https://www.irishcentral.com/roots/history/no-irish-need-apply-signs-vilified-ancestors
- The Library of Congress. (n.d.). "The great fear of the period" (1860-1869). [Image of painting]. *Library of Congress.* https://www.loc.gov/pictures/item/98502829/
- National Japanese American Historical Society. (1920). Japs keep moving—This is a white man's neighborhood. *Perfect Union Collection.* https://amhistory.si.edu/perfectunion/collection/image.asp?ID=411
- Washington, G. (1783). From George Washington to Joshua Holmes, 2 December 1783. *National Archives.* https://founders.archives.gov/?q=Project%3A%22Washington%20Papers%22%20Joshua%20Holmes&s=1511311111&r=6

Secondary Sources (the first three are found in the Immigration Data handout):

- Myers, J. (2017, Feb 1). These 3 charts explain the complex history of US immigration. *World Economic Forum.* www.weforum.org/agenda/2017/02/from-the-1900s-to-today-a-snapshot-of-immigration-to-the-us/
  - o Long-Term Real Growth in US GDP (2009)—Visualizing Economics.com
  - o U.S. Department of Homeland Security (2012)—Yearbook of Immigration Statistics
  - o U.S. Department of Homeland Security (2015)—Yearbook of Immigration Statistics
- United States Citizenship and Immigration Services. (n.d.). *10 steps to naturalization.* https://www.uscis.gov/citizenship/learn-about-citizenship/10-steps-to-naturalization

Guiding Questions

Primary Question:

- What are the "upsides," or positive aspects of receiving immigrants into the country? What are the "downsides," or challenges that stem from receiving immigrants?
- In what ways did *The Simpsons* episode "Much Apu About Nothing" mirror the history of American immigration?

Chapter 10: Civic Ideals and Practices 261

Secondary Questions:
- What is your personal story on how your family arrived in America?
- Would you consider your family history a push or pull migration?

Important Vocabulary

Cultural Diffusion: The spreading out of culture, culture traits, or a cultural pattern from a central point.

Primary Source: In the study of history as an academic discipline, a primary source is an artifact, document, diary, manuscript, autobiography, recording, or any other source of information that was created at the time under study. It serves as an original source of information about the topic.

Push/Pull Migrations: Factors which initiate and influence the decision to migrate, either by attracting them to another country (pull factors) or by impelling or stimulating emigration (push factors).

Scapegoating: A person or group made to bear the blame for others or to suffer in their place.

Xenophobia: An aversion or hostility to, disdain form or fear of foreigners, people from different cultures, or strangers.

Assessment Strategies

Formative Assessments:
- A class discussion of the following questions: *What are your present views regarding immigration policy in America today? What do you know from prior learning about America's history regarding immigration?*

Summative Assessments:
- Hollywood or History? Graphic Organizer

Sparking Strategy/Warm-Up

Lesson Introduction

Share/project this quote to the whole group:

"The bosom of America is open to receive not only the Opulent and respected Stranger, but the oppressed and persecuted of all Nations and

262 HOLLYWOOD OR HISTORY?

Religions; whom we shall welcome to a participation of all our rights and privileges …"

Ask the students: *How would you interpret this quote from President George Washington?* Have students share their answers. (5 min)

Lesson Procedures

Day 1

1. Open with the reflection questions below. Have the students share their ideas, prior learning, and personal stories of immigration. Push and pull migration may have to be (re)defined for students. (10 min)
   - *What are your present views regarding immigration policy in America today?*
   - *What do you know from prior learning about America's history regarding immigration?*
   - *What is your personal story on how your family arrived in America?*
   - *Would you consider your family history a push, or pull migration?*

2. Using the Upsides & Challenges Handout, ask students to brainstorm what might be advantages to receiving immigrants to the country, and any possible arguments about the challenges that exist. Students can do this individually, then in small groups. Collect all responses in a list from the whole class as students share. (20 min)

Day 2

1. Explain to students that they will be comparing the "Much Apu About Nothing" episode of *The Simpsons* to various contemporary and historical concepts related to immigration. After each segment of the episode, they will fill out a section of their Hollywood or History? Graphic Organizer (5 min)

2. Define the word "scapegoating" for students and have them write the definition in the left column of the "Scapegoating" section. Then play the episode "Much Apu About Nothing," stopping at the 6:14 mark. In the right column, students should

Chapter 10: Civic Ideals and Practices   263

write how Mayor Quimby's decision to create Proposition 24 was an example of scapegoating. (15 min)

3. In small groups, show the students the four primary sources related to attitudes towards immigrants from the late 19th/early 20th century. How would you describe the behavior of people in these sources? After students share what they see, explain the definition of xenophobia, and have students take notes in the left column of the "Xenophobia" section of their Hollywood or History? Graphic Organizer of the examples of xenophobia they see in the sources. (10 min)

4. Continue playing the "Much Apu About Nothing" episode and stop at the 9:20 mark. After the segment, have students write examples of xenophobia they see in the episode. (5 min)

5. Explain to the students that there are ways people view the concept of immigration. One is "assimilation" or the "melting pot," where immigrants strive to lose the customs of their home country to become American. The "tossed salad" view is that immigrants retain much of their home culture, while deciding how much of American culture to adopt or assimilate to. This allows for people's multiple identities to co-exist. In the "Immigrant Story" section of the Hollywood or History? Graphic Organizer in the left column, ask students to draw a picture representing these concepts. (5 min)

6. Continue watching *The Simpsons* episode and stop at the 15:13 mark. Ask the students to write in the right column ways that Apu tried to be a part of the melting pot and his feelings about it. (10 min)

Day 3

1. In small groups, explore the "10 Steps to Naturalization" website and take notes on the process in the left column of the "Citizenship" section of the Hollywood or History? Graphic Organizer. Discuss this question in small groups: *What steps do you feel should take place for a person from another nation to become an American citizen?* (20 min)

2. Continue watching "Much Apu About Nothing," stopping at the 19:45 mark. Students should take notes about which elements of the naturalization process was depicted in *The Simpsons*. (5 min)

3. Finish the "Much Apu About Nothing" episode. In the whole group, discuss these questions: *Do you feel Homer was accurate or inaccurate in his sentiments in his final speech? In the end, Prop 24*

264 HOLLYWOOD OR HISTORY?

passes with 95% of the support of Springfield residents. What statement do you feel the creators of the Simpsons were trying to make? (20 min)

4. Students should complete the final portion of the Hollywood or History? Graphic Organizer either in class or for homework. (10 min+)

Differentiation

Scaffolds: Teachers could take more time at each step, helping students fill out the graphic organizer sequentially.

ESL Interventions: Students could view this video of a sample lecture on the episode and the resulting questions (https://www.youtube.com/watch?v=V7Nhf6qwiGE). Students could then view the video with captions or go slower or faster at their own discretion.

Extensions:

- Students could investigate their own immigration story and share their findings to demonstrate the different waves of American immigration and the commonalities and differences that come from disparate stories.
- Students could interview a family member using Story Corps: https://storycorps.org/ These interviews are saved in perpetuity and can be an archive of family history.

REFERENCES

Cohen, D. S. (Writer), & Dietter, S. (Director). (1996, May 5). Much Apu about nothing (Season 7, Episode 23) [TV series episode]. In B. Oakley, J. Weinstein, M. Scully, J. L. Brooks, M. Groening, & S. Simon (Executive Producers), *The Simpsons*. Gracie Films; Twentieth Century Fox Film Corporation.

Hallahan. (1921, May 7). An alien anti-dumping bill. *Providence Evening Bulletin*, 13. https://www.loc.gov/resource/cph.3a44285/

Irish Central. (1910). *No Irish need apply*. https://www.irishcentral.com/roots/history/no-irish-need-apply-signs-vilified-ancestors

The Library of Congress. (n.d.). "The great fear of the period" (1860-1869). [Image of painting]. *Library of Congress*. https://www.loc.gov/pictures/item/98502829/

Myers, J. (2017, Feb 1). These 3 charts explain the complex history of US immigration. *World Economic Forum*. www.weforum.org/agenda/2017/02/from-the-1900s-to-today-a-snapshot-of-immigration-to-the-us/.

National Japanese American Historical Society. (1920). *Japs keep moving—This is a white man's neighborhood. Perfect Union Collection*. https://amhistory.si.edu/perfectunion/collection/image.asp?ID=411

Sauces' Social Studies. (2021, December 27). *Springfield and the history of American immigration* [Video]. YouTube. https://www.youtube.com/watch?v=V7Nhf6qwiGE

Storycorps. (n.d.). *Home*. https://storycorps.org

United States Citizenship and Immigration Services. (n.d.). *10 steps to naturalization*. https://www.uscis.gov/citizenship/learn-about-citizenship/10-steps-to-naturalization.

Washington, G. (1783). From George Washington to Joshua Holmes, 2 December 1783. *National Archives*. https://founders.archives.gov/?q=Project%3A%22Washington%20Papers%22%20Joshua%20Holmes&s=1511311111&r=6

APPENDIX A

Upsides and Challenges

What are the "upsides," or positive aspects of receiving immigrants into the country? What are the challenges that stem from receiving immigrants? Think about these on your own, and we'll pool our answers as a class.

UPSIDES	CHALLENGES

266 HOLLYWOOD OR HISTORY?

Hollywood or History?

Immigration

Fill in each section of this graphic organizer as you watch "Much Apu About Nothing" and are introduced to the respective sources. At the end of the episode, you will be asked to describe how true *The Simpsons* is to contemporary and historical concepts of immigration.

Scapegoating

Definition	Examples from "Much Apu About Nothing"

Xenophobia

Examples from Primary Sources	Examples from "Much Apu About Nothing"

Assimilation

Melting Pot/ Tossed Salad	Examples from "Much Apu About Nothing"

Citizenship

10 Steps to Naturalization	Examples from "Much Apu About Nothing"

In what ways did *The Simpsons* episode, "Much Apu About Nothing" mirror the history of American immigration? Use examples from each section above to defend your answer.

Chapter 10: Civic Ideals and Practices 269

"Down With Homework!"

Annie McMahon Whitlock

EPISODE(S):
"Team Homer" (1996, Season 7, Episode 12)

Grade	Subject	Topic
1st or 2nd	Public Policy Issue	Addressing a community issue

Estimated Time Needed for Lesson
TBD—could be several weeks.

State Standards

State	Standards and Descriptions
Michigan	1-P3.1.1. Identify public issues in the school community.
	1-P3.1.2. Use graphic data to analyze information about a public issue in the school community.
	1-P3.1.3. Identify alternative resolutions to a public issue in the school community.
	1-P3.3.1. Express a position on a public policy issue in the school community and justify the position with a reasoned argument. 1
	1-P4.2.1. Develop and implement an action plan to address or inform others about a public issue.
	1-P4.2.2. Participate in projects to help or inform others.
New York	1.F.2. Participate in activities that focus on a classroom or school issue or problem.
Ohio	Civic Participation and Skills
	1.8 Individuals have the responsibility to take action toward the achievement of common goals in homes, schools, and communities and are accountable for those actions.

270 HOLLYWOOD OR HISTORY?

Common Core Standards

Standard	Description
CCSS.ELA-LITERACY. SL.1.1	Participate in collaborative conversations with diverse partners about grade 1 topics and texts with peers and adults in small and larger groups.

NCSS C3 Framework

Dimension	Description
Applying Disciplinary Concepts and Tools (Civics)	D2.Civ.7.K-2. Apply civic virtues when participating in school settings. D2.Civ.11.K-2. Explain how people can work together to make decisions in the classroom.
Communicating Conclusions and Taking Informed Action	D4.6.K-2. Identify and explain a range of local, regional, and global problems, and some ways in which people are trying to address these problems. D4.7.K-2. Identify ways to take action to help address local, regional, and global problems. D4.8.K-2. Use listening, consensus-building, and voting procedures to decide on and take action in their classrooms.

NCSS Core Themes and Description

Theme	Description
X. Civic Ideals and Practices	An understanding of civic ideals and practices is critical to full participation in society and is an essential component of education for citizenship. This theme enables students to learn about the rights and responsibilities of citizens of a democracy, and to appreciate the importance of active citizenship.

Handouts/Materials/Web Links

Handout/Materials:

- Hollywood or History? Graphic Organizer

Chapter 10: Civic Ideals and Practices   271

Episode Clips and Video Content:
- "Team Homer," Season 7, Episode 12
  - o **Clip 1:** 3:42–4:38
  - o **Clip 2:** 9:00–10:00

Secondary Sources:
- Whitlock, A. M., & Bacak-Egbo, C. (Eds.). (2017). *Families and schools.* Intra-Michigan Technology Readiness Consortium.
  - o Chapter 6—Michigan Open Book Project: http://textbooks. wmisd.org/getacopy.html

Guiding Questions

Primary Question:
- How do people solve problems to make things better?

Secondary Questions:
- How can we decide on a solution to a problem?
- What is an issue we care about?

Important Vocabulary

Issue: When some people agree on one solution to a problem and others disagree.
Problem: Something difficult that needs to be solved. It can be hard to solve a problem because not everyone will agree on how to solve it.

Assessment Strategies

Formative Assessments:
- Hollywood or History? Graphic Organizer

Summative Assessments:
- At the end of the public issue project, students should reflect on how it went for a summative assessment. This could be done in an interview, by drawing a picture, or by writing. The students should address these prompts: *Did we solve the problem? If yes, how did we do it? If no, what was the reason?*

272 HOLLYWOOD OR HISTORY?

Sparking Strategy/Warm-Up

Lesson Introduction

Go over the definition of "problem" for the students. Ask the question: *What is something you would like to see change at our school or in our classroom?* (10–15 min)

This lesson was adapted from Chapter 6 of the *Families and Schools* textbook from the Michigan Open Book Project.

Lesson Procedures

Day 1

1. Project Chapter 6 from the Michigan Open Book textbook *Families and Schools*. This chapter walks students through an example of a school problem and how the students helped to solve it. This part of the lesson could take several days, depending on how much time is allotted in the elementary school day to social studies. Start by reading pages 250–251 to the students. Stop and ask: *What is the problem at Egbo School that the students want to see changed?*

2. After talking about the messy cafeteria being a problem, read pages 252–253. This is an example of how students collected data about the problem by observing it.

3. Read page 254 and ask the students: *What were the possible solutions the students came up with?*

4. Define the word issue for the students. This is where there are many solutions to a problem, but it is hard to agree on which one is the best. Ask the students to give reasons why the janitor should clean up the messy cafeteria and why he/she should not have to. Then, ask the students reasons why the kids should have to clean up the mess and why they shouldn't have to. Make a list of their reasons, then ask: *What do you think they should decide? Who should clean the tables, the janitor or the kids?*

5. Look at the charts on page 255 and page 256 of *Families and Schools*. If there are different ideas there than what the students came up with, add them to the class chart. Then finish Day 1 by reading pages 258–260. This shows that the class voted on who should clean the tables (janitor or kids), then made a plan to let others know about their solution.

Day 2

1. Review the steps to solving a public issue with the students. These are listed on p. 262 of the *Families and Schools* textbook. Or, teachers can make a separate anchor chart to keep posted in the classroom. The steps are:
   Think of a problem you really care about
   Learn about the problem by collecting data
   Think about ways to solve the problem
   Vote on a way to solve the problem
   Make and follow a plan to solve the problem

2. Explain that next they are going to watch what happened to a school called Springfield Elementary and see if they can figure out what steps the students should take. Play the first clip of "Team Homer." You may have to play the clip more than once.

   Clip 1: 3:42–4:38

3. After playing the clip, project the Hollywood or History? Graphic Organizer. In this case, the "History" part is the list of the steps to solving a public issue. The "Hollywood" part is how this issue is depicted in *The Simpsons*. Ask the students, *What is the problem at Springfield Elementary?* (They should answer that the problem is that students are unsafe and running in the halls). Put this answer in the first row of the graphic organizer.
4. Next, ask the students, *How was this problem caused?* (Students should answer that Bart's shirt created a distraction). Put this answer in the second row of the graphic organizer.
5. Play Clip 2, then ask the students: *What is Principal Skinner's solution to the problem? Why do you think he wants this solution? Do you think the kids agree with his idea?* Write their ideas in the third row of the graphic organizer.

   Clip 2: 9:00-10:00

6. Ask the students: *What do you think are other solutions to the problem at Springfield Elementary, other than school uniforms?* Write their ideas in the third row of the graphic organizer along with Principal Skinner's ideas. Have the students vote on an idea for what the Springfield Elementary students could do. Presumably, they won't vote for uniforms! Write the results of the vote in the fourth row of the graphic organizer.

274 HOLLYWOOD OR HISTORY?

7. Ask the students: *What could the students at Springfield Elementary do next? How could they let people know of their plan?* Write their ideas in the fifth row of the graphic organizer.

Day 3+

1. Ask the students to return to their ideas in the warmup from Day 1. Review the students' answers to the question *What is something you would like to see change at our school or in our classroom?* and see if there are other things they would like to add.
2. Explain to the students that they are going to attempt to solve one of the problems in their school or classroom. First, they need to choose one of the ideas from the class list. You can either help them select through a discussion or a class vote, or both.
3. Once a problem has been determined, the class should go through the five steps outlined in Day 1 and Day 2. This will take more than one day to do, so from here, the teacher should pace out how this project will work. Students should collect data on their problem, brainstorm possible solutions, vote on a solution, then make a plan to implement the solution. Refer back to the Egbo school example from Day 1 and their Hollywood or History? Graphic Organizer if students need a refresher.
4. At the end of the project, students should reflect on how it went for a summative assessment. This could be done in an interview, by drawing a picture, or by writing. The students should address these prompts: *Did we solve the problem? If yes, how did we do it? If no, what was the reason?*

Differentiation

Scaffolds: Since this is a lengthy project, teachers may need to scaffold several parts of it, much of which is unknown until the students select a public issue to solve. Some examples are that teachers can extend the lessons in small periods of time or give extra time to complete tasks by integrating social studies into reading, writing, or math time.

ESL Interventions: Students should be able to express themselves orally or in writing.

Extensions:
- Complete the Hollywood or History? Graphic Organizer again, using the book *Follow the Moon Home: A Tale of One Idea, Twenty*

Kids, and a Hundred Sea Turtles by Phillip Cousteau. Identify the five steps to addressing a public issue that appear in this book.

- If the students selected a classroom problem, have them try to address a school-wide or community-wide problem next.

REFERENCES

Cousteau, P. (2016). *Follow the moon home: A tale of one idea, twenty kids, and a hundred sea turtles.* Chronicle Books.

Scully, M. (Writer), & Kirkland, M. (Director). (1996, January 7). Team Homer (Season 7, Episode 12) [TV series episode]. In B. Oakley, J. Weinstein, M. Scully, J. L. Brooks, M. Groening, & S. Simon (Executive Producers), *The Simpsons.* Gracie Films; Twentieth Century Fox Film Corporation.

Whitlock, A. M., & Bacak-Egbo, C. (Eds.). (2017). *Families and schools.* Intra-Michigan Technology Readiness Consortium.

276   HOLLYWOOD OR HISTORY?

Hollywood or History?

This graphic organizer should be done in a whole class, where the teacher projects the graphic below and fills in the steps with students as they watch clips from "Team Homer."

Steps to Solving a Problem	Springfield Elementary
Think of a problem you really care about.	
Learn about the problem by collecting data.	
Think about ways to solve the problem.	

Chapter 10: Civic Ideals and Practices   277

Vote on a way to solve the problem.	
Make and follow a plan to solve the problem.	

For Further Viewing

With over 700 episodes to choose from, there are more episodes of *The Simpsons* that could be used to teach the theme of Civic Ideals and Practices.

Immigration

"Much Apu About Nothing" may have been the first episode of the show to address Apu's undocumented immigrant status, but the show has since shown other episodes centered around both Apu and immigration.

Coming to Homerica (2009, Season 20, Episode 21)
Displaced residents from the nearby town of Ogdenville move to Springfield, causing a xenophobic response in residents, to the point where they build a wall to keep Ogdenvillians out. (Written by Brendan Hay, Directed by Steven Dean Moore)

Much Apu About Something (2016, Season 27, Episode 12)
In Chapter 1, Ritu Radhakrishnan wrote a lesson examining the difference in experiences of South Asian immigrants using this episode, where Apu clashes with his nephew (who was born in the United States) over running the Kwik-E-Mart. (Written by Michael Price, Directed by Bob Anderson)

Civic Values

Over the years, *The Simpsons* has dealt with timeless issues of core democratic/civic values like the right to peacefully assemble, voting rights, representative government, patriotism, political parties, and many more. Here are some examples:

Itchy & Scratchy & Marge (1990, Season 2, Episode 9)
Marge takes issue with the violence depicted in the Itchy & Scratchy cartoons and organizes a protest organization to enact change. (Written by John Swartzwelder, Directed by Jim Reardon)

Sideshow Bob Roberts (1994, Season 6, Episode 5)
Bart and Lisa bust Sideshow Bob for electoral fraud during his campaign for mayor of Springfield, demonstrating the important civic ideal of protecting the right to vote in free and fair elections. (Written by Bill Oakley and Josh Weinstein, Directed by Mark Kirkland)

Chapter 10: Civic Ideals and Practices   279

Mr. Spritz Goes to Washington (2003, Season 14, Episode 14)

When the airport's flight path goes over the Simpsons' house, they go through channels to address their issue with no luck. Bart then convinces Krusty the Clown to run for Congress to help them out. (Written by John Swartzwelder, Directed by Lance Kramer)

Bart-Mangled Banner (2004, Season 15, Episode 21)

Bart accidentally moons the American flag, which leads to the family being universally hated for their lack of patriotism. This episode could be used to discuss what it means to be patriotic. (Written by John Frink, Directed by Steven Dean Moore)

The Kid is All Right (2013, Season 25, Episode 6)

Lisa befriends a new student who turns out to be politically conservative, clashing with Lisa's politically liberal views. The girls run against each other for class president but agree to set aside political differences to be friends. (Written by Tim Long, Directed by Mark Kirkland)

Practicing Civic Action

There are many episodes of the series that feature residents of Springfield protesting issues they disagree with or holding town meetings to discuss solutions to community problems. Here are examples of Bart, Lisa, and other Springfield children practicing civic action through a variety of methods.

Whacking Day (1993, Season 4, Episode 20)

In Chapter 1, Dave Johnson wrote about Whacking Day as a made-up holiday. Also, in this episode Bart and Lisa educate the town on the barbarism of Whacking Day and make a plan to save the snakes. (Written by John Swartzwelder, Directed by Jeff Lynch)

Wild Barts Can't Be Broken (1999, Season 10, Episode 11)

In this episode, the kids of Springfield are blamed for the destruction of the elementary school (actually done by Homer), and the proposed solution is a curfew. The kids band together to protest this issue through civil disobedience and media manipulation. (Written by Larry Doyle, Directed by Mark Ervin)

Treehouse of Horror XIII (2002, Season 14, Episode 1)

In the segment "The Fright to Creep and Scare Harms," Lisa organizes a ban on guns in Springfield as a response to gun violence. Since this is

280 HOLLYWOOD OR HISTORY?

a Halloween episode, the town is then defenseless when zombies rise up from their graves. (Segment written by Brian Kelley, Episode directed by David Silverman)

The President Wore Pearls (2003, Season 15, Episode 3)
In a parody of *Evita*, Lisa organizes her fellow Springfield Elementary students into striking when the school cuts music and art from the curriculum. (Written by Dan Gould, Directed by Mike B. Anderson)

The Winter of Our Monetized Content (2019, Season 31, Episode 1)
Lisa gets detention and her punishment is to make novelty license plates. To protest the privatization of detention, she organizes a strike. (Written by Ryan Koh, Directed by Bob Anderson)

CHAPTER 11

COMMENTARY ON PUBLIC EDUCATION

This chapter is slightly different from the previous ones. Up to this point, this book has shown ways to use *The Simpsons* in a K–12 social studies lesson, using NCSS's themes of social studies as a guide. This chapter features two lessons that teach about education itself. These lessons could be done with a course of pre-service teachers in a foundations of education course, or in other methods classes. Students can compare how *The Simpsons* has satirized education over the years to how close they were to capturing the real ways public schools function or how close they were to depicting real issues facing public education today.

Springfield Elementary and its group of teachers, students, administrators, and support staff have been a core part of the show since the beginning. Literally the second episode of the series features Bart cheating on an aptitude test, causing him to be mistaken for having above average intelligence. He then sees first-hand the inequities in schooling between his public elementary school and the "gifted" school he transfers to (Vitti & Silverman, 1990). This is a statement about the unreliability of intelligence testing and could be used in a classroom to discuss the use of intelligence tests today, and the history of racism involved in making these types of tests so ubiquitous in schools. And this was just the second episode of more than 700!

Tiffany Craigie authors the first lesson in this chapter using the Season 3 episode "Separate Vocations" (Meyer & Lynch, 1992). This is another episode from early on in the series' run that features aptitude tests to gauge future career choices of Springfield Elementary students and how they influence what Bart and Lisa believe themselves to be capable of. Craigie

---

Hollywood or History?: An Inquiry-Based Strategy for Using The Simpsons to Teach Social Studies, pp. 281–309
Copyright © 2024 by Information Age Publishing
www.infoagepub.com
All rights of reproduction in any form reserved.

282 HOLLYWOOD OR HISTORY?

designs a lesson to show what the purposes and challenges of aptitude testing for career goals could be.

In the second lesson, Scott L. Roberts and Kate Van Haren use the episode "How the Test Was Won" (Price & Kramer, 2009) to explore the concept and controversy surrounding standardized testing. Standardized testing has been a controversial topic since the beginning of public education. By the time students reach high school, the majority of students likely have some personal experience and knowledge of standardized testing. Using clips from the episode, students will explore the different arguments for and against standardized testing using a variety of different sources, including their own experiences. Using the lateral reading strategy, students will learn how to think critically about the purpose and how different types of data are presented in the sources. This lesson was written for high school students but could also be used with pre-service teachers who are just beginning to learn about their chosen careers.

I hope that this examination of public education issues in the show can be used to start conversations about possible solutions, using the humor and lightness that *The Simpsons* has provided for decades. For other episodes about education issues such as privatization of schooling, administration, teachers' unions, and curriculum and instructional methods, see the "For Further Viewing" section.

REFERENCES

Meyer, G. (Writer), & Lynch, J. (Director). (1992, February 27). Separate vocations (Season 3, Episode 18) [TV series episode]. In A. Jean, M. Reiss, J. L. Brooks, M. Groening, & S. Simon (Executive Producers), *The Simpsons*. Gracie Films; Twentieth Century Fox Film Corporation.

Price, M. (Writer), & Kramer, L. (Director). (2009, March 1). How the test was won (Season 20, Episode 11) [TV series episode]. In A. Jean, J. L. Brooks, M. Groening, & S. Simon (Executive Producers), *The Simpsons*. Gracie Films; Twentieth Century Fox Film Corporation.

Vitti, J. (Writer), & Silverman, D. (Director). (1990, January 14). Bart the genius (Season 1 Episode 2) [TV series episode]. In J. L. Brooks, M. Groening, & S. Simon (Executive Producers), *The Simpsons*. Gracie Films; Twentieth Century Fox Film Corporation.

"Here's Your Scientifically Selected Career"

Tiffany Craigie

EPISODE(S):
"Separate Vocations" (1992, Season 3, Episode 18)

Grade	Subject	Topic
Preservice or practicing teachers	Student Motivation and Engagement	History of aptitude tests in US schools Using aptitude tests and students' strengths and interests in teaching

Estimated Time Needed for Lesson
3–4 class periods (50–60 minutes each)

State Teacher Preparation Standards

State	Standards and Descriptions
California	TPE1. Apply knowledge of students, including their prior experiences, interests, and social emotional learning needs, as well as their funds of knowledge and cultural, language, and socioeconomic backgrounds, to engage them in learning.
Michigan	Teacher Preparation Standards P.1. Learner-Centered Supports c. Support children by using practices that engage and empower learners. d. Demonstrate the ability to build meaningful learning environments and curriculum by focusing on children's characteristics, needs and interests; linking children's language, culture, and community to early learning; using social interactions during routines and play based experiences; incorporating technology and integrative approaches to content knowledge; and utilizing incidental teaching opportunities and informal experiences to build children's development in all areas.

284 HOLLYWOOD OR HISTORY?

Texas	Standard 2—Knowledge of Students and Student Learning. Teachers work to ensure high levels of learning, social-emotional development, and achievement outcomes for all students, taking into consideration each student's educational and developmental backgrounds and focusing on each student's needs.
	(A) Teachers demonstrate the belief that all students have the potential to achieve at high levels and support all students in their pursuit of social-emotional learning and academic success.
	(i) Teachers purposefully utilize learners' individual strengths as a basis for academic and social-emotional growth.
	(ii) Teachers create a community of learners in an inclusive environment that views differences in learning and background as educational assets.
	(iii) Teachers accept responsibility for the growth of all of their students, persisting in their efforts to ensure high levels of growth on the part of each learner.
	(B) Teachers acquire, analyze, and use background information (familial, cultural, educational, linguistic, and developmental characteristics) to engage students in learning.
	(i) Teachers connect learning, content, and expectations to students' prior knowledge, life experiences, and interests in meaningful contexts.
	(ii) Teachers understand the unique qualities of students with exceptional needs, including disabilities and giftedness, and know how to effectively address these needs through instructional strategies and resources.
	(iii) Teachers understand the role of language and culture in learning and know how to modify their practices to support language acquisition so that language is comprehensible, and instruction is fully accessible.

Chapter 11: Commentary on Public Education 285

NCSS Teacher Preparation Standards

Standard	Description
Standard 4a	Candidates use knowledge of learners' socio-cultural assets, learning demands, and individual identities to plan and implement relevant and responsive pedagogy that ensures equitable learning opportunities in social studies.

NCSS C3 Framework

Dimension	Description
Applying Disciplinary Tools and Concepts (History)	D2.His.7.9-12. Explain how the perspectives of people in the present shape interpretations of the past.
	D2.His.8.9-12. Analyze how current interpretations of the past are limited by the extent to which available historical sources represent perspectives of people at the time.

NCSS Core Themes and Description

Theme	Description
V. Individuals, Groups, and Institutions	Institutions such as families and civic, educational, governmental, and religious organizations exert a major influence on people's lives. This theme allows students to understand how institutions are formed, maintained, and changed, and to examine their influence.

Handouts/Materials/Web Links

Handout/Materials:
- Vocabulary Sheet
- Hollywood or History? Graphic Organizer
- Strengths and Interests Notetaking Guide

Episode Clips and Video Content:
- "Separate Vocations," Season 3, Episode 18

286 HOLLYWOOD OR HISTORY?

Secondary Sources:

- Career Assessment. (n.d.). *Career research*. http://career.iresearchnet.com/career-assessment-old/#:~:text=Career%20assessment%20has%20been%20in,the%20Strong%20Vocational%20Interest%20Blank
- EL Education. (n.d.). *Helping all learners: Interest.* https://eleducation.org/resources/helping-all-learners-interest
- Holland-Marks, J. (2017). Using student interests as resources for instruction. *ASCD*. https://www.ascd.org/blogs/using-student-interests-as-resources-for-instruction
- Klein, A. (2021, April 26). Aptitude tests: Are they effective in opening students' minds to more career paths? *Education Week*. https://www.edweek.org/technology/aptitude-tests-are-they-effective-in-opening-students-minds-to-more-career-paths/2021/04
- Tomlinson, C. A. (2006). Teaching beyond the book. *ASCD, 64*(1). https://www.ascd.org/el/articles/teaching-beyond-the-book

Guiding Questions

Primary Question:

- How can the use of students' strengths and interests in lessons lead to increased student achievement?

Secondary Questions:

- How has the use of aptitude tests in U.S. schools evolved?
- How can aptitude tests help students make decisions about class choices and post-high school plans?
- How can we identify students' interests and strengths?
- How can we incorporate our students' interests and strengths in our planning and teaching?

Important Vocabulary

Aptitude Test: Measures a person's potential to learn and succeed.
Achievement Test: Measures actual learning of knowledge and skills.
Career/ Vocational Test: Gathers information about a person's interests, abilities, and learning potential and suggests a variety of related career paths.

Interest Inventory/ Survey: Gathers information about a person to determine their interests and suggests a variety of related career paths.

Assessment Strategies

Formative Assessments:
- Hollywood or History? Graphic Organizer
- Strengths and Interests Notetaking Guide

Summative Assessments:
- The students will create and deliver a presentation to their class. They will find at least two different activities they can use to get to know their students' strengths and interests, explain three ways to incorporate students' strengths and interests into content area lessons, identify pros and cons of using aptitude tests, and explain the benefits of using students' strengths and interests in teaching.

Sparking Strategy/Warm-Up

Lesson Introduction

In a whole group, ask the students, *What do you remember wanting to be when you were growing up? What inspired that? Did it change along the way?* Allow a few minutes for students to think and jot down their answers. Use the "Inside-Outside Circle" strategy to have students share their thoughts (Echevarria & Vogt, 2008). To do this, split the class into two equal groups, half forming an inside circle, half forming an outside circle, so that each student is facing another student in the other circle. Have students share their responses with the person they are facing from the other circle, then have the inside circle rotate so they can share with a different person. Continue for several rotations. If desired, have a few students share their thoughts with the whole group after reconvening. (15 min)

Lesson Procedures

Day 1

1. After the warm up, explain to the class that they will be learning about aptitude tests in schools. They will learn how aptitude tests

288 HOLLYWOOD OR HISTORY?

can determine students' strengths and interests and show students different career paths they may not have considered. They will also explore ways to use students' strengths and interests in their lessons to motivate and engage students. Display the Vocabulary Sheet and explain the difference between aptitude tests and achievement tests, and the different examples of each. (5 min)

2. Explain to students that they will be watching an episode from *The Simpsons* and they should pay attention to how aptitude tests are used at Springfield Elementary and the impact it has on Bart and Lisa. Show the episode. Engage in a whole group discussion about what they noticed. (30 min)

Day 2

1. Next, have students read the article, *Career Assessment*, using the "Paraphrase Passport" reading strategy (The Adaptive School, 2017). Partner 1 reads a paragraph aloud and partner 2 paraphrases. Then partner 2 reads and partner 1 paraphrases. This continues for each paragraph through the end of the reading. When they are finished reading, have partners discuss the following questions and be prepared to have one student from each partnership share out with the whole class. (25 min)

   - *How have aptitude/ career assessments evolved over the years?*
   - *What experiences do you have taking these types of assessments? What were the results? How do the results compare to your chosen career path?*
   - *How might these types of assessments be beneficial to students at any grade level?*
   - *How might they be detrimental?*
   - *How might you as a teacher use your students' results of these types of assessments to plan instruction?*

2. Have the summarizer from each partnership share out. (15 min)
3. Give students the Hollywood or History? graphic organizer and the article, *Aptitude Tests: Are They Effective in Opening Students Minds' to More Career Paths?* Have students complete the organizer in groups using their own knowledge and experience, *The Simpsons* episode, and the two articles. They should compare the history of aptitude tests in school and how they are used today to how they are presented in *The Simpsons* episode. (10 min)

Day 3–4

1. Explain to the students that most aptitude tests are designed to identify students' strengths, interests, and abilities. Next, they will be learning about different ways to use students' strengths and interests in their lessons, in order to increase motivation and engagement. They will each read one of four different texts, record important information, then share what they learned. Lead students in a "Jigsaw" (Echevarria et al., 2017) reading activity. Put students into groups of four and assign each group member a number 1–4. Have students with the same number get together, four groups total (all 1s together, all 2s together, etc.). Assign each group one of the four texts: *Using Student Interests as Resources for Instruction, Helping All Learners: Interest, Teaching Beyond the Book* (Introduction–Principle 2), and *Teaching Beyond the Book* (Principle 3–Principle 5). Groups with the same number/text should get together and read, recording key information in the notetaking guide. When all groups have finished, have them go back to their original group of four, which should contain a student with each of the four different texts. Each student in the group shares their information and the rest of the group members record it on their notetaking guide. (30 min)
2. Finally, introduce students to their final project where they will synthesize the information learned and do some research of their own. Each student will give a presentation which includes the following: (15 min+)
   - At least two ideas for getting to know students' strengths and interests
   - At least three ideas for incorporating students' strengths and interests into content area lessons at their desired grade level
   - The benefits of planning lessons using students' interests and strengths
   - The pros and cons of using aptitude tests in schools

Differentiation

Scaffolds: If needed, provide some background knowledge and front load some key information before having students read the texts. Some students may need additional support and instruction on research skills before starting their final project.

290 HOLLYWOOD OR HISTORY?

ESL Interventions: Students with limited proficiency may benefit from having key information in the texts highlighted ahead of time for them. This reduces the language load by allowing them to only read the important information. Additionally, sentence frames may be provided to assist English learners in participating in discussions. For example, "When I was growing up, I wanted to be _____" or "One important idea we read was _____."

Extensions:
- Students could extend their research by investigating how unintentionally biased questions on aptitude tests may affect the results for minority or marginalized groups of students.
- Students could investigate how the results of aptitude tests may contribute to or challenge career stereotypes, such as men in STEM careers and women in education or nursing and how teachers can address this.
- Students could interview high school counselors at various school districts to see how aptitude tests are used to help students make post-high school plans.

REFERENCES

The Adaptive School. (2017). *Thinking collaborative.* https://www.thinkingcollaborative.com/_files/ugd/6a5cc9_ed28b325ab6a4362b834f4bbf295d408.pdf

Brooks, J. (Writer), Groening, M. (Writer), Simon, S. (Writer), & Lynch, J. (Director). (1992, February 27). Separate vocations (Season 3, Episode 18) [TV series episode]. Brooks, J., Groening, M., & Simon, S. (Executive Producers), *The Simpsons.* Gracie Films; Twentieth Century Fox Film Corporation.

Career Assessment. (n.d.). *Career research.* http://career.iresearchnet.com/career-assessment-old/#:~:text=Career%20assessment%20has%20been%20in,the%20Strong%20Vocational%20Interest%20Blank

Echavarria, J., Short, D. J., & Vogt, M. (2017). *Making content comprehensible for English learners: The SIOP model.* Pearson Education, Inc.

Echavarria, J. & Vogt, M. (2008). *99 ideas for teaching English learners with the SIOP model.* Pearson Education, Inc.

EL Education. (n.d.). *Helping all learners: Interest.* https://eleducation.org/resources/helping-all-learners-interest

Holland-Marks, J. (2017). Using student interests as resources for instruction. *ASCD.* https://www.ascd.org/blogs/using-student-interests-as-resources-for-instruction

Klein, A. (2021, April 26). Aptitude tests: Are they effective in opening students' minds to more career paths? *Education Week.* https://www.edweek.org/technology/aptitude-tests-are-they-effective-in-opening-students-minds-to-more-career-paths/2021/04

Tomlinson, C. A. (2006). Teaching beyond the book. *ASCD*, *64*(1). https://www.ascd.org/el/articles/teaching-beyond-the-book

APPENDIX A

Vocabulary

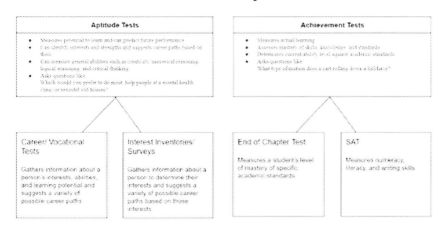

APPENDIX B

Teaching With Students' Strengths and Interests Notetaking Guide

Using Student Interests as Resources for Instruction	*Helping All Learners: Interest*

Teaching Beyond the Book *Intro–Principle 2*	*Teaching Beyond the Book* *Principle 3–Principle 5*

Hollywood or History?

Aptitude Tests

Writers of *The Simpsons* were inspired to write this episode by the actual aptitude tests many of the staff took in school. Compare the similarities and differences in the use of aptitude tests historically in US schools and Springfield Elementary School using the following sources: your own knowledge and experience, examples from *The Simpsons* episode, and the articles, *Aptitude Tests: Are They Effective in Opening Students' Minds to More Career Paths?* and *Career Assessment.*

U.S. Schools	Springfield Elementary School

Hollywood or History? How close is *The Simpsons* episode to real U.S. schools in the use of aptitude tests and other strategies designed to help students make post-high school decisions?

"Why Do We Take So Many Tests?" The Pros and Cons of High Stakes Testing in the United States

Scott L. Roberts and Kate Van Haren

EPISODE(S):
"How The Test Was Won" (2009, Season 20, Episode 11)

Grade	Subject	Topic
9-12	Civics/ History/ Sociology/ Current Events	Standardized Testing

Era Under Study	Estimated Time Needed for Lesson
Current Events	60 minutes

State Standards

State	Standards and Descriptions
Georgia	SSSocSC4 Analyze the function of social institutions as agents of social control across differing societies and times: a. Analyze the function of social institutions in society, include: family, education, religion, economy, government/politics, health care, and media. b. Evaluate the strengths and weaknesses of various social institutions.

Chapter 11: Commentary on Public Education   295

Michigan	P3.1 Clearly state an issue as a question of public policy, gather and interpret information about that issue, analyze various perspectives, and generate and evaluate possible alternative resolutions.
	P3.2 Discuss public policy issues, by clarifying position, considering opposing views, and applying core values or Constitutional Principles to develop and refine claims.
	P3.3 Construct claims and refine counter-claims that express and justify decisions on public policy issues.
	P3.4 Critique the use of reasoning, sequence, and supporting details in creating a claim and the subsequent evidence used to support a claim for credibility.
Wisconsin	SS.PS4.a.h Create arguments by researching and interpreting claims and counterclaims.

Common Core Standards

Standard	Description
CCSS.ELA-LITERACY. RH.9-10.2	Determine the central ideas or information of a primary or secondary source; provide an accurate summary of how key events or ideas developed the course of the text.
CCSS.ELA-LITERACY. RH.11-12.2	Determine the central ideas or information of a primary or secondary source; provide an accurate summary that makes clear the relationships among the key details and ideas.

NCSS C3 Framework

Dimension	Description
Developing Questions and Planning Inquiries	D1.2.9-12. Explain points of agreement and disagreement experts have about interpretations and applications of disciplinary concepts and ideas associated with a compelling question.
Applying Disciplinary Concepts and Tools (History)	D2.His.8.9-12. Analyze how current interpretations of the past are limited by the extent to which available historical sources represent perspectives of people at the time.

296 HOLLYWOOD OR HISTORY?

Evaluating Sources and Using Evidence	D3.3.9-12. Identify evidence that draws information directly and substantially from multiple sources to detect inconsistencies in evidence in order to revise or strengthen claims.
Communicating Conclusions and Taking Informed Action	D4.2.9-12. Construct explanations using sound reasoning, correct sequence (linear or nonlinear), examples, and details with significant and pertinent information and data, while acknowledging the strengths and weaknesses of the explanation given its purpose (e.g., cause and effect, chronological, procedural, technical).

NCSS Core Themes and Description

Theme	Description
V. Individuals, Groups, and Institutions.	Institutions such as families and civic, educational, governmental, and religious organizations exert a major influence on people's lives. This theme allows students to understand how institutions are formed, maintained, and changed, and to examine their influence.
X. Civic Ideals and Practices	An understanding of civic ideals and practices is critical to full participation in society and is an essential component of education for citizenship. This theme enables students to learn about the rights and responsibilities of citizens of a democracy, and to appreciate the importance of active citizenship.

Handouts/Materials/Web Links

Handout/Materials:
- Hollywood or History? Graphic Organizer

Episode Clips and Video Content:
- "How the Test Was Won," Season 20, Episode 11
    - o **Clip 1:** 3:34–5:41
    - o **Clip 2:** 5:42–6:27
    - o **Clip 3:** 7:18–8:15
    - o **Clip 4:** 10:24–11:42
    - o **Clip 5:** 14:00–14:46
    - o **Clip 6:** 18:53–21:30
    - o **Clip 7:** 16:49–18:15

Chapter 11: Commentary on Public Education 297

- Crash Course. (2019). *Check yourself with lateral reading: Crash course navigating digital information #3*. https://www.youtube.com/watch?v=GoQG6Tin-1E

Primary Sources:

- Student-developed "primary sources" concerning their experiences with standardized testing in their K–12 education.

Secondary Sources:

- Buck Institute for PBL Education (n.d). *What is PBL?* https://www.pblworks.org/what-is-pbl
- Churchill, A. (2015, April 18th) *Bless the tests: Three reasons for standardized testing*. The Thomas B. Fordham Institute. https://fordhaminstitute.org/national/commentary/bless-tests-three-reasons-standardized-testing
- DeMathews, D. (2021, March 15). Standardized testing amid pandemic does kids more harm than good. *UT News*. https://news.utexas.edu/2021/03/15/standardized-testing-amid-pandemic-does-kids-more-harm-than-good/
- ETS. (2021). *How ETS approaches testing: Purpose of standardized tests*. https://www.ets.org/understanding_testing/purpose
- Newseum. (n.d.). *Consumer questions handout*. https://newseumed.org/sites/default/files/legacy/2017/11/MLBP-Handout-Consumers-Questions.pdf
- Schaffhauser, D. (2017, November 8). Project based learning: Promising, not proven, researchers say. *The Journal*. https://thejournal.com/articles/2017/11/08/project-based-learning-promising-ut-not-proven.aspx
- Soika, B. (2021, October 29) *What will replace the SAT if it's abolished?* USC Rossier School of Education. https://rossier.usc.edu/the-sat-may-be-abolished-what-will-replace-it/
- Wright. J. (2021). Exploring satire with *The Simpsons* lesson plan. *Read, Write, Think*. https://www.readwritethink.org/classroom-resources/lesson-plans/exploring-satire-simpsons

298 HOLLYWOOD OR HISTORY?

Guiding Questions

Primary Question:
- What are the arguments for and against standardized testing in American public schools?
- How does personal experience affect one's opinions about controversial topics?
- How can a person seek out credible evidence to support ideas and opinions?

Secondary Questions:
- What is lateral reading?
- How does lateral reading help people consider multiple viewpoints and different experience cues?
- What is satire? What are the benefits of using satire to understand complex topics? What are the drawbacks to using satire to understand complex topics?

Important Vocabulary

Anecdotal Evidence: Evidence in the form of stories that people tell about what has happened to them.

Lateral Reading: The act of verifying what you're reading as you're reading it. (News Literacy Project)

No Child Left Behind: A U.S. Act of Congress that reauthorized the Elementary and Secondary Education Act; it included Title I provisions applying to disadvantaged students.It supported standards-based education reform based on the premise that setting high standards and establishing measurable goals could improve individual outcomes in education. The Act required states to develop assessments in basic skills. To receive federal school funding, states had to give these assessments to all students at select grade levels.

Project-Based Learning: A teaching method in which students learn by actively engaging in real-world and personally meaningful projects (PBLWorks).

Race to the Top: A $4.35 billion United States Department of Education competitive grant created to spur and reward innovation and reforms in state and local district K–12 education. States competing for the grants were awarded points for enacting certain educational policies, instituting performance-based evaluations for teachers and principals based on multiple measures of educator effectiveness (tied to targeted professional development and feedback), adopting common stan-

Chapter 11: Commentary on Public Education   299

dards (though adoption of the Common Core state standards was not required), adopting policies that did not prohibit (or effectively prohibit) the expansion of high-quality charter schools, turning around the lowest-performing schools, and building and using data systems.

Satire: A way of using humor to show that someone or something is foolish, weak, bad, etc.

Standardized Tests: Any form of test that (1) requires all test takers to answer the same questions, or a selection of questions from common bank of questions, in the same way, and that (2) is scored in a "standard" or consistent manner, which makes it possible to compare the relative performance of individual students or groups of students (The Glossary of Education Reform).

Assessment Strategies

Formative Assessments:
- Hollywood or History? Graphic Organizer
- Line of Contention
- Student Primary Source Essays

Summative Assessments:
- "What Do You Think: Hollywood or History?" Essays

Sparking Strategy/Warm-Up

Lesson Introduction

Students should watch at least one of the clips from the episode. Even though this beginning of the activity can be done as a whole-class discussion, small group activity, or individually, it is recommended that the teacher choose the same clip for the whole class to use. After watching the clip, the teacher should give students time to reflect on what they saw and relate to their own experiences with standardized testing throughout their school career. It is recommended that the students write down their answers because this document will make it easier for students to see their experiences and opinions. The teacher should let students know this will be used as a primary source for the next part of this lesson. (10 min)

Suggested questions to guide the creation of the primary source:
- *What is happening in this clip?*
- *What are the motivations of the school officials in this clip?*

300   HOLLYWOOD OR HISTORY?

- *What memories does this clip remind you of?*
- *What are your personal experiences with standardized testing?*
- *How closely does this clip resemble your experiences with standardized testing?*

Lesson Procedures

1. Students should begin with a quick review of the discussion of satire. Depending on student background knowledge and information, the teacher should take time to explain the value and purpose of satire. Depending on time, the teacher may wish to use lesson ideas exploring satire using other clips or ideas from *The Simpsons* (see extension activities). (5 min)

2. Students should understand that for controversial topics such as standardized testing, there are likely to be a variety of opinions and perspectives on the topic. Educated and well-intentioned individuals can take the same well-researched and creditable data and use it to support differing opinions. As consumers of media, students must be able to think critically and discern the purpose, biases, and credibility of these different types of information. Lateral reading is a technique that can be used to help consumers determine the purpose and credibility of different types of sources. If teachers and students are not familiar with the concept of lateral viewing, it might be helpful for both to view the John Green Crash Course video about how to lateral read sources. (5 min)

3. Students should conduct a lateral reading of an episode clip of their own. Students can do this section of the activity either individually or in small groups. There are a variety of different questions lists and checklists for students to use when they are lateral reading. The Newseum's Consumer Question list is a recommended suggestion. It is recommended that this part be completed as a class or in small groups so the teacher can check for understanding. Note: Lateral Reading is generally used for digital sources, but it can also be used on other sources as well. (5 min)

4. After conducting a lateral read of the clip, students should look at a variety of different articles discussing the pros and cons of standardized testing. They should conduct a lateral read of the sources as they read them. It is highly recommended that students work in small groups during this activity. The most effective learning about biases and the purpose of different sources

Chapter 11: Commentary on Public Education   301

will likely occur in student discussions. Suggested articles and sites for this section of the activity have been provided, but teachers are encouraged to find sources and articles that are specifically related to their local school district. (15 min)

5. After students should revisit their primary source created during the warm-up activity, students should discuss how their own personal feelings and experiences relate to understanding the benefits and drawbacks of standardized tests explored in the sources. Explain to students that these are examples of anecdotal evidence. When reading the message boards or comments sections often included in articles, anecdotal evidence is what readers will likely find. Have students discuss the problems with using anecdotal evidence along with scientifically supported data and evidence. Ask students if there is a place for anecdotal evidence when considering different perspectives and opinions about controversial issues like standardized testing. (10 min)

6. Explain to students several alternatives to standardized testing have been proposed over the last few decades. One popular alternative is Project-Based Learning. Similar to standardized testing, there are multiple sources in support and against the use of PBL. Show students the clip about PBL from the episode (Principal Skinner knowing to run on a storage container to save Ralph). Ask students: *What point were the writers of this clip making? What evidence, if any, did they use to make their argument?* (5 min)

Clip 7: 16:49–18:15

7. Ask students how they would go about researching and finding creditable evidence about the concept of Project-Based Learning. This is the opportunity for students to apply and use the skills they practiced in the discussions and activities about standardized testing. (5 min)

8. There are several options for this next step. The teacher can provide articles and resources about PBL for students to continue their practice with lateral reading. See the resource list above. Depending on the ability of students, the teacher may wish to send students to conduct their own research. Teachers should consider students' abilities when allowing students to search for their own sources when using a search engine like Google. It is important that students understand how Google generates its lists of sources. Students should also have knowledge about how to use keywords before beginning to search for sources on their own. If teachers feel students understand how to use search

302   HOLLYWOOD OR HISTORY?

engines, they can be allowed to find sources. If not, it is best to provide sources for students. (10 min)
9. Students should complete the What Do You Think? Hollywood or History? Essay as the summative assessment.

Differentiation

Scaffolds: The majority of this lesson should be taught in small groups. It may be helpful to have students of varying ability levels work together. The text in the primary and secondary source articles may be too technical for some students. The teacher may consider shortening the article or only using excerpts for students who may struggle with comprehension of the whole text as well as showing the images to the entire class.

ESL Interventions: In addition to the possible suggested scaffolds, teachers may wish to provide students with simplified definitions of vocabulary and key terms. As opposed to the assigned articles, the teacher may assign less technical and shorter articles to use for the comparison activity. Another alternative is to allow students to watch a video about the topics discussed. Some articles and documentaries may provide translations or subtitles, but teachers should check for their accuracy.

Extensions:
- The Read, Write, Think website has a variety of ideas that use clips from *The Simpsons* to explore the concept of satire. This website can be used to introduce students to the concept of satire or explore the concept in more depth.

REFERENCES

Buck Institute for PBL Education (n.d). *What is PBL?* https://www.pblworks.org/what-is-pbl

Churchill, A. (2015, April 18th) *Bless the tests: Three reasons for standardized testing.* The Thomas B. Fordham Institute. https://fordhaminstitute.org/national/commentary/bless-tests-three-reasons-standardized-testing.

Crash Course. (2019, January 22). *Check yourself with lateral reading: Crash course navigating digital information #3* [Video]. YouTube. https://www.youtube.com/watch?v=GoQG6Tin-1E

DeMathews, D. (2021, March 15). Standardized testing amid pandemic does kids more harm than good. *UT News.* https://news.utexas.edu/2021/03/15/standardized-testing-amid-pandemic-does-kids-more-harm-than-good/

ETS. (2021). *How ETS approaches testing: Purpose of standardized tests*. https://www.ets.org/understanding_testing/purpose

Newseum. (n.d.). *Consumer questions handout*. https://newseumed.org/sites/default/files/legacy/2017/11/MLBP-Handout-Consumers-Questions.pdf

Price, M. (Writer), & Kramer, L. (Director). (2009, March 1). How the test was won (Season 20, Episode 11) [TV series episode]. In A. Jean, J. L. Brooks, M. Groening, & S. Simon (Executive Producers), *The Simpsons*. Gracie Films; Twentieth Century Fox Film Corporation.

Schaffhauser, D. (2017, November 8). Project based learning: Promising, not proven, researchers say. *The Journal*. https://thejournal.com/articles/2017/11/08/project-based-learning-promising-ut-not-proven.aspx

Soika, B. (2021, October 29) *What will replace the SAT if it's abolished?* USC Rossier School of Education. https://rossier.usc.edu/the-sat-may-be-abolished-what-will-replace-it/

Wright. J. (2021). Exploring satire with *The Simpsons* lesson plan. *Read, Write, Think*. https://www.readwritethink.org/classroom-resources/lesson-plans/exploring-satire-simpsons

304 HOLLYWOOD OR HISTORY?

Hollywood or History?

"How the Test Was Won"

The Simpsons has regularly lampooned governmental policies. In this inquiry lesson, students will investigate the impact that standardized testing has had on students, educators, and the U.S. education system more generally. Students will use primary and secondary source materials in their analysis of the clips.

Evaluate each source provided and summarize your observations and analysis in corresponding spaces provided. In the section located at the bottom of the page, explain whether you think the scenes from *The Simpsons* "How the Test was Won" should be evaluated as accurate accounts of history, pure Hollywood satire, or a mixture of both. Use examples from your sources/documents to explain your answer.

Primary Sources	Clips from "How the Test Was Won"	Secondary Sources

What Do You Think? Hollywood or History?

306 HOLLYWOOD OR HISTORY?

For Further Viewing

With over 700 episodes to choose from, there are more episodes of *The Simpsons* that have satirized public education over the years.

Curriculum and Instruction

The Simpsons has been a proponent of real-life application of learning in several episodes. In addition to Skinner's scene rescuing Ralph in "How the Test Was Won," here are three more examples:

Bart Gets an F (1990, Season 2, Episode 1)
After failing numerous tests, Bart is in danger of repeating the 4th grade unless he completes a social studies project. He crams for the test and fails again but earns points for being able to apply his knowledge—a lesson in deep learning. (Written by David M. Stern, Directed by David Silverman)

Bart Stops to Smell the Roosevelts (2011, Season 23, Episode 2)
Superintendent Chalmers takes it upon himself to educate Bart and teaches him about Theodore Roosevelt. Surprisingly, this is a subject that motivates Bart and his friends to want to learn more. (Written by Tim Long, Directed by Steven Dean Moore)

Mathlete's Feat (2015, Season 26, Episode 22)
Lisa pushes to make Springfield Elementary a "Waldorf School" that focuses on hands-on activities (Vasagar, 2012), in order to win a math competition against Waverly Hills. (Written by Michael Price, Directed by Michael Polcino)

Administration/Teaching

The staff at Springfield Elementary have been main characters in numerous episodes. Principal Skinner, Superintendent Chalmers, Bart's teacher Mrs. Krabappel, and Lisa's teacher Ms. Hoover, have all had episodes where they are the main focus. The world of Springfield Elementary is still expanding, as new teachers, substitute teachers, administrators, and support staff are introduced as the years go on.

Sweet Seymour Skinner's Badasssssss Song (1994, Season 5, Episode 19)
Principal Skinner gets fired after one of Bart's pranks goes awry. Ned Flanders becomes principal in his place, and his administrative style doesn't

Chapter 11: Commentary on Public Education   307

work for the students either. (Written by Bill Oakley and Josh Weinstein, Directed by Bob Anderson)

PTA Disbands (1995, Season 6, Episode 21)
As mentioned in Chapter 5, this episode focuses on the working conditions for the teachers at Springfield Elementary and how they unionize to strike for better pay. Springfield residents fill in as substitutes—even Marge. (Written by Jennifer Crittenden, Directed by Swinton O. Scott III)

Skinner's Sense of Snow (2000, Season 12, Episode 8)
In this episode, Skinner decides to keep Springfield Elementary open during a snowstorm, which causes him to be trapped in the school with the students. He then has to resort to his army leadership tactics to command respect from the students. (Written by Tim Long, Directed by Lance Kramer)

Bart Gets a Z (2009, Season 21, Episode 2)
In this episode, Bart gets Mrs. Krabappel fired and she is then replaced by a new teacher named Zack Vaughn. The character of Zack is a satire of the young, hip teacher who is more style than substance—and who burns out easily. (Written by Matt Selman, Directed by Mark Kirland)

Black Eyed, Please (2013, Season 14, Episode 15)
Another episode featuring substitute teachers at Springfield Elementary! In this case, Mrs. Cantwell is a new teacher in Lisa's class—but she hates Lisa and bullies her relentlessly. A good example of how one's own experiences with school can unexpectedly manifest itself when teaching. (Written by John Frink, Directed by Matthew Schofield)

The Road to Cincinnati (2020, Season 32, Episode 8)
Superintendent Chalmers and Principal Skinner bond on a road trip to an administrator conference, even though Chalmers is contemplating replacing him with a young new principal. (Written by Jeff Westbrook, Directed by Matthew Nastuk)

The Public Education System and Educational Policy

Standardized testing and aptitude testing are just two examples of the many educational issues *The Simpsons* has tackled over the years, many times devoting whole episodes to satirizing structure and policy of the public education system. In some cases, the satire seemed so over-the-top at the time the episode aired, but later came to fruition closely to the depiction. These kinds of episodes are great for a Hollywood or History?

308   HOLLYWOOD OR HISTORY?

comparison, and also adds to the lore that *The Simpsons* can predict the future (Whitlock, in press).

Lisa Gets an A (1998, Season 10, Episode 7)
Lisa cheats on a test and gets an extremely rare A+++ which qualifies Springfield Elementary for more state funding. Lisa, of course, feels guilty for cheating but pressure to keep it to herself to get money for the school. This episode is a great commentary on state funding tied to student performance and the pressure to cheat to maintain funding status. (Written by Ian Maxtone-Graham, Directed by Bob Anderson)

Grift of the Magi (1999, Season 11, Episode 9)
Once again, Springfield Elementary is in danger of shutting down for lack of funds. A private company buys out the school and turns the curriculum into serving corporate interests—making Funzo toys in time for Christmas. This episode is a commentary on privatization in education, and given that it aired in 1999, was an interesting prediction for privatization efforts to come. (Written by Tom Martin, Directed by Matthew Nastuk)

Bart vs Lisa vs 3rd Grade (2002, Season 14, Episode 3)
When Bart does poorly on a standardized test and Lisa does well, Bart is demoted to 3rd grade while Lisa is promoted … also to 3rd grade. They end up in the same class, competing with each other. Another great commentary on not only standardized testing, but the consequences of being "held back" in school and "skipping grades." (Written by Tim Long, Directed by Steven Dean Moore)

Girls Just Wanna Have Sums (2006, Season 17, Episode 19)
Springfield Elementary becomes segregated by gender, and Lisa realizes that the boys are getting more rigorous math instruction than the girls. A great episode to talk about sexism in education. (Written by Matt Selman, Directed by Nancy Kruse)

Waverly Hills 90210D'oh (2009, Season 20, Episode 19)
Homer and Marge lie about where they live in order to get Bart and Lisa into Waverly Hills, a better school district than Springfield. This is a great episode to study how a child's zip code impacts the quality of public education they receive. For a full lesson using this episode, see Chapter 3. (Written by J. Stewart Burns, Directed by Michael Polcino)

A Test Before Trying (2013, Season 24, Episode 10)
Another episode on high stakes testing—Springfield Elementary closes when their test scores are not high enough—and another criticism of the

amount of testing in school that replaces proper school funding. (Written by Joel H. Cohen, Directed by Chris Clements)

The Caper Chase (2017, Season 28, Episode 19)

In a parody of "Trump University," Mr. Burns starts his own for-profit college and hires power plant workers (Homer) as professors. Clearly a comment on for-profit institutions of higher learning that may or may not be a scam. However, Yale University is also revealed to be a scam in this episode. (Written by Jeff Westbrook, Directed by Lance Kramer)

REFERENCES

Vasagar, J. (2012, May 25). A different class: The expansion of Steiner schools. *The Guardian*. https://www.theguardian.com/education/2012/may/25/steiner-state-funded-free-schools

Whitlock, A. M. (in press). Can *The Simpsons* predict the future? In S. L. Roberts & C. Elfer (Eds.), *Hollywood or history? An inquiry-based strategy for using cartoons to teach topics in elementary and secondary social studies*. Information Age Publishing.

ABOUT THE AUTHORS

Annie McMahon Whitlock, Editor, is an Associate Professor of History/Social Studies at Grand Valley State University and a former middle school social studies teacher who teaches elementary and secondary social studies methods courses. Her research is centered on teaching elementary social studies through civic engagement, place-based inquiry, and curriculum integration. Annie is the editor of the peer-reviewed *Great Lakes Social Studies Journal*, a Michigan Council for the Social Studies publication, and is a past member of the member of their Board of Directors and National Council for the Social Studies Board. Her favorite episode of *The Simpsons* is "You Only Move Twice."

Erin C. Adams is an Associate Professor of Elementary Social Studies Education at Kennesaw State University in Kennesaw, GA. Her primary areas of inquiry are K–12 economics education and social studies teacher education. "The Miseducation of Lisa Simpson" combines her interest in grocery stores, labor theories, and the power of economic discourse. Erin is new to *The Simpsons*, as she was not allowed to watch the show as a child. She is looking forward to watching the episodes featured in the book.

Amy Allen is an Assistant Professor of Social Studies in the Elementary Education Program at Virginia Tech. Throughout her time as an elementary school teacher, Amy focused on engaging young students in complex and thoughtful dialogue and integrating social studies concepts throughout all subject areas. These experiences served as a catalyst for many of her teaching and research interests which broadly include elementary

312   ABOUT THE AUTHORS

social studies, place-based learning, and in-service teacher professional development. Her favorite episode of *The Simpsons* is "Margical History Tour"—of course!

Martin Castro began his pedagogical career as a Peace Corps Volunteer teaching English in Ukraine (Слава Україні!). In 2022, he began his 10th-year teaching high school social studies in the Bronx, specializing in educating recently-arrived immigrant youth. He believes in ensuring that his students are prepared for their lives after graduating high school. Aside from any episode written by Conan O'Brien, Martin's favorite episodes of *The Simpsons* include "Lisa the Iconoclast," "Radioactive Man," and "Flaming Moe."

Timothy Constant is the Lead Curriculum and Instructional Coach for Clarenceville School District in Livonia, Michigan, a part-time Lecturer for Eastern Michigan University, and a board member for the Michigan Council for the Social Studies. Prior to his current position in Clarenceville Schools, Dr. Constant was the Associate Director of Teacher Education and Outreach at the Zekelman Holocaust Memorial Center and a principal/assistant principal for multiple districts. Prior to being a school administrator, he was a middle and high school Social Studies and English teacher.

Tiffany Craigie is an English Learner coach at the Ottawa Area Intermediate School District in Holland, Michigan. As a coach she works with teachers throughout the county to better serve and educate English learners. Her passion is advocating for high quality, equitable learning for all students. She received her Masters of Education in Differentiated Instruction from Cornerstone University, K–12 school administrator certification from Eastern Michigan University, and K–12 English as a second language certification from Western Michigan University. She taught 6th–8th grade language arts and mathematics, 3rd 5th grade ESL, and was a K–8 school administrator. Her favorite *Simpsons* episode is "Lisa Gets an A."

David A. Johnson is an educational consultant and coach specializing in Social Studies, Secondary Literacy, and SEL. While only 8 years old when *The Simpsons* made their debut on Tracy Ullman, he honestly can't remember a time when America's favorite yellow family wasn't on the airwaves, and hopes he never lives to see the day it's off. His favorite character is Sideshow Bob, and his favorite episode is Cape Feare.

Daniel G. Krutka is a citizen, monorail enthusiast, and Associate Professor of Social Studies Education at the University of North Texas. His research concerns ideas about technology, democracy, and education ... but they're more of Shelbyville ideas. If that peaks your interest, you can learn more at the Civics of Technology project (https://www.civicsoftechnology.org/) and the Visions of Education podcast (https://visionsofed.com/). His favorite episode from his childhood is probably "Homer the Great," also known as the Stonecutters episode. He even remembers laughing with family and friends at the first *Simpsons* episode when it aired.

Jeffrey Koslowski is a Nobel Foundation NSHSS Educator of Distinction award winner. He teaches World and Advanced U.S. history at Henry Ford Academy in Dearborn, Michigan (on the grounds of the Henry Ford Museum and Greenfield Village). His favorite *Simpsons* episodes include "Homer vs. the 18th Amendment," "Lisa the Vegetarian," and "Lost our Lisa." This is his second contribution to the *Hollywood or History?* series and fourth published chapter. He is married with a daughter and lives in Canton, Michigan.

Timothy Monreal is an Assistant Professor in the Department of Learning and Instruction at the University at Buffalo. Tim's research explores the intersection of space, place, and Latinx (teacher) identity and subjectivity. Partly due to his love of baseball, his favorite *Simpsons* episode is "Homer at the Bat."

Ritu Radhakrishnan is an Associate Professor and Chair of the Department of Curriculum & Instruction at the State University of New York at Oswego. She is the coordinator of the Adolescence Social Studies education program and teaches courses in Literacy, Curriculum Studies, Culturally Relevant Teaching, and Elementary & Adolescence Social Studies Methods. She also serves as the Chair of the School of Education Diversity Committee. Her research focuses on incorporating critical pedagogy and aesthetics in social studies curriculum. Specifically, she examines how the integration of aesthetic practices, including children's and young adult literature, in social studies curriculum affect student engagement, voice, and agency. Her favorite *Simpsons* episodes are "The Crepes of Wrath" and "Lisa vs Malibu Stacy."

Scott L. Roberts is a Professor of Social Studies Education at Central Michigan University. He teaches elementary social studies education, educational technology, and research methods. He has served as a board member of the Michigan Council for Social Studies, on several committees for the National Council for the Social Studies, on the editorial board of *Social Studies and the Young Learner*, and was named the Georgia Council for the Social Studies' Gwen Hutchinson Outstanding Social Studies Educator (2012). He is the author of multiple publications concerning history

314 ABOUT THE AUTHORS

education and is the co-editor of the *Hollywood or History?* book series. His research interests include state history, discussion-based strategies, history education, and educational technology. His favorite *Simpsons* episode is "How the Test Was Won."

Anthony Salciccioli, has taught U.S. History, Government, Sociology, Law, Big History, Philosophy, and World History. During his tenure he coached football, wrestling, and track and field. Anthony served as the President of the Michigan Council for the Social Studies from 2012–2014 and has been awarded the McConnell History Educator Award in 2014, the Fishman Prize Honor Roll in 2015, and the Gilder Lehrman Michigan History Teacher of the Year in 2016. In 2017, he was awarded the Clarenceville Schools Teacher of the Year as well. His favorite episode of *The Simpsons* is "Lisa the Iconoclast."

Kate Van Haren is a fourth and fifth grade social studies teacher at Pittsville Elementary School, a small, rural school in the state of Wisconsin. She is currently starting her PhD journey at Penn State University. Her ultimate goal is to provide teachers with the resources and confidence to teach and advocate for quality history and civics education for all learners. These efforts include creating curricula that encourage students to engage with primary sources and consider multiple perspectives at the very beginning of their social studies careers. Her favorite *Simpsons* episode is "Lisa's Substitute," way back from Season 2. It's a great reminder of what kids remember most about the teachers they encounter.

Kymberli Wregglesworth is a veteran social studies teacher at Onaway Secondary School in Onaway, Michigan. She is a James Madison Fellow and was a finalist for Michigan Teacher of the Year in 2018-19. She was the 2022–23 Michigan Council for the Social Studies President and is active in a number of social studies groups nationwide, including serving as a member of the Michigan Teacher Leadership Collaborative and the iCivics Educator Network. She enjoys spending time in the outdoors with her husband and daughter. Her favorite episode of *The Simpsons* is "Treehouse of Horror XXV."

Printed in the United States
by Baker & Taylor Publisher Services